RELIGIONS OF THE WORLD

A QUESTION OF FAITH

JAY LAMB

Religions of the World: A Question of Faith

Copyright © 2021 by A. J. Lamb Jr.

Triple Fire Press

Cover design by Amy Chae Designs

All rights reserved. No part of this publication may be reproduced, stored in a retrieval system or transmitted in any form or by any means, electronic, mechanical, photocopying, recording or otherwise without the prior permission of the publisher or in accordance with the provisions of the Copyright, Designs and Patents Act 1988 or under the terms of any license permitting limited copying issued by the Copyright Licensing Agency.

Dedicated to my first religion guru Huston Smith and the many, many people who have shared their knowledge, understandings and points of view about their faith with me.

Thank you also to my bright and beautiful daughters, Sheila, Sara, Rebecca, and Jenna, and my loving wife, Sandy, for their edits and technical assistance.

CONTENTS

Introduction	ix

PART 1
UNDERSTANDING RELIGION

1. The Ultimate Question	3
2. A Searcher is Born	5
3. Why Religion?	8
4. Why Religion Confuses Us	14
5. Making Sense of World Religions	19
6. The Single Definition Fallacy	25
7. Faith and the God-Like Force	29

PART 2
THE RELIGIONS

8. Hinduism	37
9. It's Karma Baby	43
10. Working the Karmic System	49
11. Hinduism the Religion	54
12. Ways to God	59
13. Buddhism	65
14. The Noble Eightfold Path	71
15. The Buddha's Teachings I	76
16. The Buddha's Teachings II	81
17. There Is Not One Buddhism	86
18. Zen and Nirvana	91
19. Chinese Beliefs	96
20. The Gods of China	102
21. The Wisdom of Confucius	107
22. The Man With A Plan For Today	112
23. Confucius' Legacy	115
24. Taoism (Daoism)	119
25. The Wu Wei Way	124
26. Religion in China Today	129
27. Abrahamic Faiths	135
28. Judaism	140

29. Practicing Judaism	145
30. Who Is A Jew, Etc.?	149
31. Rules And Scripture	154
32. Rules and Holidays	159
33. Christianity	164
34. What Christians Believe	170
35. More Beliefs	176
36. Jesus And Paul	181
37. Biblical Scholarship	186
38. The Roman Catholic Church	191
39. Protestants	197
40. The Orthodox Churches	202
41. Islam	207
42. Muhammad's Life	212
43. The Big Split	218
44. Sufi's And The Five Pillars Of Islam	224
45. Issues With And Within Islam	228
46. True Islam	238
47. Fear Of Islam	242
48. Shari'ah And Scriptural Interpretation	247
49. The Heart Of Islam	252

PART 3
THE MAJOR MINORS

50. Jainism	257
51. Zoroastrianism	260
52. Baha'i	263
53. Sikhism	266
54. Indigenous Primal Religions	269
55. Modern Paganism	274

PART 4
A QUESTION OF FAITH

56. Key Questions About Religion	285
57. The Pi Process	296

PART 5
THINKING ABOUT...

1. What Do We Know?	307
2. What Reality Is	313

3. If There Is An Afterlife	318
4. If There Is Free Will	322
5. Prayer And God	328
6. The Problem Of Evil	332
7. Is God In Our Future?	336
8. God's Plan	348
9. God's Will	352
The Religion Teacher's Bookshelf	357
Notes	379
About the Author	385

INTRODUCTION

Sometimes when we consider religion, we think about the loving compassion of the infinite something we might think of as God. Our minds fill with images of a beautiful heavenly realm where everyone is good and kind, nothing is ever boring, and we are happy and loved all the time, forever. We might feel some compassion for those who did not make it to this place but we know in our hearts that God is just so some things are just the way they have to be. If reincarnation is our preference, we might imagine a line of our lives stretching from the distant past to the present, with each incarnation seeming to be wiser, kinder and more compassionate than the one

INTRODUCTION

before. Looking toward the future, we envision the line ending in a golden glow of liberation. Bliss, pure bliss.

Sometimes when we consider religion, we see a world torn apart and suffering because of the violence and discord motivated by emotions run amuck, inflamed by differences in religious faith. During any moment in time, have we ever had a world where no one was being persecuted because of their religious beliefs? In reality, any combination of mass murder, ethnic cleansing, violent mobs or just day-to-day discrimination against those whose religion is different or "wrong" or "evil" can be found in the news almost every day. Why does this happen?

First, people's emotions and egos can become tied to their faith as religious belief is usually absorbed through culture and family. Unfortunately, while many people are able to coexist peacefully with those of other beliefs, some cannot, and in certain situations, their emotions will get the best of them. A zealot might say, "My religion is God's religion so that unbeliever who disagrees must be wrong and evil." Unfortunately, such angry views have been coopted by religious and political demagogues to persecute religious minorities within a country, or to supercharge emotions against a perceived enemy outside. Any effort to find compromise or common ground is seen as a deal with the devil.

Second, the vast majority of American citizens and, I would argue, citizens of most countries, are religious illiterates. In his 2007 book, *Religious Literacy: What Every American Needs to Know- and Doesn't*, this is how Steven Prothero described our country. He was and is 100% correct. Understanding other religious views is almost impossible if you don't know what they are or, even worse, believe wildly inaccurate stereotypes. Citizen ignorance translates into public policy ignorance. Mistakes and errors in judgment create ugly divisions at home and harm our global interests. However, a Pew Research Center survey found Americans who personally know someone in a religion different from their own – or who have at least some knowledge about that faith – are more likely to have positive feelings about them than those who don't[1]. Knowledge and familiarity are key for a peaceful religious world.

I started writing *Religions of the World: A Question of Faith* as a way to present what I had learned after twenty-one years teaching a World Religions class to very smart students at the Thomas Jefferson High School for Science and Technology. During that time, I crafted a way to present religion by highlighting the underlying philosophy of each faith without excessive terminology or cultural confusion, which made it easier to understand.

When I finished writing about the religions, however, I found the writing was not finished with me. Teaching those classes and writing this book has been part of my lifelong search to discover the truth about religion and God. I realized by just providing information I had not advanced that search, even for myself. If I don't have the faith that would connect me to an existing religion, how could I find those answers? What did I believe to be true?

I decided to engage with that question to see what set of beliefs and practices make the most sense to me. It is my belief if more of us had religious views that reflected our rational thinking we would certainly help reduce or eliminate the violent events from the past caused by clashing religious faiths. While most people may still decide to follow their family faith, no faith, or combine in new like-minded groups, they will do that because it makes the most sense to them.

This book examines two religious subjects. First, for most of the book, I explain how to approach the concept of religion and the beliefs and practices of the major world religions in a way that is easy to understand. Second, I try to model a process to discern a personal understanding of God and religion, using rational thinking. You may follow this process by reading about the religions, going through the questioning, and compare your answers to mine. Your results will almost certainly be different but that is to be expected.

PART 1

UNDERSTANDING RELIGION

1

THE ULTIMATE QUESTION

"There is either an intelligent and purposeful force of some sort (God) in this universe or there is not. I want to know the truth."
- Jay Lamb

All my life I have wanted to know the answer to this question and its logical follow-up: *If yes, then what is it and what does it mean to us and which religion, if any, is true?*

I was fortunate to find a position in the Humanities Department at the Thomas Jefferson High School for Science and Technology for the last twenty-five years of my teaching career. Science and Math kids need the Humanities too, contrary to some opinions. I also taught World History and Advanced Placement U.S. Government, but the subjects I had the most passion for were my electives, Philosophy, and especially, World Religions.

I had two goals for my world religions class. First, find a way to teach so my bright high school students could clearly understand the essentials of each faith and how that faith is practiced. I worked on that from day one until my last day, when I retired. Second, I used the class content as a springboard to help me learn and understand not just what each religion believes, but how their experiences and evidence could answer those ultimate God questions. That process continues.

2

A SEARCHER IS BORN

"I know that everyone dies, but I always thought an exception would be made in my case."
- Mark Twain

On warm summer nights when I was a kid, we would ride our bikes under the streetlights in our suburban subdivision and throw stones in the air to watch the bats dive on them. On rare occasions, before we were called in to bed, a few of us would put down a blanket in someone's back yard, lay on it with our heads together and look at the stars. Gradually, in the warm quiet, we would stare hard and start to talk about what was going on out there. Our stream of consciousness discussions usually circled around God, religion, what we knew about science, and our mishmash of speculations about how it all worked out in the cosmos. For some reason I found these meandering discussions in the dark absolutely fascinating. However, we ended up with more questions than answers. Later I discovered the short cut metaphor, courtesy of Douglas Adams' *The Hitchhiker's Guide to the Galaxy*, which describes what we were trying to figure out.

That is, what is the answer to the meaning of "Life, the Universe, and Everything." I don't think the answer is really 42 but if it isn't, what is it?

Because I was raised by parents who were fairly devout Roman Catholics, it took me years of struggle and much annoyance to several nuns and CCD teachers (Catholic Sunday school on Tuesday nights), to realize my questions were going to be answered by these folks in essentially the same way, "That's what we believe." That answer was not and is not good enough. I needed to know not what "we" believe, but what is true.

Here we are today. What I want is not to "believe" in an answer, or have "faith" in it, but to KNOW I have found it. My heart, my soul and my mind all have to be in agreement. Whether it's the Great Frog God Alvin pulling all the strings in the universe or there is nothing intelligent and purposeful running the show, I want to know that. Of course, things get in the way of this search. It can't go full speed ahead 24/7. Life and love go on, money has to be made, children have to be raised, and complications occur. I love to spend time at the beach and in the mountains and sometimes, for short periods of time, I want to put all this out of my mind and take a breath. I also realize I may never actually find the answer. But, what can I say? Trying to figure out the ultimate picture about life, the universe and everything is a real mystery that calls me and I am hooked on this search. You may think this is hopeless and I am wasting my time but as the saying goes, it's not the destination, but the journey.

For me, there has never been any doubt there is a correct answer to these questions. Not one that is just right for me but not for you or one that can be interpreted in a million different ways, but the real one, the true one. Whatever is true and whatever is, going to happen will happen, whether everyone or no one believes it. However, if I can't find an answer I can prove to be true, I want to find one that makes enough sense to me that it should be true.

As I search, I like to think I am a diligent philosopher, open to whatever the answer might be and alert for my own prejudices. Is one religion correct? Do they all have value? Is some combination of beliefs correct? Are there bits and threads throughout religious experiences which can be put together in a new way to provide a clear insight, or are the atheists right and there is nothing going on out there besides natural, mindless, processes with no higher purpose? I cannot think of any intellectual endeavor more important or exciting than making progress toward understanding this. Besides, it's fun.

To date, I have met many people who think they already know the truth about religion and I am convinced they really, sincerely, believe. But their profession of faith, by itself, is just not enough for me because I know someone down the street who feels just as strongly about a different view. I am the guy who, when religious groups knock on doors in the neighborhood to convert folks, and everyone else hides behind their curtains hoping they will go away, invites them in to talk. Almost everyone is happy to share their beliefs if the request comes from a sincere desire to learn and understand and not an attempt to start an argument or make fun of them. As a result, I consider myself to be a serious investigator of religion. It is my avocation.

I will focus on world religions because these are the folks who claim to have the truth. Some believe only their point of view is true but others will admit, while they prefer their own faith, they don't see any reason why any good person cannot be saved. Saved for what? Why? There are many questions to be answered and I have to begin somewhere. I had better get started because this is a big job and I won't live forever (or will I?). Let's get focused.

3

WHY RELIGION?

"Millennia of history have shown that religion is not a 'small difference' but probably the most profound difference that can exist between people."
- Samuel P. Huntington

My atheist friend once said, during one of our many discussions about religious beliefs, that "Big claims require big proof." Therefore, he pointed out, religion cannot be true because, not only do religions contradict each other on their claims but they also offer no empirical evidence. In his mind, this lack of evidence means religious claims are false. He believes lack of evidence is evidence of God's nonexistence.

I don't agree. I do agree some particular religious beliefs do not appeal to me but I am not able to trash the whole concept because of that. Speaking to my agnostic friend the other day we both agreed when a religion says "You have to believe what we believe or you will go to hell" this is both intellectually insulting and untrue.

After all, if you were God and you were designing a religious system for people to base their lives and actions on would you come up with a peek a boo system where people had to guess which of many proffered beliefs was true? Especially if their choices doomed or rewarded them for the rest of eternity? That's nuts, and I am operating under the assumption if there is an intelligent, creative, force running the universe, it is not crazy.

Both my atheist and agnostic friends do pick the most obnoxious examples that can be found as their primary evidence contradicting religious validity. They focus on Evangelical/Fundamentalist Christianity because their pronouncements are most often in the news, but they do not know much about other religions or even other Christian points of view. When one mentioned a scientific idea that the universe, in its continuing expansion, will eventually curve back around to become a big bang type of singularity again, he was very surprised when I said how that seemed to agree with ancient Hindu thinkers. To another I mentioned several conversations I have had recently with some mainstream Christians about the "believe or go to hell" point of view. These Christians were shocked by that statement and said this was not part of their denomination's beliefs. They said their faith grew over time but such absolute beliefs were not required for a good afterlife.

I have come to the conclusion, based on my conversations, research, what I read and hear in the media, and my twenty-some years teaching about world religions, that most people don't know very much about religion, sometimes including their own. Yet religion has a tremendous impact in the world. If we are going to investigate the value of the claims religions make, we should make sure we understand their beliefs correctly so we know what we are talking about.

I know people so sure of their religious point of view they do not wonder about religion at all. They "know." My atheist friend and several of my religious friends seem so certain what they believe is true they do not feel the need to speculate about or investigate other possibilities and alternatives. The atheist scoffs at any religious perspective and the religious friends wonder why I am interested in other religions when they already know the right answer.

There are also those for whom religious questions are just not important. Those folks are either content with the answers they were raised with and don't have the need or desire to question farther, or they don't want to rock the boat, or they think it is just too complicated and confusing, or, for whatever reason, they don't care. For them, the energy they would expend wondering about religion just does not trump the attention required to live their daily lives. After all, the world is filled with many ways to distract us and for some, religion can be ignored or at least put off until later. Not for me.

However, as zealous about this search as I may sound, I have discovered a personal bias that creates a conundrum I have not found a way to solve. Speaking metaphorically, if I am presented with two doors to choose from, and one door leads to a universe where my existence is essentially purposeless and random, where events occur with no more reason than tossing a handful of dice, and where I (physically, intellectually, spiritually and any other way I may not know about) will eventually, totally cease to exist, I will take the other door. The other door leads to a universe and an existence that reflects individual and universal meaning and purpose. Through this second door, my decisions seem important because living is not just a temporary physical process but a long-term spiritual one too. Here, when my body dies, the essential part of what is me lives on in a spiritual realm run by a benevolent force or forces or it might incarnate again in the physical, but it will continue to exist, learn, and evolve. That sounds good to me. I like existing. Who, besides me, would also pick the second door if the choice of doors were real and meaningful? I think just about everyone would.

My desire to have door two as my answer makes me suspicious of that as ultimately being true. How nice reality should end up to be exactly what I most want it to be. Isn't this just the sort of after-life existence I would invent if I could? I am suspicious. On one hand, just because it is what I would most want, does that prove in any rational way it is not a candidate for true? On the other hand, how can I be sure my underlying psychological desires are not skewing my thinking? Like Tevye in *Fiddler on the Roof*, it seems I am always (unfortunately?) able to see the other point of view.

In our world, religion causes excitement. There are few subjects that will get people as exhilarated, happy, kind, contentious or crazy, as religion. Sometimes it is concern about their own religion and sometimes it is their concern about yours that sets them off. There are so many attitudes about religion, pro and con, relaxed and ecstatic, live and let live, and in your face, it makes it almost impossible to generalize. But when it's all added up, the safest generalization is that religion can have a big impact in this world, not just on individuals, but on the policies of nations, and this can have a seismic effect on all of us. The other safe generalization is this impact is becoming more important. Despite the predictions of some twentieth century sociologists that religion would wither away as the world modernized, that does not seem to be happening. Certainly, they don't seem to have considered (who did back then?) the impact of globalization. While studies show there are some countries where religion is less important than in the past, it is the opposite in other places. In many parts of the world Fundamentalist faiths are on the rise. For at least the foreseeable future, religion, as an essential part of the human equation, is here to stay.

Human beings have found a dizzying variety of ways to exercise their religious instincts. Religion is never separate from the larger culture of a people and it is our culture that socializes us into our beliefs about the way we live, what we believe, and how we act. Many thousands of years ago, when all religion was tribal and later, regional, people were usually widely separated and each group would have different gods. The fact that our group had our gods and other people far away had their own, different gods surprised no one. In a way, ancient polytheism promoted tolerance since it was clear to everyone these are our gods and those are yours. Gods were associated with groups and you would no more worship another god than you would change your ethnicity. It was a package deal. However, when ancient globalization began, for instance, when Alexander the Great conquered the Persian Empire and introduced Greek ideas and gods to that part of the world, groups began to mix, and local identities began to disappear. Traditional concepts of our gods and your gods began to erode. As the winners, the conqueror's gods might seem much more appealing, and besides, there were now more choices, especially in the cities where different peoples and their gods mixed readily.

In both domestic and foreign policy, international politics, economics, civil rights and liberties, and the environment, religious views influence opinion and policy decisions. But what if, as is the case, people know either only a little or inaccurate information about other religious beliefs and practices? Most people's religious attitudes usually come from their gut but what if their gut is wrong? We know that for democracy to function well, we should have a literate and knowledgeable electorate. The decisions voters make on issues and candidates will be more accurate if those decisions are based on what is really happening in the world. If our religious worldview is made up of bigotry, fantasy or ignorance then our political decisions will reflect that and we will be susceptible to inaccurate media, and political and religious demagogues. Then, our policies and our leaders will reflect our disconnect with reality and we will make mistakes.

Does it matter whether or not anyone in the United States today knows anything about the religions of other people in the world? Doesn't it make sense to focus on our own concerns and let people in other countries worry about theirs? No, it does not. Anyone who has been paying attention for the last ten or twenty years knows, like it or not, the world is changing and globalizing in ways that affect everyone. Religion is a key topic in almost every foreign or domestic dispute in the news today.

You can't swing a cat in the public policy world without hitting a religious issue. The question for each of us is, do we know enough about religion to sort out the reality from the hyperbole? And, perhaps more importantly, since we live in a democracy, to what degree is the other guy's inability to comprehend these issues going to affect us when he goes into the voting booth?

4

WHY RELIGION CONFUSES US

"Religion consists in a set of things which the average man thinks he believes and wishes he was certain of."
- Mark Twain

I remember watching a television special on Hinduism or India when I was a teenager. I don't recall much, but two images have stuck with me over the years and help explain my early confusion. First, I saw a parade of elaborately, colorfully decorated elephants ambling down the streets of a city in India, and I was impressed. They don't have decorated elephant parades where I come from.

The next scene was of an ornate temple overrun with monkeys. Monkeys were scurrying everywhere and it did not look like they had just escaped from an overturned monkey cage. They looked very much at home. This seemed to me to be very cool because no one where I lived allowed any live animals, let alone monkeys, to have their way with their church.

Everything I knew about religion in India for years after was they had painted elephant parades and let monkeys live and scamper around in their churches. That was about it. I did feel our local denominations could pick up some clues from these Hindu folks on how to run a religion if they wanted to jazz up their services and increase attendance. However, I did not have the slightest idea why those people did these things or how this related to what they believed. The meaning behind these actions was totally incomprehensible.

Later, when I learned a little more about Hinduism it occurred to me why my earlier experience, however visually impressive, lacked any meaning. The more I thought about it the more I identified this as the same sticking point I had found in trying to understand other religions. The problem is this. Rites, rituals, celebrations, ceremonies, art, music, dance, and other religious activities conducted and explained in a foreign language, are culturally based and only have meaning to the outsider when he can experience them with cultural understanding. For these activities to make sense the outsider must be aware of their cultural context and how they reflect that groups' understanding of the way their religion explains the world.

From outside a culture, you can watch and appreciate the skills and beautiful ornate costume of the pretty girl dancing, but you might miss the meaning of the elaborate hand gestures, or that the dance is depicting aspects of the eternal dissolution and rebuilding of the universe. Most of us are first introduced to other religions visually, but unless we understand what it all means in the context of that culture and its history, we are most likely going to feel lost. However, while confusing cultural differences may often defeat our attempts to demystify ritual, philosophy is a universal language of understanding. We humans have brains that work pretty much the same way and despite how we may speak and act, our inner thought processes are essentially identical. Once someone explains, without the cultural overlay, what it all means and how a people's religious expression connects to their larger beliefs about how the universe works you begin to get it.

Recently, a new acquaintance who had toured several Asian countries mentioned she found Buddhism impossibly confusing. In each country she visited she went to Buddhist temples to see what it was all about. In each location something different was happening and she couldn't make heads or tails out of it. When I tentatively offered to discuss this with her, she looked me straight in the eye and said, "I've given up trying to figure out Buddhism."

Not to pick on Buddhism, but in a conversation with friends, I mentioned I had seen an exhibit of paintings of Buddhist Bodhisattvas. One asked me what a Bodhisattva was. In order to answer that, I briefly outlined the major divisions within Buddhism, between those who believe spiritual progress is primarily the job of the individual and those who believe there is compassionate spiritual help available. I also mentioned how each of those major groups has split, over time, into many smaller sects, each with somewhat different points of view on matters of theology or practice. My friends seemed surprised there were so many different divisions within Buddhism. They had always assumed one Buddhist believed the same as another. Curiously, as Christians, they were aware there are hundreds of Christian denominations and many points of view even within their own church, but they were not able to automatically make the leap to the idea that other religions might share similar divergence.

No member of any faith believes what they think is illogical or irrational. Something they believe or do may seem crazy to you but their faith has an underlying explanation of how things work and what we are supposed to do with our lives, which makes absolute sense to them. Of course, any religious philosophy is based on assumptions that may not seem logical or reasonable to an outsider who might examine them, but once we know those assumptions and the logic that holds them together, we can understand where they are coming from, why they do these things, and how their beliefs make sense of what they do.

This doesn't mean we agree with what they believe or even find merit in what they do, just that we understand how they got there and what it means. We learn what these people believe about humans, God, and the universe that makes sense to them and whether these assumptions come from revealed scripture, enlightened masters, or philosophical contemplation. Only when we figure out this aspect of a religion can we begin to understand the beliefs supported by these concepts. Once this is accomplished, we can more easily make the connection from those beliefs to the rituals and other physical manifestations. Because we understand the underlying philosophy, making sense of the decorated elephants and the temple monkeys comes more easily.

Another difficulty in trying to understand religions is the sheer volume of information. There are so many sacred texts to read, so many schools of thought and so many points of view in every religion that it is absolutely impossible to understand and reconcile all of the disparities. At cocktail party years ago, I met a professor whose expertise was Vietnamese Buddhism. While she had an amazing depth of knowledge in this area and about Buddhism in general, on other religious subjects she did not know much more than I did. The same limitation is true, of course, if one is discussing world history or mathematics (I suppose). Since there is so much material, no one, in or outside of the religion, can know it all.

As this is the case with all religions, it is also the situation within any particular religion. Even though they might agree on a few basics, there is no religion of any size that does not contain disagreements and different interpretations between its own members, even within smaller sects, on what it all means and what they are supposed to do. This can complicate our task of trying to figure out what these folks believe, especially if we are trying to find the one "right answer." For instance, finding out what Hindus believe and do depends on which Hindu you ask.

Early in my teaching career, a Muslim student came to me with one of the textbooks we used and pointed out a section of the text he said was incorrect. I took this very seriously and researched the subject industriously. What I found should not have surprised me, but it did. I discovered the student had highlighted one of the key disagreements between Sunni and Shi'ite Muslims. We can easily imagine how someone outside of a religion can misrepresent it, but it often happens people in the same religion contradict each other on important points of belief or practice.

This makes it hard to be sure what is true about a religion. It makes you wonder if there actually is a "right" answer. The result is that this lack of absolutes yields over-broad generalizations about religion in the press, our politics, and in the opinions of barber chair philosophers. Not knowing what is correct, people's attitudes and impressions about religion can be influenced by demagogues using overblown rhetoric, false premises, and the latest internet fallacy. Since even pronouncements by people in the same religion can disagree and give you contradictory information how can we get it right? It all depends on how we approach the subject.

5

MAKING SENSE OF WORLD RELIGIONS

"There are two ways to be fooled. One is to believe what isn't true; the other is to refuse to believe what is true."
- Soren Kierkegaard

Understanding any religion accurately requires two connected approaches: First, know the underlying philosophy of each religion and second, develop a correct understanding of how beliefs and practices are actually lived by the religion's adherents. Think of this as the physiology of the religion, how it lives and breathes.

While all religions have a structure or anatomy of some sort ranging from very organized, hierarchical and formal to very loose and casual, what teaches us the most is to understand the physiology, how it functions as a living system. As every cell and organ has a job in a body, so does every religious adherent and faith community have a place in the extended identity and process of their system of religious beliefs and practices. However, unlike organic systems, which only change very slowly, using evolutionary time frames, religious organisms can change relatively quickly and often, unpredictably.

Approaching religion with this in mind is the key to seeing through prejudice, ignorance, misinformation and contradictions.

This idea was introduced to me in an article written by Dr. Michael C. Weber of Gettysburg College, titled *Teaching Religion in the World History Class.*[1] The crux of Dr. Weber's argument is that we should understand a religion not as a single monolithic entity where all adherents believe and practice exactly the same way, but to see it the way it is actually lived. To demonstrate this difference, Dr. Weber distinguished between the textbook definition of religion "...an intellectual system of thought or belief that somehow seems to exist without flesh and blood human beings defining and enacting the requisite cults and rites," and the "embodied" religion as it is lived by human beings, on the ground, during any particular time period, in any particular geographic location. Seeing the difference between these views of religion is crucial to understanding. The textbook might say one thing but the ways individuals actually believe and practice their faith is our evidence for what is really happening and tends to be extremely varied and complex.

What Weber describes as the "essentialist" view of religion, the way it is usually taught, sets up a narrow understanding of the religion, through the sort of broad generalizations that might be found in any religion textbook. Misunderstanding arises when we learn those generalizations and then always expect the living religion to fit. It doesn't work. With so much complexity and differing points of view in any faith, textbook writers and teachers must clip off the extras and generalize the rest. Even if the authors are thoughtful enough to warn us about this, the take away knowledge by readers is often compressed in their minds over time and internalized to register as, "All Buddhists believe this," or "all Muslims believe that."

Weber suggests religions can only be accurately defined if we take into consideration what every person in that religion believes and does. It is individuals, usually in accord with their local religious community, who decide, through their own social calculus and traditions, what is important, what is believed, what is meant by that belief, and how that belief should be demonstrated both in religious practice and in daily life. It is that mass of living, breathing individuals, with all of their variations, points of view, and differences in interpretation, that most accurately defines a religious faith. Adherents of the same religion separated by distance, culture, or time will make different decisions that could differ markedly from each other. If we pretend broad religion-wide generalizations are the only correct descriptors of a faith, we are doomed to an inaccurate understanding. While such generalizations have their uses in controlling a large amount of information, they are, at best, approximations, and do not reflect the living nature of the religion.

Years ago, when researching information about Native American tribal religions, I found an author who said essentially, yes, we can say a few things in general about these religions. However, he also said because each tribe had significant differences from other tribes, in order to be accurate, he either had to write a book highlighting the distinguishing spiritual characteristics of every tribe, one that would be extremely long and probably not read, or he would have to use broad generalizations and hope everyone would remember the limitations of such a method.

As I pondered this, it occurred to me the most accurate way to understand any religion is not to see it as a single definition or a monolithic entity but as an organic organization with, within a fairly broad spectrum, significant diversity in both beliefs and practices. If I could design a visual representation that would show these variations within that faith, and every faith, what would it look like? I decided it would look like a scatter diagram. (See next page)

Think of this as a graphic metaphor, an image that illuminates a conceptual idea, not based on actual data. Considering a religion, when viewed this way, allows us to grasp its diversity of beliefs and practices more accurately, as it really exists. Every religion, through its unique scattering of dots, has its own pattern but shares this diverse nature with all other faiths.

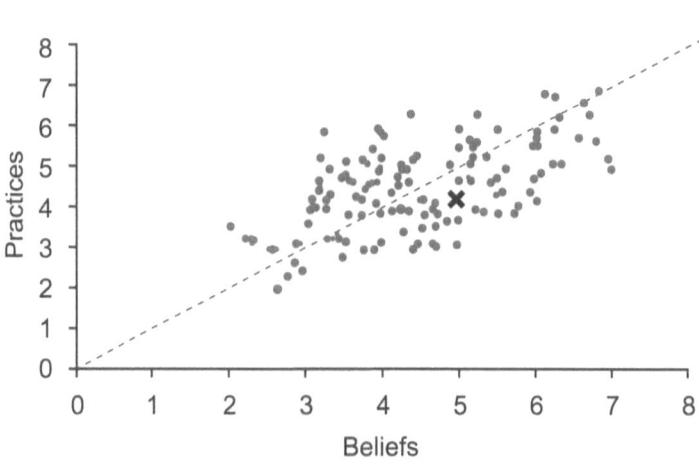

In this example, the different locations of the dots, relative to each other, show the scope and variation of the practices and beliefs of this faith, indicative of either geographical and/or theological distance, while the dots represent adherents' faith communities. The diagonal line is the average of the different points and can be thought of as the generalized "textbook definition" of the religion. The other important idea to keep in mind is these dots are not locked in place. Over time, religions evolve and so, the dots can move.

While generalizations are important to understand the broad basics of a faith, problems arise when people short cut their thinking, assuming that is all they need to know instead of seeing this as just a starting place. The most accurate representation of any religion would be its unique spread of dots on the graph. What is most important to understand is the organic nature of the living religion as an ongoing process, not an unchanging product.

If we mistakenly take the diagonal as the only right and true definition for the religion, see how many adherents would be considered to be lapsed, hypocrites, or at least, out of the mainstream.

According to Weber's view, we would find relatively few members of this religion accurately reflecting the defined values. Yet, each one of the people who might appear to be an outlier probably considers himself to be a member of this religion in good standing, believing and practicing this faith as he/she or their community believes it should be done. The diagonal line is only the line of best fit. It has value as a sort of mathematical average of points and shows a higher level of consensus on religious beliefs and practices along its length than another line would, but it is not defining.

Let us consider an adherent to this faith marked by the "X" on the graph. While this person's beliefs and practices are close to the diagonal line, they do differ to some extent. Dots close to X probably represent the local community or X's particular sect within the larger faith. Further dots are probably representative of different sects or geographically separated groups. As evolutionary theory demonstrates, groups of humans who are physically separated will, over time, develop divergence in language, culture and religion. Based on his beliefs and personality, our person, X, may show a certain degree of tolerance for disparities with those adherents represented by dots nearer to him. At some more distant point on the graph though, he may decide those people are too mistaken in their beliefs and practices and are not really true believers.

The reality is that through time and over geographic distance religions keep changing and the dots keep moving around and the diagonal line keeps shifting. Religions are a process in motion. As difficult as herding cats, this diversity defeats our ability to develop an accurate, unchanging, simple definition for any religion. The generalizations we create to make this easier will often be inaccurate when applied to specific people and situations.

For instance, a recent Pew Research Center survey showed that when asked if society should be accepting of homosexuality, 76% of American Catholics said yes, 45% of Polish Catholics agreed but only 6% of Nigerian Catholics thought this was a good idea. Imagine how the dots on the Roman Catholic scattergram would be all over the chart if this were one of the beliefs being graphed.

When presented with a situation where we do not know sufficient facts, there is something in the human subconscious that "fills in" the empty areas with subconscious assumptions (connecting the dots) that seems satisfactory but may be wildly incorrect. Because of this, people assume their view of a religion is correct. If asked, they would admit they do not know all of the facts, but believe their general understanding is right. Unfortunately, if they see that religion as a single undifferentiated belief system their view is inaccurate. Then, if they acquire more knowledge, they may know more facts but will be confused if this new information does not fit with what they think they already know. If this is the case the religion will seem confusing and incoherent to them, but it is not the religion that is incoherent here. Broad generalizations cannot be accepted as truth statements. Accepting one simple definition for any religion is what I call the Single Definition Fallacy.

6

THE SINGLE DEFINITION FALLACY

"All generalizations are false, including this one."
- Mark Twain

The biggest and most common mistake people make in their understanding of religion is to think, often subconsciously, that everyone in any faith believes the same and acts the same. They apply a single definition to every religion. While some may later study world religions and develop a deeper, more accurate understanding, most will not. Since most people don't know much about various religions, whatever knowledge they have, whether from reading an article, the media, or an ancient classroom, will be filed away some place in their minds to, in most cases, morph into a hard and fast absolute definition. If this happens, the person has fallen victim to the Single Definition Fallacy. Whether watching a story about religion on T.V. or meeting someone of a different faith, the Single Definition Fallacy will skew the person's understanding. This is a problem because now, fortified by the misplaced belief they correctly understand the religion (Hey, I read an article!), they will make inaccurate assessments and judgements. To keep this from happening, they must disable the Single Definition Fallacy. This can be done by adopting the "There is not one *(insert name of religion)*" concept.

I first heard this "not one" statement used at an Islamic conference hosted by the George Mason University Center for Global Islamic Studies and the Virginia Foundation for the Humanities in the spring of 2011. In discussing the difficulty American Muslims have had in defending their religion against charges of terrorism, the speaker reminded the audience there is not one Islam, but many points of view, interpretations and practices within that faith system. Everyone nodded their heads knowingly and the speaker moved on, but I was making furious notes. It struck me this term was the key to understanding not only the reality of Islam as it is practiced differently around the world, but also of every religion. To be accurate, we must always be aware there is not one Christianity. There is not one Hinduism. There is not one Islam. There is not one Judaism. There is not one Buddhism. The correct understanding is the scattergram not the single definition. Understanding this about all faiths is the key to inoculating ourselves against the Single Definition Fallacy (SDF).

Though this was my last year of teaching, I made the SDF part of my introduction to each religion. For instance, in my opening remarks about Hinduism I mentioned we would be discussing a number of concepts such as Karma, Reincarnation, and Moksha. While I would be explaining these concepts to the class as I believed a Hindu would, based on my experience and reading, we could probably find a Hindu somewhere who would disagree with some aspects of what I was saying; and then we could find someone to disagree with him. Would that be because one of us was right and the others were wrong? No. Though any one of us could be in error on a matter of fact, as far as the correct meaning of beliefs and practices were concerned, we simply had different views on the subject. The fact my view was backed up by the textbook and our guest speaker did not mean any more than a difference of custom or interpretation, and that was OK and normal within the context of that religion. "See kids, there are many different points of view. There is not one Hinduism."

For the next religion we studied I wrote, "There is not one Buddhism." This became the organizing principle to explain everything we learned in the class. We studied central content and generalizations but the students understood (I hope) that each religion, as it was believed and practiced, had many different points of view and, except in the case of extreme outliers, or matters of fact, we could not judge the correctness of a person's beliefs. After all, their beliefs as members of that faith, are their personal beliefs and may not only differ more or less from the understanding of the person of the same faith living next door but, also and especially, across time and territory. Even with adherents of the Roman Catholic Church, where all tenets are clearly spelled out by hierarchical authorities, I have heard Catholics say, "Well, I don't agree with the pope on that."

Remembering the many speakers on each major religion, I brought to my classes over the years, and their often-differing points of view about the same religion, convinced me this understanding of religious belief and practice was correct. One year, a Muslim speaker told us it was not essential to pray at an exact time of day if you had a business meeting or other important event. You could make it up later and God would understand. A later speaker was adamant about the timing of prayer. One Christian speaker insisted those without a belief in the death and resurrection of Jesus, as the son of God, could not enter heaven, while another, a minister, said she believed we could not determine the answer to such questions and God would sort it out. She came close to saying there was no hell.

To pretend each or any religion is absolutely "one" in its convictions and has only one "right way" in its practices is to perpetuate an inaccuracy of the highest order. Yet statements by politicians and articles in the media often sound that way. When people whose minds are blinded by the Single Definition Fallacy hear inaccurate public remarks, all that sticks with them is the falsehood. The "There is not one way of thinking about religion" can help us all develop a more accurate mind set. If there is only one thing you remember from this book, please remember this.

7

FAITH AND THE GOD-LIKE FORCE

"It ain't what you don't know that gets you into trouble. It's what you know for sure that just ain't so."
- Mark Twain

Each Religion, if nothing else, claims to have an accurate view of reality. This idea is also shared with science. Science has shown many times our perceptions of the world are limited and reality is deeper than we can observe with our senses. The fact that science has occasionally been wrong does not bother scientists because self-correction is built into the scientific method. It is commonly believed the scientific process, over time, is leading us to a more accurate understanding of things as they really are.

There are those who say such scientific information, based on evidence and reasoning, is the only accurate source of knowledge. They are believers in what has been called Scientism. While sometimes used in a pejorative way, I like the term and feel it fits my atheist friends who feel religious "truths" are just a collection of fairy tales. Since science cannot prove the falsity of religion or the existence, or lack thereof, of God, Scientism, as many follow it, seems to me to also be a faith, a faith science alone has valid truths.

While many religions are able to coexist with scientific claims, some insist science's understanding of reality simply does not go far enough. Science must use empirical evidence, lots of math, and a rigorous method of reasoning to obtain its results. Religions, while usually not rejecting those tools outright, see the criteria of empirical knowledge alone as limited. In addition to occasional adherence to various interpretations of scripture, religions utilize a combination of faith, intuition, and personal experience as the ultimate criteria of knowledge, and the way this works varies from religion to religion and person to person.

Faith is the belief that something is true without sufficient empirical evidence to rationally deduce that truth. According to St. Paul, "Faith is to be sure of the things we hope for, to be certain of the things we cannot see." However, individuals have different levels of faith in different things and each individual's degree of faith can vary. Studies have shown that few people are able to maintain rock hard, unyielding, unquestioned, religious faith over a long period of time. For most people their faith graph would be like a sine curve of high faith, followed by a trough of doubt, followed by renewed faith, and so on.

Faith aside, scientific evidence for spiritual experiences is hard to come by. An interesting combination of science and faith can be found in *Proof of Heaven: A Neurosurgeon's Journey into the Afterlife*, by Eben Alexander. Alexander, a neurosurgeon and once the poster child for the "science is always right" point of view, had a near death experience while in a coma and came out of it transformed by what he says happened to him. He has now set up a non-profit to spread the word that there is a creative, loving, divine force in the universe. Sudden enlightenment, charlatan, or a brain malfunction anomaly? Which makes the most sense?

Like Alexander, many people, across all cultures and from ancient times to the present have claimed to have had mystical experiences they cannot explain rationally. Though this type of evidence is anecdotal, there are so many assertions it is hard to dismiss them out of hand. Author Barbara Ehrenreich, a long-time atheist, wrote a piece for The New York Times in which she described an experience she had as a teenager.

"There were no visions, no prophetic voices or visits by totemic animals, just this blazing everywhere. Something poured into me and I poured out into it... I felt ecstatic and somehow completed, but also shattered."

For years Ehrenreich thought she might have had a mental breakdown until she became aware of other cases like hers. Still an atheist, she now suggests the frequency of these moments may not be caused by a mental aberration but might be real, possibly an encounter with other forms of consciousness. With so much current and historical testimony involving various experiences with spiritual phenomena, it's hard not to believe something is happening to these people, but what? It seems facile to casually brush them all away as brain aneurisms or hoaxes.

Faith adherents cite intuition as giving them an internal validation that their beliefs and experiences are true. Intuition is an instinctive feeling of knowing that arises without the need for validating rational or empirical considerations. Based on intuition, we know something to be true as surely as we know we exist. Especially in Christianity, Islam, and Orthodox Judaism many have a strong faith that certain information contained in their respective scriptures is correct. Adherents believe these words and the interpretations they have either deduced or been taught, reflect a more accurate view of reality than science can ever find. In the absence of empirical evidence, their intuition confirms for them this is so.

Where does such steadfast faith come from? Why is it easy for some people to believe so deeply while those of other faiths or no faith can look at the same words and just not get it? In *The Faith Instinct: How Religion Evolved and Why it Endures*, Nicholas Wade asserts the attributes of religious belief have been so useful for human beings in an evolutionary sense it has become part of our genetic code. However, it developed, it seems to some degree faith is endemic in human nature; we simply have different views on when, where, and how to apply it and what value to give to it.

I have faith, for instance, my wife has never cheated on me even though I do not have sufficient empirical evidence to back that claim. After all, I cannot account for her whereabouts and activities for long stretches of time, except through what she tells me. However, it doesn't matter to me I don't have evidence; I believe my statement to be true.

Someone might call this wishful thinking and point out that while the vast majority of married couples also think this way, data shows there are cheating husbands and wives out there and naive spouses who are going to eventually be devastated. In such situations, their faith has clearly been misplaced. I feel sorry for those people and cannot explain how the faith they had in their mates could have been so wrong. Were they blind to the facts? My faith is not. I have a first-hand intuitive understanding of the person I married based on the 34 years we have been together. I know my understanding to be as true as anything in life can be. My intuition supports my faith in the relationship and provides a certainty that does not need other proof, even though I could cite numerous examples of her honesty and commitment to our life together. I am not wrong on this. As I think about it, I also cannot prove we do not all exist in the *Matrix* but I don't think we do and I don't need proof to make this assertion. Same deal with my wife. Does that sound like a religious faith? Not really religious of course, but faith nonetheless.

While there is an element of faith in Buddhism and Hinduism, they rely much less on belief in scripture or specific theology for their authenticity, even though they have that, but on personal intuition based on results and a tradition of those who have achieved a deep mystical/meditative awareness. The Buddha, for example, said not to follow his teachings if you find what he advises does not work for you. Your intuition about your situation before you discovered Buddhism, compared to the changes in your life after you have followed the Buddha's teachings, will give you an answer to that question. To someone on the outside, this might seem to be a subjective, slippery way of knowing, but to you, based on your intuition, it probably seems spot on. Even though Hinduism is deeply tied to Indian culture, it provides many different ways to approach spiritual development and tells us progress is measured by actions not beliefs. Zen Buddhism and Taoism, focus on an intuitive understanding of reality, based on introspection and meditation, as the best way to see things as they really are. There is a belief here that the intuitive heart (in a sense) can understand reality more clearly than can the rational mind.

Does the God-like Something Exist?

It seems clear either a "God-like sort of something" exists or "It" does not. What is not clear is the answer to the question. Blaise Pascal, in the 16th century, said, "If there is a God, He is infinitely incomprehensible, since, having neither parts nor limits, He has no affinity to us. We are then incapable of knowing either what He is or if He is." I like that response even though it doesn't really answer the question. However, that may be the best we can do. After all, when we talk about things existing, we are talking about just that, "things." We can know if things exist or do not exist since they are limited and physically definable. Through science, we can examine their qualities, measure them, and devise criteria to determine if they are real or not.

Unfortunately, God (including related notions such as the Great Spirit, Brahman, Nirvana, Tao, Logos, etc.) is not empirically knowable given what we have to work with. Physically measurable properties only apply to physical things. If God/Brahman/Tao/Nirvana exists as a non-physical something (which every religion I know agrees with), that Something cannot be measured in a way to either prove or disprove Its existence. God may exist in a form or dimension or nature that is absolutely inscrutable to the human mind and senses. After all, our perceptive and cognitive abilities evolved in this world and there may be other types of reality in the universe.

Therefore, God, at the present time at least, does not exist in any way we can empirically understand. Our view on God's existence and definition, then, can only be a matter of personal opinion, intuition or faith.

With that rather indefinite definition, let's move forward to see how, given their own internal differences of opinion, religions try to answer these questions.

PART 2
THE RELIGIONS

8

HINDUISM
THERE IS NOT ONE HINDUISM

"Creation is only the projection into form of that which already exists."
- Bhagavad-Gita

To those raised outside the culture of India, Hinduism can seem confusing. If we try to understand Hinduism there are so many different faces that present themselves as "genuine Hinduism" in the 1.2 billion people who identify as Hindu, that the casual seeker might not know what to select as the genuine article. But the mistake is not in looking, but in trying to find one belief, one practice, and one way of dealing with the spiritual. Western religions are often all about the "one true belief," and the right worship or action to get the seeker into the correct relationship with God. Sometimes in different denominations of Western religions, you can find the idea that the particular beliefs or actions of "my" faith are correct and all others are wrong. Applying this sort of mindset to a study of Hinduism would be very frustrating because, from the Hindu point of view, there are many ways to understand the spiritual, many ways to view God, and a wide variety of methods to increase one's spirituality. The idea of one right belief and one correct practice for religion would be confusing to a Hindu because he knows perfectly well that people are different, and in a spiritual search the goal is not to find the one "Right" answer but the answer that best suits you. In this religion, as in most eastern religions, it is your actions in life, not your particular beliefs that count.

I have related the story about my introduction to Hinduism as a teenager, so if you recall the level of confusion and misinformation that incident laid down with me you might appreciate the difficulty I had in trying to understand Hinduism when it came time to teach it to a class.

With all of the gods and rituals and ceremonies and points of view in Hinduism, I was having a hard time identifying a central organizing principle. The grand diversity of Hindu practices still left me very confused. Fortunately, early on, I was able to find a guru (a guide to spiritual understanding, a very Hindu concept). Sometime during the first year I taught World Religions, a parent gave me the phone number for Dr. Vilas Nene, who was to lead me from the confusion of my ignorance. Dr. Nene, an engineer for Mitre Corporation, looked at his religion from a scientist's point of view and helped me to see the logical, philosophical side of Hinduism. From that first year until my last year of teaching no one took better notes, asked more questions, or learned more than I did from Dr. Nene. I applied his method to other religions and found that they became much more comprehensible when seen through the logical eyes of the scientist/philosopher. His book, *The Logic of Hindu Thought*, a more detailed version of the lecture he delivered to my classes every year, is an excellent guide.

Hindu Thought

In order to understand Hinduism from outside the culture of India it helps to consider Hindu thought as the result of centuries of accumulated philosophical disputation. For thousands of years Hindu thinkers pondered the deepest questions, meditated, responded to the views of those who came before them, and left their own thoughts for the consideration of later generations. They asked, "Given the world as it seems to us and a few logical assumptions about the most ultimate questions, what can we rationally say to be true?" and "What is the correct dharma (principles of the spiritual state of existence) and how can I best apply this dharma to my life?" At its core, Hinduism, if it is nothing else, is an ongoing, evolving, search for answers that make sense. Hindu thinkers looked around the world at everything they could perceive and decided to begin with the assumption that the universe is rational and is ruled by laws. After all, if everything is totally random and stuff just happens, there is nothing to figure out. To begin the process of understanding those laws, they started with creation.

It is easier to comprehend the Hindu view if we compare it to a view that is more widely known here. How do the Abrahamic religions (Judaism, Christianity, and Islam) understand the creation of the universe? The traditional belief is that God existed before everything else as an unexplainable singular entity. For some reason, God decided to create everything that is not God. Essentially, God said Shazam! (or whatever God did) and the whole universe was created at once from nothing. Then there existed both God and God's creation and the process of developing life, and everything else began in the way God wanted it to happen. The views of religious folks differ as to whether God's process was the six-day literal biblical variety, a God motivated type of evolution, or something else.

Western religions believe we have a dualistic universe containing God (singular undefinable entity) and God's creation (us, stars, worms, etc.) that are not to be confused with each other in any way.

Some believe that every action on earth is ordained by God while others believe that God gave us free will, set the system in motion and rarely, if ever, interferes except in the most subtle ways. However, the actual separation of God and his creation is thought to be complete and absolute.

This theory would not have made sense to the Hindu thinkers. Early on, they accepted the notion that things like the physical universe cannot be created from nothing, just by wishing them into existence. Rather, they thought it more logical that Brahman (the Hindu term for God, the highest reality- I use both words interchangeably) in creating the universe, transformed his own spiritual essence into the physical universe that we are all part of now. The primary difference between this and the Western view is that Brahman (God) was the raw material used to create the universe. Everything in the universe (us, stars, worms, etc.) is a manifestation of Brahman from Brahman. There is no real separation between God and his creation but a transformation of the same God stuff from a spiritual aspect to a physical form. Matter was not created from nothing, but from God. Brahman is both outside of creation and an intimate part of it. Every particle of the universe is then, in some form, Brahman.

With thanks to Dr. Nene I will use one of his favorite examples to illustrate this transformation. First, I show you that I have a giant bag of cotton. Then I turn my back and then show you I now have a big pile of thread. Then I turn my back and then show you I have a shirt. You say, "Hey man, what happened to the cotton and what happened to the thread?" I say, "Big dummy, the cotton became the thread and the thread became the shirt. The cotton is still in the shirt, it just looks different and you did not see me process it from one state to another." You say, "Oh."

So, Brahman is the basis of everything that exists in the universe. This means, of course, that at the highest level of existence, there is nothing that is not Brahman. If things seem different from each other, that is only part of the illusion of the transformation process. For example, I open my hand wide facing you. With the other hand, I hold a book half way up my fingers so you can only see four pink finger tops above the book. If you were new and focused only on the book and the fingers, you might say it looks like there are four separate independent pink things sticking up over that book. But we both know that this perception would be an illusion, and that really, the fingers are four parts of one hand that is part of one person.

Likewise, there is no real separation between Brahman and Brahman's creation. The world, however, presents a day-to-day view that contradicts this. All we usually see are the pink finger tops. "Hey look, there are four separate little pink things." This is *Maya*, the illusion of separation that life seems to show us.

It's not that the world doesn't actually exist, it does. But our belief, based on our limited perceptions, that the physical world is the ultimate reality is the illusion. We have forgotten that ultimate reality is the spiritual reality, that we are spiritual beings created from Brahman and, ultimately, everything is Brahman. Hindus would agree with Tielhard de Chardin's statement, "We are not human beings having a spiritual experience, but spiritual beings having a human experience."

As limited human beings, we can attempt to understand Brahman in two ways. The first is Brahman Nirguna. This is the limitless, unknowable, incomprehensible, actual Brahman, or force. Is it like a person or is it like energy? Both and neither? The essence of the creator of hundreds of billions of galaxies is far beyond the grasp of our wildest imaginings, and probably too subtle and intimate to understand. As when contemplating other names for the unexplainable, the Tao, God, Nirvana, etc., we just do not know. The second concept of Brahman, Saguna, is our understanding uses the hints and bits and pieces of Brahman that we think we can perceive and, in a small way, comprehend in the world around us. This is where the many Hindu gods come in.

The idea behind the gods is that since Brahman is infinitely multifaceted, we can slice off a facet of Brahman and assign that quality to a deity. Each deity, in the multitude of Hindu gods and goddesses, represents and helps us focus on some aspect of Brahman. These often shows up in stories and mythology. So Brahman is our universe, and every physical, intelligible and unintelligible thing in it. The ways we are able to understand Brahman are only limited by our imagination. There are many, many gods and goddesses to fill this void. More on this later.

9

IT'S KARMA BABY

"When you see a good person, think of becoming like her/him. When you see someone not so good, reflect on your own weak points."
- Confucius

How do we human beings fit into the big picture from the Hindu point of view? What is our role in this great cosmic creation drama? In both Christianity and Islam, the most prevalent idea of the human role in God's process is roughly this: God created our souls because he loves us, and put each soul into a human body sometime at or after conception. We live our lives as best we can, given our personal and environmental assets and liabilities, using our free will to make decisions. When we die, our life is judged, based on some calculus of actions and beliefs, and our soul is then assigned to another realm. It may be either the happy joyous one, heaven, or the painful, sad one, hell, to spend the rest of existence. Roman Catholics, who are not perfect but not too bad, can also have a delayed holding pattern in Purgatory. While some believe judgement occurs at a certain "end of times," the result is basically the same.

In terms of God's fairness, a Hindu thinker might ask how people born into wildly different circumstances and situations can be judged relative to each other? One lucky person might be born into a wealthy, loving, family, have a sweet life, unperturbed by major issues, easily live an upright and virtuous life, and die calmly and peacefully. Another person might be born into horrible conditions with extreme environmental, physical or psychological limitations that cause them continuous struggle and strife, where they never see anything but the worst side of life. This person might make many questionable decisions, and have few opportunities to know or practice virtue.

In the West, the religious response to this question is usually some version of "God will sort it out." After all, it is argued, God knows each person's situation, and he knows the events and processes that went into our life decisions. God will be the judge. There is also a second, Calvinistic version of this theory, which explains that all humans, being sinners, actually deserve the "negative" judgement. The fact that God happens to choose a few of us to get the "positive" judgement that we don't deserve, is God's business and inherently inscrutable. These days most people in Western religions like the first version best.

Hindu thinkers would reject both of these theories. First, they reject the concept of an eternal hell as not making sense if we are dealing with a loving, rational God. Then they would look at the great diversity of people and situations. If the rules of the universe are rational it is absolutely unfair to judge people in different situations against each other. In one life, why should one person be born in a situation to suffer while another lives the good life? Is God just messing with us? The Hindu thinkers searched for an answer that would be logical and would explain, in a way that made sense, the great variation of quality and opportunity in human experience.

Our existence, they said, is part of a grand cosmic process. Brahman has transformed into all of the separate things of the universe. One of those things is my soul (atman). While my body (the one I have now, for instance) only lives one lifetime, my soul, being spiritual and not physical, is immortal and acquires a new body sometime after the end of a life. Then it is born again. It is that soul that is the real me since the body I have in any particular lifetime is only its temporary vehicle. My body is a particular collection and arrangement of whatever it is that makes up atoms. A blade of grass is also just a particular collection and arrangement of the same stuff. Eventually my bodily collection will dissipate and become parts of other collections. So will the blade of grass. This process is a manifestation of Brahmin.

There are a variety of theories to explain soul progression. I like this one: Souls evolve slowly and naturally through a mineral state, a plant state, and an animal state, until reaching the human state. Through many successive transformations, a soul advances automatically to a more complicated, sophisticated, and eventually, self-aware human state where free will comes into play. Hindus believe the time on earth for each soul does not begin and end with one bodily birth and death as Western religions believe, but through a process called *Samsara* or reincarnation, a continuing existence through many births, lives, and deaths. Our ultimate goal is to achieve Moksha, to be liberated from this cycle of reincarnation, and return to God.

The quality or nature of our future lives is determined by the actions of our soul, during this life and our past lives. This is Karma, the spiritual law of cause and effect. We learn in physics that for every action, there is a reaction. As it is in the physical world, this principle is said to also be true in the spiritual one, and ensures that the actions of every lifetime are reflected in the design, and details, of later lives. In other words, the great variety of human situations we observe in the world, are not happening the way they are because God is rolling dice with each of our lives, arbitrarily making some of us suffer while others are happy. The actions of our past lives, based on our free will at that time, have determined the sort of life we have now, which in turn, will help determine the quality and content of our future lives. God has provided us this opportunity to learn and advance, but is not responsible for any perceived injustices and troubles we might encounter. We are.

Reincarnation

To the Hindu thinkers, this hypothesis makes a lot of sense, but to folks brought up with Western ways of thinking, it takes some getting used to. To see this more clearly, let's hypothesize that each of us is not really just the body we see in the mirror when we drag ourselves out of bed each morning. That is the body we have for this life, but we didn't have it for our last life, and we won't have it for the next one. We have had many bodies through many lives, and it helps us to understand that any one of those bodies (including the one we have now) is not who we really are, any more than the costume I wore for Halloween was the real me. Our current body is a temporary identity, a temporary physical existence. Our soul is who we really are. Just as we go through the many days of our physical lives, the soul goes through many lifetimes. Our actions in our past lives have, through the law of karma, determined the parameters of our life right now, and our actions in this life will set the stage for our future lives. But, if true, what is the point of this process? Why is it happening and what can we do to control it?

There are many views on this. It is thought by some, that our soul is drawn through this process of many lives by, first, an instinctive, and later, a volitional desire to reunite with Brahman. Remember, our souls and everything in the physical world, is a transformation of God. Given that, it is as if God is a magnet of love and perfection that deeply impels us over lifetimes to return. This gives us an internal compass that leads us to emulate the qualities of God in our lives. Each soul, in striving to return to Brahman should, ideally, live a life that ultimately reflects the qualities of Brahman, i.e., to act more God-like, which is the goal of almost every religion. The life decisions that lead us in this direction can be found by following what many consider to be the best way for a human to live: a life of virtue, compassion and selflessness. Your soul, as a transformation of Brahman, is trying to learn its way back. The problem we have in doing this, is that the distractions of the world, combined with our undisciplined free will, lead us to often make selfish decisions that do not lead us to God. Quick advancement through fewer lifetimes is more easily said than done.

Free will can provide opportunities to make bad decisions but it can also help us to accelerate our spiritual progress. In any pre-human state, progress must happen slowly and automatically, because the entity has either no choice, or instinct alone, as a basis for actions, yielding very few real opportunities to make decisions. Somewhere along the way, in the development of the soul, the use of will comes into play more and more. The very good thing about our human state is that advancement can happen at a rapid rate, because we humans can rationally understand our situation and focus our will to bring about good results, if we want to.

While many Western students are fascinated by the whole karma/reincarnation concept, since it is an exotic alternative view of reality they have never before considered, I have been asked a lot of practical questions. For instance, someone always asks, "Why can't I remember my past lives?" In response I ask, "Can you remember what you were doing a year ago today?" "Well, no." "Then how do you think you can remember events from a past life?" I read once that the lack of memory from one past life to the next is a blessing, because if you remembered everything that happened then, it would mess up this life. Imagine you remember that Timmy from work pushed you off a cliff two lifetimes ago, and you decide to get back at him by pushing him off a cliff today. Explain that to the judge at your trial. It would be like trying to act in a play today, but you fumble your performance because you keep remembering all of the lines from the previous plays you were in. If I was designing this system, I would probably make sure that past life memories were very hard to access.

However, there are people who claim that evidence of past lives exists, and that hypnosis can induce past life memories. The late Dr. Ian Stevenson, who was Carlson Professor of Psychiatry at the University of Virginia, published *Children Who Remember Previous Lives: A Question of Reincarnation*, after forty years of studies. To the best of my knowledge, science does not give afterlife theories a lot of credence. However, I once attended a so-called past-life regression, which involved hypnotizing a person to bring out past life memories. Later, I spoke to the person who had been hypnotized. She seemed convinced that the things she had described from a past life had not been made up by her, but had come into her mind just as memories would. I don't think she was lying, but was she mistaken? You can make your own decision about such claims.

10

WORKING THE KARMIC SYSTEM

"How people treat you is their karma; how you react is yours."
- Wayne Dyer

Humanity's big problem, from the Hindu point of view, is that even though we are from Brahman (God), and in an ultimate sense, are Brahman, we don't act like Brahman. We perceive ourselves as single egos living our lives as totally separate individuals in a world that is only physical. I take what I see in the mirror each morning as the sum total of what is me- one body, one personality, one life. My ego, right now, defines who I think I really am. Focusing only on this view of reality, all of our day-to-day decisions revolve around what makes sense in our individual lives, but only for this lifetime. We forget to see the big picture. We forget that everything that exists is a transformation of God; so all humans and plants and animals and galaxies are God. We forget that who we perceive ourselves to be in this life is not really who we are.

How would our present lives function if we thought we existed only for today, forgetting that we have had many days in the past and will, hopefully, have many days in the future? In that case, our friends would see us making decisions that do not make sense and they would try to find out what was wrong with us. They would want to help us to realize that life was not for one day but many days. Hinduism suggests that life is not just one life, but many lifetimes.

When we refuse to act like God, we do things in our lives that kick in the law of Karma and set up a situation, after we die, to boot us into another life to learn the lessons we have flubbed in this one. This could be interpreted to mean that we are trapped in nearly endless cycles of reincarnation. At times in Hindu history, many people have felt this way and have reflected their belief by adopting a "who cares about anything, it's all hopeless" attitude. But, as I understand it, this system should not reflect such a fatalistic point of view.

K-12 Reincarnation

Some of those who believe in reincarnation look at the multitude of lives we have had, and see the difficult aspects of each new life as punishment for the mistakes we have made in past lives. Some believe if we are horribly bad, we will be reincarnated as an animal or a bug and have to work our way up again. Being a teacher, I think we won't have to worry about the punitive nature of that point of view. To me, it makes more sense that each life becomes an opportunity to learn new lessons. My basic teacherly assumption is that we all make mistakes, but do we learn from our errors or do we do the same dumb thing over and over again? Since the goal of the karmic process is to achieve Moksha or liberation, we reach that goal when we have learned all of the lessons that life (or many lives) can teach us, and there is no longer a reason to return.

So how do we get to that point? Again, from a Hindu point of view, God is not in a hurry. We can take as many lifetimes as we want to complete this process, since our advancement is not based at all on what we believe, but how we act. It helps me to think of the entire process as a kindergarten through twelfth grade school, but with lifetimes substituted for each school year. In this school, however, each of us is free to pick our own area of study and to determine how fast we wish to proceed to graduation, through many lives or fewer, rather than advancing with our age cohort.

We can spend many lifetimes, metaphorically speaking, playing in the sand box and swings in kindergarten, which, as everyone knows, is a lot of fun. At some point, however, we will probably get tired of sandbox and look for something else to do. Eventually we learn how the school works and that we can continue to play around, or we can strive to learn the harder lessons. However, there is nothing inherently wrong with just playing around. It is believed that living for wealth, pleasure, fame or power, even over many lifetimes, when done ethically, are simply stages we may have to work through to get those desires out of our systems.

Each life, then, is like a karmic classroom where lessons of what we need to learn to become more God-like are presented to us through experiences. How we respond to those challenges helps determine our progress and the set of lessons in future lives. Clearly, if we are just reacting to each life in a mindless, unthinking way, the odds of our making real progress are lessened. However, if we apply ourselves, live ethical lives, meditate and make good decisions, we will greatly accelerate our spiritual growth. There are students in every school who, despite their teachers' exhortations, never look beyond today to see the long-term value of their education. How many more years would it take those students to graduate if they simply stayed in school on their own schedule and at their own pace? Better students come to understand the value of school, hard work, and learning their lessons to get through in a reasonable amount of time, to prepare themselves for greater advances after graduation.

It is clear that graduation comes more quickly for those who are focused. And what is graduation in the school of karma and reincarnation? That is when all of the lessons are learned and there is no need to go back to school, no need to come back for another life. Our soul is allowed or is able to slip the bonds of separation from God. Moksha. What are we like in that existence? God knows.

The End of the Road

Hindu thinkers believe that eventually, way off in the future, Brahman will bring the universe to an end and then, when Brahman wants to, will recreate it and start over. They believe that existence really consists of an unending series of creations and destructions, over many billions of years. The universe, in that sense, has always existed. This coincides nicely with the Big Bang theory. Scientists believe the universe started with the "big bang" about 14 billion years ago, continues to expand, and has a number of possible fates. I think the two most popular are that it may continue expanding on and on for many billions of years, until it eventually runs out of fuel, fizzles out and ends as a lot of cinders floating further away from each other. Or, at some point in the expansion, if there is enough total mass, it will cease expanding and begin contracting. Eventually, as contraction continues, there will be a "Big Crunch" as the universe may return to the sort of singularity that led to the Big Bang. Hindu thinkers, who also postulated a "Crunch" like theory, felt that once the "Crunch" happened the process of creation will begin again, part of an unending cycle. While there are additional scientific hypotheses about the fate of the universe, to the best of my knowledge, science has not yet decided which of them is most likely.

This is the way Hindu thinking is clear to me. There are undoubtedly Hindus who have different views or would disagree with this explanation. The great thing about being a Hindu thinker, though, is that everyone can take a shot at it. The goal is to come up with an explanation that is rational, logical, and fits the facts of the world as we know them. Beyond some basic assumptions, all thinkers are looking for the answer that makes the most sense, and there are many, many schools of thought in Hindu philosophy. A lot of ideas are shared in a syncretistic way. You might be discussing different views on these questions with another person, and they might really disagree with you. But while such disagreement might make them illogical from your point of view, it doesn't make them evil or a sinner. The reason is that in Hindu thinking, ultimately, the details of what you believe don't matter. The spiritual system is what it is, whether we understand it correctly or not. What matters most is how you act, lifetime after lifetime.

11

HINDUISM THE RELIGION

"Indian religion has always felt that since the minds, the temperaments and the intellectual affinities of men are unlimited in their variety, a perfect liberty of thought and of worship must be allowed to the individual in his approach to the Infinite."
- Sri Aurobindo

There is a famous Ben Franklin saying, "Experience is the best teacher," which has a lesser-known ending, "but a fool will learn from no other." Following Hindu thinking, we have the opportunity to go from lifetime to lifetime experiencing and learning from all that a wide variety of lives have to offer. After all, in many ways, for many people, life is fun. Also, there is nothing inherently wrong with being slow about our spiritual progress since, once again, "God is not in a hurry." But at some point, it is thought, we begin to realize that the temporary ephemeral nature of life on earth is not ultimately satisfying. Perhaps we begin to wonder what our many lives really mean, and what the ultimate goal of our existence actually is.

If, at some point, we decide we want to focus on spiritual progress, what do we do?

This is where Hinduism the religion comes in. The word "Hinduism" is actually a western label for what is best described as a vast umbrella covering many different ways of expressing religion, based on the history and culture of India. With tremendous energy, excitement, beauty, and variety, Hinduism provides help, assistance, lessons, and encouragement on our karmic path. Today there are at least ten major schools of thought, and the active worship of many gods. What all of these expressions have in common is their existence in Indian history and culture, and a general belief in the principles described here. Realizing that human beings have different personalities and respond best to different motivations, Hinduism provides several different ways to help us progress spiritually. Generically they are called yogas, because each one involves some degree of discipline and commitment.

The first, most visible, and overwhelmingly most popular way, both in Hinduism and throughout the world, to feel closer and connected to God, is Bakhti yoga. This is a yoga that uses the emotions and involves loving God through worship services and prayer. Many people, regardless of their religion, find deep meaning and comfort in the practice of traditional worship-based rituals. Hinduism does not skimp on this. Since there is a vast Hindu mythology with many gods and goddesses, each one reflecting a different way to understand Brahman, there are a great variety of ways in which they are worshipped. This includes many different types of individual and group devotional ceremonies or pujas. The thinking here is that our love and devotion to a god will translate into better, more compassionate actions on our part.

The question is sometimes asked whether Hinduism is monotheistic or polytheistic. Certainly, with so many gods the easy answer is polytheistic. But that would be incorrect. As Dr. Nene explained to me, the answer is monistic. God is all. But, if our intent is to have a devotional, loving relationship with God, how can we do that since God is so ineffable and indescribable? The God of the whole universe is really too big and abstract to focus on. Hindu's find that assigning a particular quality of God a name and a personality rooted in mythology helps to concentrate our attention on the aspects of God represented by that god or goddess. Most Hindu's worship through the image of a god or goddess to connect with the facet of Brahmin that God represents. (See chart showing some of the most popular gods and goddesses).

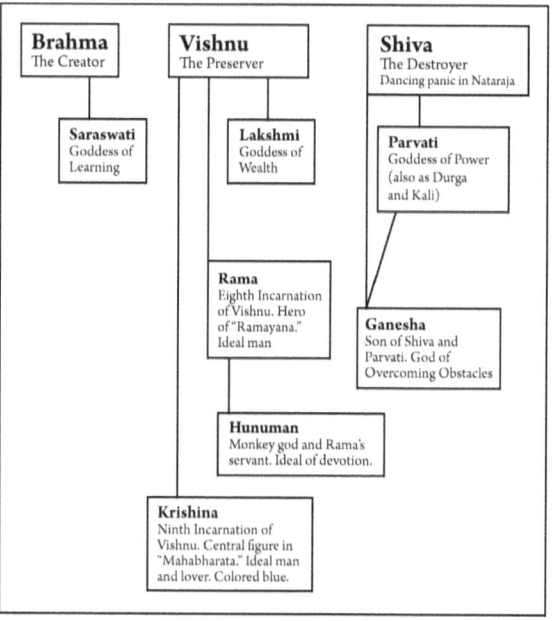

For instance, I have a picture of the goddess Saraswarti on the wall by my desk. Among other things, Saraswarti is the goddess of teachers, students and learning. Looking at her picture makes me think of how I will try to be the best teacher I can be, since this is what she represents to me. If I was Hindu, I might do a daily devotional service at home, or weekly at a temple, that would help to reinforce what I want to accomplish. I would be asking God, through the aspect represented by Saraswarti, to help me become a better teacher. If I was Hindu, she would be my deity. My goddess has meaning for me, but what she means to anyone else is beside the point. If she works for me and helps me accomplish my goals or to be a better person, more God-like if you will, that's what counts.

Many Hindus will pray to the elephant headed god Ganesha before starting new tasks or projects, since he is the god identified with that sort of help. If I did that too, it would not take anything away from my "goddess" because I know that all of these gods and goddesses are facets of the one God, Brahman, who is everything anyway. So, as Hindus worship their many gods, they are worshipping different aspects of the one God. Of course, given their diversity of beliefs, there are Hindus who believe that the gods are real beings, created by Brahman for somewhat the same purpose as some Western religions believe angels were created. Whether this is true or not doesn't ultimately matter. Whatever the vehicle we use to get there, the goal is to find a way to connect with God, in the way that works best for us.

In a like manner, many Christians focus on the image of Jesus as an easier, more personal way to approach God. Catholics often pray to Mary and both Catholics and Orthodox Christians utilize a wide variety of saints (often based on occupation or situation) to intercede with God for them. It is believed that when petitioned, the saints will pray for us. When praying before a cross, crucifix, picture or statue, no one is worshiping that physical object, but is using it as an icon to direct their thoughts and emotions through the image to help them connect with Jesus/God/or a saint. Using this focus to become more Christ-like, i.e., a better person, is another example of Bhakti yoga. Hindus are using the same process and have their gods and rituals as a method to help focus on an aspect of God. It helps humans to take God on in bite size pieces, and frankly almost anything that has meaning to us could be used to make this connection. I have a friend who feels the most spiritual when he is alone in the wilderness. You could focus on a blade of grass with the thought that this too, is a transformation from God, and use that realization to advance your spiritual consciousness.

One of the most interesting ideas in Hinduism for Westerners to consider is that you don't have to worship God, or any of these gods, to make spiritual progress. The worship is for your benefit, not God's, to help you focus on being a better person. Since spiritual progress is determined by the actions we undertake to reduce our karma, progress comes not from attending temple services or identifying with one God or another, but by how these activities encourage and lead us to perform good actions. Certainly, there is a belief that worship helps bring about such behavior, but not everyone likes religious ceremonies and rituals or responds well to them. For those folks, Hinduism provides other ways to progress.

12

WAYS TO GOD

"I have learned so much from God that I can no longer call myself a Christian, a Hindu, a Muslim, a Buddhist, a Jew."
- Hafiz

Besides Bhakti yoga, Hinduism suggests several ways to get closer to God. For instance...

Jnana yoga involves following a reflective, intellectual, path to understanding, which might involve learning about religious scriptures and commentaries, thinking, discussing, or philosophizing about finding the source of existence. This is not a casual activity but a serious, focused attempt to find ultimate reality through a rational process. A hypothesis is laid out and the mind is used to track the answer to its source. Jnana Yogis report finding "the infinite Self that underlies one's transient finite self." There are not a lot of people who can give the time to or have the interest in such deep and serious work, but for those who do, Hindus believe the spiritual results are very rewarding.

Karma yoga is the path to God through work. Yes, you can find God on the job. Work is one of the most significant aspects of the human condition, and can bring us income, satisfaction, and recognition. In this path, a person would work with the sincere mindset that she was doing it not for her own profit or aggrandizement, but for God. Getting beyond the ego opens the worker to approach each task not as their finite selves, but as their infinite selves. She will be able to find and identify with the self that is below our outer mask. A good example of this might be the great value found at auctions for genuine Shaker furniture. The most influential leader of the Shaker faith Mother Ann Lee, instructed followers to "Put your hands to work and your heart to God." Furniture and other crafts were produced with God in mind, not profit or pride. You don't skimp on materials or workmanship if you are making this end table for God.

Raja yoga

Regular meditation is highly recommended, in both Hinduism and Buddhism, as a great way for everyone to make spiritual progress, though many who meditate do it for its own benefits, not for any religious purposes. The goal is to try to clear the mind of distractions and to reach a state where we are able to be, to watch thoughts go by but not be a part of them. It is not hard to learn how to do this, but the major difficulty is trying to calm our "monkey" minds that always seem to have lots of activity going on. Success in meditation, however, is about the experience, not any particular goal. If I approach meditation in a Western mindset, the way I would approach preparing myself over six months to run a marathon, with goal points that must be checked off by this or that date, I will be very disappointed. However, if I approach it the way I might approach a habit of long walks, so that even though I know this is good for me and will increase my long-term health, that is not why I do it. My daily goal is to enjoy the walk. I have no immediate expectation, but if I think about it at all, I imagine the long-term effects will be good. Meditation is said to make us calmer, maybe see things in our lives more clearly, and perhaps understand the world and our fellow man just a little bit better.

Then there are those, through discipline and with guidance, who are able to go much deeper in meditation, practiced here as an arduous psychological self-experiment requiring great effort. More like a full-time job, when deeply engaged, this will hopefully lead to a mystical awareness of the true self that lies below. This is Raja Yoga where the self drops out entirely and there is only focus on "something being known." This is where words fail, and we can only substitute poetry from the *Upanishads*, "That verily, That thou art."

This variety of ways to approach spiritual advancement are meant to accommodate people's different personalities and inclinations. You can pick one or any combination, and later, switch to suit changes in your life and interests over time. Given your good ethical actions, no one needs to judge your intensity or devotion because the results are the product of your own efforts, and the only measure comes from your actions. From this perspective, one could reasonably say that everyone is a Hindu. A Muslim devoutly praying, a Roman Catholic at confession, a Hindu conducting a puja to Krishna, or a Wiccan participating in a coven ritual, if each is striving for good ethical lives, all are making spiritual progress through their rituals. Even an atheist who doesn't believe any of this religious nonsense, but who is trying to be a better person, will die one day, find out she was wrong about religion, and will reincarnate based on the Karmic actions in her life. It doesn't matter what she believed, or whether she was right or wrong about her beliefs, because the only real measure is her actions.

Scripture

If you really want to dig into the primary sources of a religious belief system, you should read some of its scriptures. Hinduism does not disappoint in that category, having vast collections of religious literature that range from the adventures of the gods in comic book editions, to profound discussions on the nature of existence. My favorite is the *Bhagavad Gita*, which can be read from start to finish in a few hours, takes a long time to think about. In this story, just as a battle as is about to begin, the famous warrior Arjuna has his driver pull their chariot out ahead of the ranks so he can survey the opposing armies. Seeing friends and relatives on both sides, he becomes despondent and doesn't want to fight. Little does he know that his charioteer is really the god Krishna in disguise. The conversation that ensues about life, death, God, and duty is fascinating, informative, and to the point. As a portion of the much larger *Mahabharata*, the *Bhagavad Gita* is a compelling story that lays out many of the ideas of modern (last 2000 years) Hinduism. There are also excellent teaching and learning stories in another set of readings, the *Upanishads*, which get to the heart of Hindu thinking.

The *Vedas*, the most ancient scriptures going back more than 4000 years, were memorized by priests and passed on for generations, before being written down. While many Hindus give the *Vedas* the greatest respect as the spiritual core and source of Hindu beliefs, they have less connection to modern Hinduism. The religion described in the Vedas served tribes of Indo-European herders and raiders, as they moved through, and eventually settled in India. This religion seems more like the polytheistic practices of the Greeks and Romans, focusing on the worship of distinctive individual gods and goddesses with strict rites, rules, and a controlling priestly caste, the Brahmins. Because of this, scholars often refer to this earliest incarnation of Hinduism as Brahmanism. While there are hints of the Monist, understanding of God in the Vedas it is hard for the outsider to see. Somewhere along the way in its historical development, as the Indo-Europeans settled down and found agriculture more profitable than cattle and raids, India became an advanced society with growing cities and civilization. During this process, the ancient polytheism began to change and all those gods and goddesses were seen as aspects of the one, not as separate, distinct, entities.

Purpose of Existence

I remember the catechism we used when I was in first or second grade in Catholic school. In a very early section, in a question and answer format, it asked, "Why did God make us?" The answer was, "Because God loves us." This didn't make a lot of sense to me at the time because as I looked around my classroom, I saw lots of kids who I did not believe were particularly lovable. Why would God create them? Later Sister Bernadette mentioned that God had created us so we could worship and adore Him, which made even less sense. I considered myself pretty self-centered, but even I had enough of a balanced personality not to create beings just so they could hang around and worship me. That sounded pathetic. A friend suggested God was lonely and wanted to have people around to occupy his time. Nah. I'd been lonely at times, and was the God of the universe that bad off?

So why does everything exist, which it does, since, clearly, here we are? What could God have been thinking? I have always thought that if there is an answer to this question, it is either so deeply complex that we just don't have the brainpower to grasp it, or is so subtle, elegant, and simple that we just overlook it. The Hindu thinkers, considering the journey of reincarnation through lifetimes and what they had deduced about creation, came up with a very sublime answer. God does this spontaneous creation thing over and over because it is fun, it is sport, it is play. While I have to admit that I generally just give up when trying to figure out the motivations of God, this notion intrigues me.

This answer is simple, intellectually appealing, and rational. Brahman does this because it is fun. Living through the lives of billions of beings throughout the universe, for billions of years at a stretch, each one developing over lifetimes, must be endlessly fascinating even to God. It's what God does for amusement and, from the Hindu point of view, everything, including us, is ultimately derived from Brahman and will ultimately return. Maybe we are all playing a very big long term cosmic game and have just gotten so wrapped up in it we have forgotten that it is a game.

13

BUDDHISM
THERE IS NOT ONE BUDDHISM

"You only lose what you cling to."
- The Buddha

Buddhism was started by a man. Twenty-five hundred years ago he saw a world of suffering, from which there seemed to be no escape, and decided to do everything in his power to end that misery. Even though he was a prince, a husband, and a father, he left his kingdom, wife, and child to answer this question: How can suffering be ended?

What he reported discovering are not deeply complex theological answers, but explanations simple enough for the average person to clearly understand. Since his death, around 483 or 400 BCE (Scholars disagree as to exactly when he was born and died. The scriptures say he was 80.), those answers have spread around the world and have been interpreted in many different ways. What he said has been viewed liberally and conservatively, and how people understand and respond to his words in their religious practices and their daily lives is demonstrated with tremendous variety. His influence on the history of the world has been so great that he is universally known not by his name but his title: The Buddha, the enlightened one.

Buddhism can be a practiced as a philosophy of life, or it can become a many-layered religion, with heavens, hells, good and bad spirits, gods, and complex rituals and theology. At the simplest level, the story of Buddhism is the story of a man who felt that there was something not right about life, and decided to search out the causes and solutions for this problem. In a way, the Buddha was the original self-help master. His discoveries are meant for each of us to help solve the problems that come with life. If he had done this work in today's world, his findings might have ended up as a book, *Eight Steps to a Better You*. Oprah and Ellen probably would have interviewed him.

According to the traditional story (try the film, *Little Buddha*), the Buddha, Siddhartha Gautama, aka Shakyamuni (Sage of the Shakya clan) spent his early life as a pampered, sheltered prince in what is now Nepal. In what must be one of the classic child raising blunders of all time, his father, the local king, was determined to keep his son from all knowledge of suffering and death so that he would be the next king, and not a spiritual redeemer as had been earlier predicted by a soothsayer. I have always wondered what dad was thinking when he decided on this course, because he couldn't have set up a better situation to not get what he wanted. When Siddhartha eventually saw old age, death, and suffering, he was shocked with the realization that life was not the bowl of cherries as he had thought. He also realized, as a bright young Hindu man would, given a belief in reincarnation, that this suffering went on lifetime after lifetime after lifetime.

This is what he wanted to change. He wanted to discover how we humans could end this suffering by eliminating our seemingly endless reincarnation recycling. Siddhartha threw himself totally into this effort and tried various, sometimes harsh, spiritual disciplines to find the answer. The story is that one day, while meditating on a riverbank, he heard a music teacher on a passing boat speaking to his student about tuning his instrument. He said, "If you tighten the string too much it will break and if you make it too loose, it won't play."

This made sense and convinced him that some methods, such as extreme asceticism or a normal life, wouldn't work to solve the problem. One is too much and the other is too little. After years of effort, Siddhartha decided to meditate, sitting under a tree, until he reached enlightenment, which, according to the stories, he did. He called his system the Middle Way and spent the rest of his life teaching and preaching his philosophy and gathering followers who also spread his ideas. These followers, it is believed, scrupulously memorized everything the Buddha said, and passed it on orally for several hundred years, before it was finally written down.

His basic realization of the human condition is explained through his philosophical summary about life, the Four Noble Truths. Newer translations use the term "unsatisfactoriness" instead of suffering. That works for me too.

1. Life is suffering. Throughout most of world history and in most places, people would need no further explanation for this statement. Hunger, disease, injuries, and early death from a host of afflictions have been the lot of most folks. While there are almost always some happy and joyful moments in life, no one would have denied that, overall, an unsatisfactory life was the bottom line. However, there is more to this than physical suffering. For many of us who have access to generous quantities of food, shelter, clothing and medical care, the traditional idea of physical suffering does not necessarily resonate. While we understand the concept intellectually, our lives are generally devoid of frequent, gratuitous, physical suffering. However, suffering does not have to be physical but can also be mental. This is now understood as depression, alienation, angst and mental health problems, as described by both existentialist philosophers, and modern psychiatrists and psychologists. It can also be found in our concern that we humans might succeed in making our planet uninhabitable. These are more likely to be the primary sources of suffering in prosperous modern societies.

Suffering also arises from our clinging nature. One of the basics of Buddha's teachings is that nothing is permanent. There is no permanence because all things are in flux, and we and everything around us, are constantly changing. As a rule, we like things to stay as they are, but even before we get used to them, they shift again. We try to hold on to people, places, situations and objects as they are, but they always change. Sometimes the transition is fast, sometimes incredibly slow, but it is just as inevitable. Everyone and everything is not concrete permanent "things," but processes in motion. If we try to hold on to what is changing all of the time, we can't do it and that fills us with frustration and disappointment, i.e., suffering.

2. Suffering comes about because of desire. We are attracted to what we cannot have, and have aversion to things we cannot avoid. We want life to stay the same, or at least to adjust in the ways we want it too. We tend to see ourselves as the center of the universe and can be very selfish. Selfish desires can become limitless, and life can be pretty disappointing when we want and want. Even if we satisfy some of our desires, we immediately find new things to want. We are like a hamster in a wheel trying to get to our "goal," but never finding an end to our running. Our ego is one of the main motivators of our desires. So much of what we want is connected to our conception of who we are, and what we think we deserve, but are not getting. This generates annoyance and anger with how unfair life is. It is our unsatisfied desires that set up the karmic situations that keep bringing us back lifetime after lifetime. After all, from the reincarnation point of view, dying does not solve one's life problems; it just passes them on to our later lives.

3. Suffering can be ended by overcoming desire. Easy to say, hard to do. The Buddha says that if only we can rid ourselves of desire, our suffering will end. If we can control our ego and rid ourselves of those desires, we will not be discontented and exasperated with life. Unfortunately, we are saddled with lives that do not make that easy to accomplish. It is so easy to become caught up in life, that we treat all of our transient everyday desires as the "most important things" and bend our efforts to achieve them. It is really our ignorance of what is true, what is real, and what is in our long term best interest that keeps us blind to how we should act. However, if we can end our ignorance, we can learn how to beat desire. In the process of overcoming desire, we will have learned and applied all of the lessons we need, and will not need, to return for another life. There will be nothing to pull us back.

4. Desire can be overcome by following the Noble Eightfold Path (N8FP, explanation to follow). Even if we understand the Four Noble Truths intellectually, the habits of our lives, and the cultures we grow up in, do not provide us much leverage to make spiritual progress. However, the Buddha has left guidance for us. By applying the principles of the N8FP to our lives with discipline and industry, it is believed that we can make progress in eliminating desire. Not only will our current life be happier, but we will significantly reduce our number of rebirths. Instead of blindly wandering through lives filled with ignorance and greed, we will have a plan and a direction that will more quickly bring about the results we want.

Unsatisfactoriness (suffering)

Why is life so often unsatisfactory as the Buddha describes it? Some religions insist that we humans are all sinners, and messed up (through the actions of Adam and Eve) the chance we had to live in paradise. However, a few years ago I read *Why Buddhism is True*, by Robert Wright, who suggested an answer based on science that makes more sense. By the way, in explaining the title of the book, Wright says that he is not endorsing Buddhist metaphysical claims like reincarnation. However, he finds the Buddha's description of what ails us aligns closely with the findings of evolutionary psychology and, from his own experience, mindfulness meditation seems to help us straighten that out.

Any life form, in any given environment, has to find ways to reproduce successfully, if its species is going to continue to exist. Individual organisms, to reproduce successfully, have to compete with the environment and with other members of their own species. Natural selection will allow those who find ways to propagate their genes into the next generation to continue. Those who are not successful will not have descendants. Natural selection "rewards" the actions, beliefs, and mindsets of those whose actions make them successful gene spreaders, regardless of how they do this. These winning qualities are retained and passed on. There is no morality involved in this process, just success or failure. Most species that have ever existed are now extinct.

The evolution of the human mind was guided by natural selection over millions of years in this way. All of the actions, beliefs, habits of mind, ways of thinking, development of consciousness, feelings, emotions, and ways of seeing and understanding the world, developed in us because those qualities were successful at putting genes into the next generation. Natural selection did not help humanity become a paragon of rationality, virtue, happiness, or wisdom, just a successful gene spreader. We were not created perfect and messed up our big chance, or created flawed, we have been responding to the mindless evolutionary dictates of natural selection. Those who did not succeed, did not pass on genes. Our ancestors did, and Wright suggests, since evolution has not had enough time for us to adapt to the cultural changes of the world we live in today, our evolutionary operating system, which runs our minds and reactions, is not in sync with today's world. We receive stimuli from the world around us, but we respond using our ancient response system and it often doesn't work well. We react in an overly emotional way, we can't think clearly, we lose our temper, and we do something stupid. Wright does believe, through his personal experience, that mindfulness meditation, as recommended by the Buddha, will help us to control our minds, see situations more clearly, and reduce our ignorance and suffering.

14

THE NOBLE EIGHTFOLD PATH

"If with a pure mind a person speaks or acts, happiness follows them like a never-departing shadow."
- The Buddha

What is it we really want? The Buddha says we want to end our selfish, ignorant desires, replace them with unselfish goals and perceive life as it really is. This will make us happy. If we agree, we can follow the Buddha's Noble Eightfold Path (N8FP), his guidelines for happiness in life. The theory is, as we practice this discipline, following it becomes a natural part of our lives, and we gradually reduce *wanting* to follow it. Even though desire motivates us to begin, as we make the N8FP a part of our lives, it leads us to understand that cravings are not needed. In other words, as we mature "spiritually," there are fewer places for greed in our lives, and eventually it dies a natural death. When desire departs, there you are.

So, how does someone proceed if they want to follow the N8FP? The Buddha's directions are relatively straightforward and easy to understand, and despite different interpretations on how they should be applied, it would be hard to stray far from the spirit of his plan. The N8FP is not intended to be a step-by-step, eight-point program since, after the first few steps, they believe it can all be worked into life, more or less simultaneously. However, patience is cautioned to temper one's initial exuberance. As with most serious undertakings, improvement is said to come with time, practice, and dedication. For instance, someone who wants to run a marathon, and has not run competitively before, will not try to cover 26 miles on their first day of training. They will work gradually, over many months, to reach their goal. If they did try the whole marathon on the first day, they would end up laying on the road in complete agony, cursing the whole idea. So it is with the N8FP.

As a preliminary consideration before beginning this discipline, the Buddha suggests that we will be more successful if we surround ourselves with like-minded people. Think about the friends and acquaintances you spend most of your time with and how their influence can either help or hinder your efforts. Are these the sorts of folks who will be supportive of your spiritual goals or not? After all, it's hard to lose weight if you hang out with people who eat Twinkies and Ho-Ho's all day long, or to do well in school, if you are always with the students who don't do their homework. Find the ones who can support you.

The Noble Eight Fold Path

1. Right Knowledge- Understanding of the problem we face (suffering) and its cure
2. Right Aspiration- We must want to seek this goal and do it for the right reasons.
3. Right Speech- Truth and charity in our speech
4. Right Behavior- Selflessness and charity, including the Five Precepts- do not kill, steal, lie, or be unchaste (restraint for the married) or drink intoxicants (see a modern discussion of this in *For a Future to Be Possible: Buddhist Ethics for Everyday Life* by Thich Nhat Hanh).

5. Right Livelihood- Choose an occupation that promotes life and benefits others rather than one that destroys life or is selfish.
6. Right Effort- Willpower and appropriate timing. Developing skill, paying attention
7. Right Mindfulness- Alertness, self-awareness and self-analysis.
8. Right Concentration- Meditation.

Each of these steps has generated a wealth of commentary in both the ancient and modern Buddhist community, and there are plenty of books and web sites that can flesh these out in detail. Notice that the first two have to do with our mental state before we make any changes. Three through five have to do with how we live our lives in the larger community, and the last three focus on the proper working of our mind and will.

Those who have decided to follow this teaching as closely and sincerely as they can, really as a full-time job, usually become Buddhist monks. They give up family life in society and, either individually or in a group, work on understanding themselves, meditating, and often helping others through example, and by teaching and preaching. Those who buy into the basic Buddhist ideas, but are not ready to give up the day-to-day aspects of family, home, and work, incorporate those aspects they can, and are Buddhist lay people. Traditionally, the lay people hope to gain merit by supporting the monks and living virtuous lives so they can be reborn in a better life, or maybe in a life where they will be able to become monks.

An important part of gaining "salvation" is meditation. As was mentioned about Hinduism, meditation is an important part of the journey toward liberation in Buddhism too. Practitioners report that regular meditation makes them calmer, helps them understand life better, and leads to better personal and life decisions and actions. While there are many ways to meditate, there are three main types. Vipassana, is for psychologically minded folks involving mindfulness meditation; visual imagery, used by Tibetan Buddhists, which is said to be good for artistic personalities; and those methods used by Zen Buddhists, which include either passive observant meditation (Soto) or meditation to solve a Koan (Rinzai), said to be agreeable to the poetic mind.

This is the core of Buddhist teaching. Everything is changing and you have to work your way out. Meditate. There is much more to Buddhist thinking but, while not meaning to denigrate its value, it is primarily commentary and interpretation.

From the discussion above, it is clear why some critics see this teaching as "just" a philosophy and not a religion. After all, there is no mention of God (or gods), worship, rituals, beliefs, or theology (though many Buddhist sects offer these), and little that can be defined as a religion, in the Western sense. Some have said Buddhism is best understood as an "atheistic" religion. I can see why they might say that, but Buddhism does deal with the spiritual world and our afterlife by advising us on what needs to be done to halt our rebirths, which sounds religious to me. However, a creator God, especially as understood in the western religions, is definitely not part of the discussion. Buddhism deals with the human spiritual condition, but does not see that process as a subjective one, where success or failure depends on holding certain correct beliefs. Rather, Buddhists believe that our spiritual results come from what we do, and how we act, in a process that is as real and as natural as our breathing, or the working of the water cycle. The universe is a system, it works a certain way, and if we want to work with it, there are certain things we need to do. Want to run that marathon? Successfully? There are certain things you need to do, in the proper order, to prepare. Same thing here.

The Buddha said that it was a waste of time to try to figure out answers to all of the big questions I like to contemplate such as: What is the nature of the universe? What is the spiritual realm like? What is a soul, and where does it go after death? He felt our time would be much better spent working on our own salvation, rather than on questions that our knowledge of, or lack thereof, would have no impact on our results. The Buddha is said to have told the story of a man shot with a poisoned arrow who asks all sorts of questions that must be answered about the type of arrow, and who shot the arrow, what caste was he, what tribe was he from, what kinds of feathers it had, etc. before he will allow the arrow to be pulled out. Why would anyone need to know all of that, when what was really needed was to have the arrow removed?

15

THE BUDDHA'S TEACHINGS I
NO SELF/NO SOUL

"The sad part is the reminder that no matter how high you go in life, and no matter how many accolades you win, it's never enough. The desire for even more admiration races ahead."[1]
- David Brooks

The Buddha wanted us to use our minds to decide what was true and how we should live. He applied this rigorous rationalistic methodology even to his own teachings:

"Rely not on the teacher/person, but on the teaching. Rely not on the words of the teaching, but on the spirit of the words. Rely not on theory, but on experience. Do not believe in anything simply because you have heard it. Do not believe in traditions because they have been handed down for many generations. Do not believe anything because it is spoken and rumored by many. Do not believe in anything because it is written in your religious books. Do not believe in anything merely on the authority of your teachers and elders. But after observation and analysis, when you find that anything agrees with reason, and is conducive to the good and the benefit of one and all, then accept it and live up to it (according to the Kalama Sutta).

However, people are people and they want to know the answers to their questions, so, following is a discussion of a few Buddhist concepts that might help explain Buddhist ideas in more detail.

No Soul (or No Self) Concept

What is a soul? In the West, people generally think of a soul as created by God. Most would agree that it is a non-physical manifestation of the part of me that remains when my body dies, at the end of this life. Many believe that the soul contains the intellect, personality, and mind of the person. However, it is constituted, most believers would identify it as "the real me," as opposed to the "physical me." From the Hindu point of view, the idea of a soul is similar, but because of the belief in reincarnation, it is thought that the soul is maturing, growing, and developing over many lifetimes. It is still seen as the "real me," but has those many lifetimes to experience and learn from, rather than just this one. As I am the grown-up, in relation to the child who was me earlier in this life, a Hindu might see his soul in this life as more mature, in relation to his soul in an earlier life. From both points of view, despite whatever changes and developments might take place to the soul over one lifetime or many, there is still the belief that at its core, my soul is always "me" and that doesn't change.

But what is that "me" I keep referring to?

In Buddhism, there is an interesting modification to this concept. Because of the belief in impermanence or the continuous change of all things, it follows that there is nothing that can be identified as an unchanging thing. By unchanging, I mean an object, whether physical or spiritual, that is always and forever exactly what it is right now. Can we find something that does not change? No. If everything is changing there can be nothing that does not change, and therefore, no unchanging soul. The soul, rather than being something that I can identify, in some way, as always being me, is always in the process of changing too. Because of that, my definition of me must be modified since, as we can see, what I identify as me is not a constant thing, but an ever-changing process. I only know the "me" from this life, and even that has been constantly changing. If this is true, there really is no constant me or constant soul, but an evolving collection of physical and mental experiences that pass from one existence to the next, known as the Five Aggregates. To call this collection "a soul" does not seem accurate in the way the term has been used in other religions. There is nothing here but a process. Thinking about the common definition of a soul, in this case "no soul" might be more accurate.

The 18th century Scottish philosopher David Hume proposed what is called the Bundle theory. Hume asserted that all objects consist of a collection of attributes, properties and relationships but nothing more. There is not an actual thing, just this collection. Hume sounds a lot like the Buddha.

The best way to describe the relationship between you in this life, and you in past lives, is the traditional 'candle line up' example. Line up 10 candles and light the first one. Use the first to light the second, the second to light the third, and so on until they are all lit. What is the relationship between the flame on the first candle to the flame on the last candle? They are clearly not the same flame since they exist on two separated candles, but they are clearly related to each other in some way. What they have in common is a causal historical relationship. One flame led to the existence of the other, and that one to the next, but they are not the same flame.

It is believed that this collection of experiences is the spiritual essence of each one of us. The state of our spiritual existence in this life, came from the karmic decisions made during past lives that came from the same process in lives before that. The decisions and experiences resulting from each lifetime led to the composition and situation of the next. However, so much change has taken place over many lifetimes that, if we could analyze a life we led in a past existence, we might find little in common with ourselves today. The main point to understand is that the entity we generally define as ourselves, is really a process in motion. Every day of our lives we are changing in very small ways and usually do not notice the shift until times goes by. How did my brown hair get so gray and thin? It wasn't like that before. We are not definable, because some transition is always taking place, whether from one moment to the next, or from one lifetime to the next. Each of us, including our soul (or not soul), have a causal connection to the past and to the future, but that is all. The process continues.

Once, I was one year old. Since then, every cell in my body has been replaced, and I have evolved dramatically both intellectually, emotionally, and in every way that can be measured. Other than through a causal historical connection and memory, it seems absurd to say that the one year old is me. That was me many years ago, but that is not me now. In fact, as you may have already guessed, from this point of view, there is actually no objective "me" since I am continuing to be revised, in many ways, through every moment of every day. Popeye the sailor frequently said "I yam what I yam." But from a Buddhist point of view (if Popeye was a real person), as soon as he said it, he was inaccurate. In the next moment, he no longer was what he had been. Something changed.

You can see how this causal connection makes us think nothing actually changes, if you examine an old movie on real film. Each frame is a separate, discrete picture minutely different from the one before and the one after. When we run the film at the proper speed, a continuous visual experience is created because we cannot look fast enough to see each frame anymore. The many small frames now appear to be a continuous image so, as we watch the movie, we are easily drawn into the illusion. Such is life.

Try to point at the real me. If you point at my arm, that is just an arm. If you point at my chest, that is just a chest. If you point at my head, that is just a head. I cannot find "one single thing" that is me.

JAY LAMB

I am a collection of continuously changing physical, intellectual and spiritual parts, in relationship to each other that I *call* "me" to make life simpler. These are less accurate, especially if such generalizations encourage me to forget my true nature. Do you have a soul? When you reach enlightenment, let me know.

16

THE BUDDHA'S TEACHINGS II
ATTACHMENT

"The Only Constant in the Universe is Change."
- Heraclitus or the Buddha or Einstein or the *Tao te Ching*

Nothingness/ Formlessness

The absence of permanence extends from concepts of "me and the soul" to everything. We live in a universe that is a mass of interconnected processes, all of which affect and are affected by others, and that keeps everything interacting all the time and at many levels. There is no independent unconnected thing here. Every "thing" is a collection of processes and ingredients that come together for a period of time, and then eventually depart. Whether we are looking at a star or a human being, each is a collection of elements that did not exist together, at one time, and will not exist together at some point later. While they exist, they are always in the process of change. The universe consists of no unchanging things. No things.

Attachment and Detachment

Probably the biggest problem we have, according to Buddhist thinking, is attachment. We are attached to things- to our beach cottage, to our car, to our new big screen TV, to our home, to our neat new t-shirt, and generally to all of our possessions. We like to get new stuff, and often feel bad over the loss, destruction, or theft of our old stuff. We part with it wistfully, even if it is old and worn out. Everyone in my family was sad when we traded in the twenty-year-old family van. What great memories! No one wants to let it go. Of course, buying new to replace old makes us feel better. In general, many of us have more than we actually ever need, and sometimes our accumulation becomes an end in itself. For instance, I don't understand why certain persons need so many shoes. I know this because I have questioned it, and have been told that I just don't understand. Maybe it is the same reason I have so many teacups or books. Most of us would be very disappointed if we could not continue to acquire. Of course, we need money to do this, so we work a lot, and probably feel that the more money we can earn, the better. Perhaps the Amish, with their horse drawn, minimalist material life style are on to something.

We are also attached to other people. We have a spouse or lover, children, relatives, and friends who we love in a variety of ways, and whom we truly enjoy. We generally become very sad or depressed if anyone dies or moves away. I was sad for several days when Leonard Nimoy died in 2015, and I had never met the man. We want our relationships to stay secure and happy. We don't want them to change. My wife and I have discussed where we will live later in retirement and that conversation always includes a consideration about where our children will live. We like them and want to see them often. Forever.

We are also attached to ourselves. We are usually the center of our attention and the center of our universe. We are attached to who we are, to our personalities, and to our continuation. We may or may not like who we perceive ourselves to be, but whichever way it works out, we pay a lot of attention to ourselves, our plans, our wishes, our desires, our looks, our dreams, how people treat us, and how we treat ourselves. We have memories of ourselves in the past and see ourselves as continuing personalities. That is a lot of attachment.

The problem, as described by Buddhism, is that attachment creates frustration because while attachment is what we do, the universe doesn't go along.

The past no longer exists and the future does not yet exist. All that exists is now. However, we become attached to the past and look forward with apprehension or longing to the future, and by focusing on those, we forget to focus on today. Attachment has only an illusion of permanence, because nothing, not even our own selves, can continue indefinitely. If we try to attach to things that we expect will last, we will only continue to make ourselves frustrated and unhappy. The answer, of course, is to not become attached in the first place. Be detached.

Unfortunately, to be completely detached from everything we would have to live in a cave, not have anything, and never see people. We could never love someone. But that just does not seem right because we are human beings, and we have to have some attachments or we cannot really be human. What a quandary. Living in the world is like having been dropped into a candy store, with many tempting delights that we both want and need, yet we are being told that the candy is bad for us, and we should not have any.

The Stoic philosophers of the Hellenistic period and Roman Empire saw a similar problem with life, and came up with some advice. Epictetus, one of the most accessible Stoics, said that we should always be prepared every day in case what we most love is taken from us. The key, he said, is understanding that nothing in our lives is under our personal control, except how we react to events. Everything that happens to us, that really counts, is the result of the decisions and actions of others or random events. In almost every case, we are helpless to affect the outcome. When we are faced with events beyond our control, the only real question is how we react. Most of us can get over the loss of our things, but what about the hardest part, our loved ones? We could come home tomorrow and find our spouse and children are dead. We could spend the rest of our lives mourning that event, drinking too much, losing our jobs, and ending up in the gutter, but what good would that do us, or our departed loved ones?

What Epictetus wants us to do is to realize the true state of the world, not the world as we would like it to be. We should use our reaction to tragic events, the only thing we can control, to make the best of the situation. He recommends detachment. It's not that we shouldn't love our spouse and our children, with all of our heart and ability, but we should not become attached to the emotion of love. We should be able to have a period of mourning, then pick ourselves up and carry on. This is not easy, but I think the Buddha would agree with Epictetus.

My wife and I used to volunteer with a local SIDS (Sudden Infant Death Syndrome) support group. Losing an infant like this is one of the toughest things. While most parents were eventually able to get over the loss of their baby (you never forget, you are just able to move on), a rare few could not. In a way, their inability to stop mourning became a permanent negative memorial to their child. It was so sad to see people whose decisions made them feel worse. They could not detach. I hope by now, those few have.

The realization that each of us is not a permanent entity is scary for some, but liberating for others. It is scary because we begin to wonder who or what we really are. This might set a few moorings adrift since it is so much more secure to be sure. On the other hand, some see this as an opportunity to continuously recreate ourselves. We are always who we are right now. We are not that person remembered from our past, and we are not the person we might predict for the future. Our evolution is always in motion and we are free to be who we choose to be. For somewhat different reasons, this is in agreement with existential philosophy. We have total freedom to create ourselves, and the denial of that freedom, the insistence that we are only a previously created locked-in-place form, is bad faith, like lying to ourselves.

17

THERE IS NOT ONE BUDDHISM
THERAVADA AND MAHAYANA

"The past is already gone; the future is not yet here. There's only one moment for you to live."
- The Buddha

There is not one Buddhism as it consists of a number of distinctive sects and, perhaps hundreds of local options. Within a few hundred years of the Buddha's death, disagreement arose over what he really meant when he talked about this or that. The most conservative follow the core beliefs outlined above and little else. The most liberal have gods and demons, heavens, hells, past and future Buddha's, helpful spiritual beings, salvation, elaborate rituals and more. However, all of these groups base their interpretations on the core teachings of the Buddha. Everything derives from that.

Eventually Buddhism began to expand from its birthplace in India. Over time, it spread into Southeast Asia, central Asia, East Asia, and Japan. As Buddhism moved into countries that already had their own long standing, sophisticated religious and philosophical points of view, it adapted to the prevailing cultural norms, added local religious and cultural conventions, and eventually made a home wherever it appeared. Because Buddhism has no absolute theological requirements, being a creed of actions, not required beliefs, it was able to adapt and thrive in many places. Concurrent with this spread and translations of Buddha's teachings, there arose new interpretations that created disagreements about what the Buddha really meant. Thus began the spread of different Buddhist views from the most conservative to the very liberal.

Books have been written comparing the various branches of Buddhism, and much can be said about this, but I will try to melt this much longer discussion into a nutshell. There are many, many sects within Buddhism. However, they can be roughly divided between those that are more conservative, identified under the umbrella term Theravada, and the more liberal sects known as Mahayana. There is also a case to be made for Tibetan Buddhism (Vajrayana), the Dalai Lama's, as a separate branch, and Zen Buddhism as a unique form of Mahayana Buddhism, which stands outside the liberal to conservative axis. Within each of these syncretistic umbrella groupings, there is still a great degree of diversity, but all of these groups, again, see the teachings of the Buddha as the source and inspiration for their beliefs, however they interpret and practice them.

The conservative groups focus on a strict interpretation of the Buddha's teachings. In doing this, they emphasize the importance of the monks and their efforts to reach enlightenment and ultimately Nirvana. Ceremonies, rituals, and abstract theological beliefs are minimized and personal effort is maximized. The lay community supports their local monks with food and gifts that allow the monks to focus on their spiritual goals. By doing this, the community members hope this support will give them good karma that will aid with their next incarnation. Perhaps they will even be reborn in a situation where they can be monks. Most lay people are too busy with family and jobs to become heavily involved in full time religious activity. This is Theravada Buddhism, sometimes referred to as the 'little raft' because only a few can make it over to enlightenment at a time. This point of view is supported by the Buddha's final words encouraging his followers to get busy working on their own salvation. On his deathbed, the Buddha is reported to have said, "Behold, O monks, this is my last advice to you. All component things in the world are changeable. They are not lasting. Work hard to gain your own salvation."

However, some later Buddhists thought deeply about this and developed a different understanding, which came to be called the 'big raft'. Their thinking might have gone something like this:

The Buddha was Mr. Compassion, right? He was all about helping everyone reach enlightenment. Does it make sense then that upon his death he would say, "you are all on your own," and zip off to Nirvana where he could no longer help anyone? No way. In fact, the Buddha is probably still available to help us. In fact, if there was one Buddha, there may have been other Buddhas in the past or scheduled for the future. In fact, probably the most spiritual souls are not going off to Nirvana, but forgoing their ultimate bliss to stay behind to help everyone else be successful. Isn't that what truly compassionate people would do? There must be lots of help out there.

This interpretation is justified in two ways. First, as later writers commented on Buddhist thought, they were inspired with ideas and points of view that seemed to make Buddhism more compassionate and capable of helping lay people also reach Nirvana, not just the monks. This thinking spread and became very popular, as you might imagine, with lay communities. It expanded until it became the majority belief within the Asian Buddhist community. Second, it was widely thought that these elaborations were a valid expression of Buddhism because, as humanity matured, people were able to better understand these more sophisticated concepts.

There is a story that while the Buddha was preaching to his followers in the forest, he reached up and grabbed a handful of leaves. While gesturing to all the leaves in the forest, the Buddha said these few leaves of knowledge, out of all the truth there is (the forest full of leaves), is all I can really tell you about, because it is all you can understand. See, said the liberals, what we are discovering are some of those other leaves. Folks in the past couldn't grasp all the truth, but now it is coming out.

The conservatives are not wrong, they said, just very limited in their understanding (of course the conservatives disagreed). This is Mahayana Buddhism, the big raft because many people can make it to enlightenment, not just monks.

Mahayana Buddhism is a very popular big raft/ tent. Since it has interpreted the Buddha's words in various ways, its history is somewhat like Protestant Christianity, split into many different groups. While they all have the Buddha's teachings at their core, they also have widely varying beliefs about what it all means, and what one should do. In the broadest sense, the idea is that everyone can make spiritual progress. The role of the monks is more to help the community advance rather than just focusing on themselves. While Theravada Buddhism most admires the monk who makes his own spiritual progress, Mahayana, developing from an emphasis on the Buddha's compassionate role, admires the being, known as a Bodhisattva, who is dedicated to helping others advance spiritually.

The story is told that the struggle for Nirvana, through many lifetimes, is like climbing a ladder up an extremely high wall. The Bodhisattva is the advanced being who comes to the top of the wall and can see over it into Nirvana. All she has to do, metaphorically, is to put her leg over the top and she is there. However, before she does this, she looks down from these heights and sees all other beings struggling up the wall, way down below on their ladders. With an intense burst of compassion, she decides to forego Nirvana, and descends the ladder back to earth to help others. The Bodhisattva's vow is to not reach Nirvana until all other beings have been helped to reach enlightenment. The Mahayana belief is that with the Buddha, past and future Buddhas, and Bodhisattvas, there is grace available to help all of us, if we would just access it. Grace for the asking, beats tough, difficult, self-effort, twelve ways to Sunday as a way to reach enlightenment.

Many Mahayana sects have elaborate rites and rituals, based on gods that appeal to many people. The Buddha is worshipped by some, not because he is a god, but as a sign of respect. There are past Buddhas, Bodhisattvas, and various self-born celestial beings that are popular. Traditionally Buddhism, as it exists in patriarchal cultures, has taught that women must reincarnate as men to reach enlightenment. One popular goddess (or bodhisattva, depending on choice of origin story) in Tibetan Buddhism is Tara, one of the rare female deities, who guides followers on the path to enlightenment.

Hinduism found out a long time before this, as other religions have discovered, that most people just don't get the deep theological and philosophical aspects of their religion. Frankly, they either don't have the time for it, or they don't have the mind for it. They do, however, like rituals, especially if the worship of spiritual beings is involved. Familiar rituals that they have done since they were kids, feel good and give them assurance. They have busy lives, and want to know that by going to a service, and praying or chanting or meditating, and donating, they have done religious good for themselves.

You can see why Mahayana is more popular. There is plenty of help to achieve enlightenment and progress is not just for monks but laymen too. A variety of methods and practices is no hindrance in Mahayana. There are Buddhists who pray to gods to get the favors they need in this world, but those gods are more like powers of nature, and certainly not anything like the creator God of Abrahamic faiths. After all, while those gods are powerful and live much longer than we do, they are part of our existence and are also searching for enlightenment. Many Buddhists believe in different levels of heavens, earth, and hells that we migrate through between lifetimes, like either a tough love boot camp, or a vacation, depending on our life's actions. In Pure Land Buddhism, adherents believe that by doing the right things, one may be reborn in a perfect paradise where enlightened masters show us the way to Nirvana. Not meaning to take anything away from these concepts, it seems that people are often very clever in discovering easier ways to achieve their spiritual goals. Who is to say they are not right?

18

ZEN AND NIRVANA

"Nirvana is not the blowing out of the candle. It is the extinguishing of the flame because day is come."
- Rabindranath Tagore

Zen

It is said that one day the Buddha was about to preach a sermon to his followers, but instead he held up a lotus blossom. Everyone was probably saying, "What's going on? What's the Buddha doing?" Except for one guy. He got the Buddha's message and so went off to start what would eventually be, with a little Taoist influence, Zen Buddhism. Zen, known as Chan in China, is fairly popular in the U.S. and stands out because of its lack of religious trappings, and the perception that it is very intellectually and psychologically deep. On the way to enlightenment what Zen Buddhists do, first and foremost, is seated meditation. The Rinzai school ponders insolvable riddles called *koans*, while in the Soto school, one sits counting breaths and observing thoughts.

The idea behind the koans is, that if we really want to understand the nature of reality, not what everyday life fools us with, we have to change our mindset. Koans are used because it is believed that our minds must be forced to operate beyond the rational and logical, to the intuitive level, if we are going to see life and the world as they are. Focusing on a koan puts our mind at odds with itself. Since we were born, we have been trained to use logic and rational thinking to solve problems. While many of us still do not do that well, it is the method we most depend on, as our minds are grooved by thousands of experiences, in our culture to act in certain ways. When we try to solve a koan, our mind uses its best set of tools, the logical and the rational, to find the answer. But koans are riddles that do not have rational solutions. So, when our mind gets cranked up to solve a koan, it slams up against the unsolvable. Yet, our assignment is still to solve the riddle. If we are persistent, and perhaps are lucky, our mind will tire of smashing itself on that unanswerable riddle, give up on the rational method, and find another way to the answer, using the intuitive. Perhaps in a flash of insight or in a growing realization, the student comes to the solution. If you are not sure if you have it right, your Zen master will let you know and, if needed, give you a hint.

In the Soto school, as in most other forms of meditation, the more passive sitting and observing meditative technique is said to bring about more gradual changes in perspective and understanding. My friend John, who spent several years in a Soto Zen monastery, told one of my students, that meditation made his day a little brighter, his life a little happier, and his tennis game more fun.

So, what is the value of this discipline? A Western student who had been in training for many years is reported by Huston Smith in *The World's Religions* to have answered, "No parapsychic experiences, as far as I am aware. But you wake up in the morning, and the world seems so beautiful you can hardly stand it." Sounds like John.

When I introduced this concept in class, I told students about the famous koan, "What is the sound of one hand clapping?" Many of them immediately started opening and closing one hand quickly, making that sad little sound of slapping fingers on palm, and looked up with the expectation that they had solved the riddle. "No," I said, "a clap is made with two hands, what is the sound of one hand clapping?" "But Mr. Lamb, you can't clap like that with one hand." "Ah," I said, trying to sound inscrutable, "that is the riddle."

Nirvana

If life on earth, through many lifetimes, is suffering, what is the alternative? What is the something else I am striving for as I follow the N8FP, lead a good life, and try to end my cycle of rebirths? I assume that this something is without suffering and will make me happier, but what is it? What more is there? The answer, young grasshopper, is Nirvana.

The first thing to understand about Nirvana is that there is no way we can actually understand Nirvana. We can talk about it, and use lots of descriptive words and examples and stories, but if we think we will understand what it is, we are wrong. Curiously, if we understand those stories, we will at least know why we don't understand. Needless to say, there are a number of slightly different flavored beliefs about this term, but this is the one that makes the most sense to me.

There is the story of the frog who came back to visit a group of tadpoles in his old pond. He tried to tell them about his adventures on dry land, but the tadpoles kept asking questions because they could not conceive of "dry land." All of their short lives had been lived in the water. Every word the frog used, and every explanation he concocted, left them even more confused. Trying to explain dry land to tadpoles, who had no concept of life outside the pond, was impossible. By the time the frog was finished, the tadpoles were only sure that this dry land was a negative nowhere place, because it contained no aspects of existence that they knew, could comprehend, or imagine. Nothing in their experience helped them to understand this.

So, Nirvana is to our lives. Buddhists believe that Nirvana is our ultimate goal or destination, but we do not have the concepts, like the tadpoles, to understand it. The best explanation I have heard is

"Bliss, pure bliss." Yet, in trying to understand bliss, I can only conceive of it in terms of my human experience. Also, as much as I try to use words to understand, the Buddha teaches that ultimately there is no "me" and ultimately no "there." Or, to not understand it another way, once I become enlightened, I will know that "I", "it", and "everything" is indistinguishable and ultimately "one" anyway. Nirvana is not distant, but here, I just don't realize it. Perhaps if I stopped for a few years of deep mystical meditation, I would get it. But if I did and then tried to explain it to you, I might find that words just cannot convey the message.

That makes it tough to get a real grasp of the concept. Is it a place? Is it in my mind? Is it somewhere different from either of those? When you find out for sure, drop me a line. In Western religions, everyone talks about the afterlife, and there are numerous examples of heaven in story, art, and scripture. Cultural artifacts like *New Yorker* cartoons or the daily comics, depicting people in heaven with robes, wings and fluffy clouds are a common caricature. But is that really what it is like? I don't think so but I don't know, and I suspect that no one else knows either. What does it mean to be close to God in heaven? Again, I suspect that no one really knows, but everyone assumes it is good since every religious person wants to go to heaven.

Same deal with Buddhists. They are supposed to be making progress on ending the cycle of reincarnation, so there will be no reason to be born again, so they can reach Nirvana. Maybe Buddhism could use a heaven like metaphor to try to describe Nirvana, something people can grasp and feel comfortable with, like a *New Yorker* cartoon. The delights of heaven laid out in the Qur'an are certainly described in terms that are attractive and meaningful to human beings, whether that vision is metaphorical or actual. But the basic teachings of the Buddha are just too philosophical and straight forward for that. No mumbo-jumbo or 'play pretend' allowed. So, we are left with non-descriptive descriptions. But Nirvana must be good, right?

. . .

HISTORICAL FOOTNOTE: In *The 100: A Ranking of the Most Influential Persons in History*, Michael Hart ranks the Buddha as the fourth most influential person in world history, just ahead of Confucius. The difference, he states, is because Buddhist thought has traveled the world, while Confucius' ideas have had little impact outside of East Asia.

19

CHINESE BELIEFS
TRADITIONAL CHINESE THINKING

"Fish forget they live in the water; people forget they live in the Tao."
- Confucius

From a Western point of view, it can be difficult to talk about Chinese religion. In fact, a few scholars have said there actually is no Chinese religion, only philosophy. There is much in Chinese thinking that looks like religion, but it is based on philosophical concepts. When the rest of the world began to investigate China, it turned out there was no Chinese word that directly corresponded to "religion," as it is defined and practiced in the West, so one had to be invented. If you have to invent a new word to describe what you do that they don't, but you think they might, something is very different.

Part of this divide in understanding seems to be cultural. In *The Geography of Thought*, Richard Nisbett suggests that Asians and Westerners perceive and reason in different ways. He recounts how an Asian student told him, "You know the difference between you and me is that I think the world is a circle, and you think it is a line." Westerners seem to think in terms of logic, specific rules and categories while Asians focus on the broad context and complex interrelationships.

Yin and Yang

This can be seen by examining the traditional Chinese understanding of how the universe is organized and operates which is rooted in the concept of Yin and Yang. The cosmos was originally a swirling chaos. Then, out of this, one thing developed. That one thing existed in relationship to now another thing, its opposite. These two opposing forces did not attack and destroy each other, but existed together as complementary opposites in a continuous harmonious flow, a rise and fall that makes the universe work. Each is dominant at the right time and place, but Yin's moment of greatest dominance leads invariably to the dominance of Yang, and vice versa. Existence and non-existence, life and death, flow into each other in a cycle, and each will always contain, at its center, the essence of the other. Though they are opposites, each one sets the stage for, and has a role in fulfilling, the existence of the other. This is a lot like my wife and me. While Westerners see themselves as independent individuals who want to stand out, traditional thinking leads the Chinese to see themselves as part of a harmonious whole, and they want to fit in.

This is the context, then, in which the working of the universe, the forces of nature, and the world of human beings, made sense to the Chinese. There is a continuous rhythm of opposing processes increasing from, and then yielding to, each other. Everything is changing all of the time, but it is moving back to a previous state. The universe can only exist and continue as long as there are these balanced, dynamic relationships. Stars are created and later destroyed. There is winter and there is summer. There are men and there are women. There is hot and there is cold. There is life and there is death. Even though they are opposites, the existence of one is essential for the existence of the other. One is not good and the other bad, as both are part of the process that makes everything happen. Balance and harmony in these relationships are what is good, and imbalance and disharmony are bad. Things work well only in the proper relationship with everything else. You can't understand the part, without understanding the whole.

There is a story told about a farmer. One day his horse runs away and his neighbor comes over to commiserate about such bad luck. The farmer replies to his friend, "Who knows what is good or bad?? The next day, the horse returns leading six other horses into the corral. The neighbor comes over to celebrate such good luck. The farmer replies to his friend, "Who knows what is good or bad?" The next day, the farmer's son tries to ride one of the new horses, is bucked off and breaks his leg. The neighbor comes over to commiserate about such bad luck. The farmer replies to his friend, "Who knows what is good or bad?" The next day the magistrate comes around to draft soldiers for the army. The son is not drafted because of his broken leg. On it goes.

I am looking at a D battery sitting on my desk. It has a positive pole and a negative pole. One of those poles is not bad, and the other good. If I cut the battery in half to separate them, I will have no power. I can only have a useful battery if both the positive and negative poles are working properly. One cannot work without the other because they are opposites, and their opposition, in terms of physics, gives the battery its power. Expand this example to the way a person's life works, the way the country's life works, the way nature works and the way the cosmos works. Each one is a dance of complementary opposing forces. Nothing will go right if harmony and balance are not maintained. If you want to be a happy, productive person, have an honorable family, or a happy country, you, peasant or emperor, have to maintain the balance because that is the way reality works best. All Chinese beliefs, practices and actions flow from there. Some of these practices could be called religion.

The most important relationship of complementary opposites to maintain is the relationship between heaven and earth, the realm of the spirit, and the realm of the living. Heaven, in this sense, is not the Western religious idea of the place that God has created, inhabited by the souls of worthy dead people who have earned their position. While many people in the West believe that heaven exists, it is very distant and there is not much, if any, communication or connection between those who occupy heaven and those living on earth.

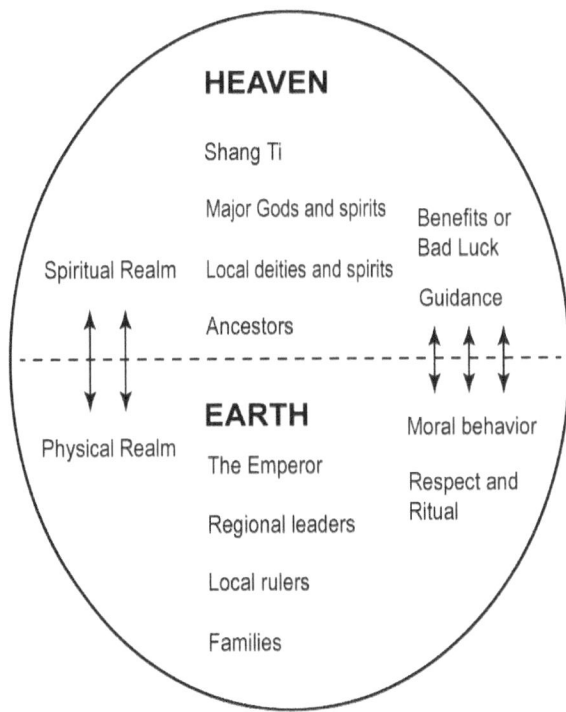

The Chinese heaven and all of its inhabitants have a direct, intimate relationship with earth and all of the people who live here. Within the cosmos, all heavenly beings and humans, both living and dead, exist in their proper place in an integrated system as part of the whole. Heaven is occupied by everyone's ancestors, including yours, some of whom are in a hierarchy of gods and goddesses, along with a variety of spirits, all at different levels. Each is intimately connected with the earth in some way. The name of the highest God, Shang Ti (Shangdi), eventually became synonymous with Heaven (Tian). The heaven-earth connection is that of an interactive system with strong, constant, relationships between the two realms.

Reinforcing this, some Chinese families have records of ancestors, going back thousands of years. It's not that these ancestors are worshiped, like worshiping a god, but it's more of a deep respect for the cultural and family connection running from your ancestors, through you, on to your descendants. No one feels right unless they are comfortably immersed in that long chain of beings. You want to feel harmoniously connected to the whole family.

In both heaven and earth, all inhabitants have the responsibility to maintain the harmony and balance of the cosmos through the proper operation of their relationships. Society in China has traditionally been based on patriarchal and hierarchical political and social systems, which are congruent with the structure of heaven. The emperor was at the top on earth, with merchants at the bottom (since they don't do anything useful, just buy and sell things), and everyone else someplace in between. Each person has a place in the hierarchy, and duties that are required, if harmony and balance are to be maintained. Requests go up from the bottom, while decisions and favors come down from the top. Both the emperor and everyone else must do their duties correctly, regarding both heaven and earth, or chaos ensues. The expectations are similar for heaven. The highest-level gods relate to the highest levels on earth. But there are also lower level occupants of heaven, as there are lower level folk on earth and their relationships are similar up and down the line. You, as a peasant farmer, for instance, relate to the local village god, the god of your field and your own ancestors, but not to higher levels. That's someone else's job. Traditionally, most people could not imagine another way to do things and no one in China seriously challenged this process until modern times.

You get the sense in this system that what is important is not right and wrong, or good and bad, but doing the right thing in the right way, at the right time. Maintaining harmony and balance is good, allowing chaos to happen is bad. We provide the gods with respect and ethical behavior that honors ourselves and our ancestors. They, in turn, provide us with benefits (good rainfall for instance, but not too much) and advice. And, as we can be punished for transgressions by the authorities in the human world, we can also be punished by the spiritual authorities. Remember though, the punishment is not so much for doing a particularly bad thing, but for doing whatever upsets the balance. You have a place and a role in your family, your village, and your society. If you fulfill your role, that is good. If you fail to fulfill your role properly, that is bad.

20

THE GODS OF CHINA

"Let the states of equilibrium and harmony exist in perfection, and a happy order will prevail throughout heaven and earth, and all things will be nourished and flourish."
- Confucius

The heavenly realm of the Chinese gods is not unlike earth, in many ways. There are hierarchies, but merit is rewarded, and gods have moved up and down in the rankings over time. Your village god is the equivalent of a local government official, who has the job of insuring the well-being of his community. On the correct day at the correct time, you will show respect by worshipping the god, using the proper ritual, making offerings, and requesting whatever it is you need. The god has no personal or practical need to be worshipped, and certainly does not take away your offering placed in the shrine or temple. The fact that you do these things shows respect on your part and thankfulness for the benefits the god will provide. It's a lot like the scene from *The Godfather* where someone asks for a boon from Don Corleone and kisses his ring. Though Don

Corleone talks of their friendship, it is clearly not the friendship of equals. It is the show of respect and the proper ritual that makes the relationship work.

What are the gods? One professor told me that heaven was ancestors from top to bottom, from the mythical emperor Shangdi, believed to be the originator of Chinese civilization and the ancestor of the Chinese people, to Uncle Fred who died last year. There is no Big "G" creator God, only small "g" gods, who have the power, at their level, to grant favors, but also expect to be treated with respect. There are many different points of view on this.

Gods can be replaced. If the people are doing the correct rituals and showing proper respect, the god should provide benefits. If the god does not come through, a village may replace their god with another or temple worshipers may change their allegiance to another temple. Gods who provide benefits are seen as rising powers in heaven while those who do not are seen as falling powers, which is why, over time, the ranking can seem dynamic, as these shifts in power occur. Human beings who live great, notable, or unusually tragic lives can be "promoted" after they die and become gods too.

Most larger villages and cities constructed temples that included at least one, but often a number of currently popular gods. The gods don't mind sharing the space. Local people will revere the gods, often at home or in a temple, and participate in ceremonies (as mentioned above), but will also avail themselves of the other services offered by a temple. These might be a combination of such things as divination, astrology, channeling, faith healing, and advice on how to deal with problem ghosts.

The most significant relationship you have with heaven is through your ancestors. They are not alive in the bodily sense, but they are certainly believed to exist, and are the most important (and numerous) part of your family. Sometimes after death, spirits of the deceased might be angry and resentful. If you treat your ancestors with sincere respect, they may be mollified, settle down, and become an asset to the family. Do you remember the scene from *Mulan* (Disney, 1998) where the ancestors found out that she ran off to join the army and disgraced the family? If not, watch it. I am not sure how the ancestors really are supposed to operate, but I bet the Disney cartoonists at least captured the spirit of concern and potential family dishonor in the relationship between the ancestors and the living family.

Ancestor worship shows a respectful relationship between you and the ancestors. You are supposed to fulfill your role in life correctly and with virtue. This brings honor to you on earth, and to your ancestors in heaven. You show respect to the gods and to your ancestors by completing the appropriate rites, rituals and obligations correctly and with humility. Then, everyone is happy, everything works out, and the system of harmony and balance continues. However, if you mess up, bad things will happen. Your ancestors will be angry with you, bring bad luck your way, and maybe even sic a hungry ghost on you. Everyone will be on your case until you straighten things out.

Mandate of Heaven

Traditionally, at the highest levels of society, since at least the Zhou Dynasty, the concept of the Mandate of Heaven has reflected the belief that Heaven approved the political leadership of China. Theoretically, the emperor, serving as the earthly representative of heaven, the "son of heaven," is all powerful, but his all-powerful decisions in running the government are supposed to be for the good of the people. If, over a period of time, the government makes decisions not in the people's interest, heaven gets upset. Through various signs and portents, heaven lets its displeasure be known, and this may encourage rebellions. Eventually, it is thought, heaven will assist a worthy rebellion to victory. The new dynasty will make decisions in the interest of the people, and will continue to have heaven's approval. After all, if heaven didn't approve, they wouldn't have won, right? This is not so very far from the old European notion of divine right of kings, which goes like this. "I'm the king. If God didn't support me, I wouldn't be king, right? Therefore, God wants me to be king and opposing me is the same thing as opposing God, right?" Isn't logic wonderful?

There is probably an argument that could be made that the current Chinese Communist Party is the latest dynasty. Like the emperor in the old days, they have total power and want to keep it, but they also seem to be interested, at least to some degree, in making the Chinese people happy and prosperous. It remains to be seen how long the CCP will last before something different comes along. Most dynasties have lasted a few hundred years.

Belief Systems

So far, we have not said a word about Confucianism or Taoism, which most people think of as the "religions" of China. To see the place of these belief systems, it is important to understand the historical, cultural matrix from which they (with the later inclusion of Buddhism) arose. The belief in the concept of Yin and Yang, the importance of harmony and balance, the relationship of heaven and earth, and the hierarchical nature of things with complementary responsibilities, created a society that reflected these ideas in day-to-day life. As hundreds of years go by, most people, as peasant farmers, are growing their crops, worshiping their gods, revering their ancestors, and fulfilling their responsibilities to maintain harmony in the interlocked, hierarchical system involving both the earthly and the heavenly facets of life. As they do their part for the happy existence of their family, their village, and their country, so they also, and simultaneously, are satisfying the requirements of heaven. In this way the ebb and flow of everyday life is, in a manner of speaking, religious.

It is out of this matrix of traditional Chinese belief that Confucianism and Taoism arose. Buddhism may have arrived in China as early as the 3rd century B.C.E., but didn't start to spread widely until the 2nd or 3rd centuries C.E. Over time, Buddhism contributed greatly to Chinese culture, and was adaptively absorbed into the larger traditional religious system. Like Yin and Yang, Confucianism and Taoism are complementary opposites, and while individual people might choose one based on personal preference, there is no idea that one is right and the other wrong. In Chinese thinking, the idea that one of two opposing points of view might be wrong is not accurate. What we have here is syncretistic thinking. All possible ideas and philosophies are part of the cosmos and therefore do exist. Rather than what is right and what is wrong, the question should be which actions are most appropriate for a situation. The Chinese are more practical than they are ideological. Sometimes Chinese religion is called the "Great Faith" because it contains every Chinese belief and practice. The wise person knows when it is best to be a Taoist, best to be a Confucian, best to be a Buddhist, and when it doesn't matter. It would not be out of character to act as a Confucian at one time, a Taoist at another, to worship the local god, or pay respects to the ancestors. This would never be seen as wishy-washy or indecisive, but wise.

While most peasants don't have the time or interest for all of this, so they stick to their ancestors, the local gods, and the time honored rituals that bring them satisfaction and practical results. However, there are many options, and combinations of religious observance to select as most appropriate, for a given situation. Your family would teach you the particular set of observances and rituals that they perform, and you would carry this on.

This sets the stage for understanding the relationship between Confucianism and Taoism, which are usually studied as separate religions. Traditionally, the upper classes in China were less likely to be interested in the emotional, ritual filled practices of popular folk religion. They focused on more rational and austere beliefs, like Taoism and Confucianism that attempt to answer the big questions. While, in a Western sense, these beliefs are separate systems, they and Buddhism are, from a Chinese point of view, seen as aspects of a larger religious and cultural whole.

21

THE WISDOM OF CONFUCIUS

"The superior man understands what is right; the inferior man understands what will sell."
- Confucius

In 5th century BCE China, the Zhou dynasty was going downhill fast, and predatory feudalism was running amuck. With a weak central government, power devolved to the states, and lords squabbled violently and incessantly with each other, in a way that qualifies this time period to be accurately dubbed "the time of warring states." Just the name provides the clue that this era was not known for peace, happiness, and prosperity. Times were bad, and traditional beliefs and values seemed to have been forgotten.

What I like most about Kung Fu-tze (Confucius is the western translation of his name) is that he was a teacher. He was also a man with a plan. Born in 551 BCE, he saw what a mess China was becoming, and figured out a way to solve the problem by focusing not on individual rights, but on the well-being of society. Here's how he did it. During Confucius', time those who knew about China's history, pretty much agreed that in the mythological ancient days of sage kings and cultural heroes thousands of years before, China had been a great place. All of the kings were good, clever, and great leaders; all of the people were virtuous and things were wonderful. One day a king invented agriculture and everyone cheered. It was that kind of place. However, it was also agreed everything had gone downhill since that golden age. All of the ideals, values, and virtues of the past had been forgotten. Confucius saw that everyone just did whatever they wanted and didn't follow the old rules. The ways things had been done in the past, and had been followed from generation to generation, were not being passed on. People's actions had become spontaneous. When faced with a problem, they did whatever occurred to them, which might or might not help society be a better place in the long run. Any good idea that did come up would not be saved, since the cultural habit of accumulating and passing on the wisdom of the past seemed to be broken. Confucius could see this was not working. He might have thought:

Clearly, to have a happy nation, some sort of system must be established to improve relationships so people can have the best chance for a good society and happy lives. Focusing on what's good for the group will create the best opportunity to bring about what is good for the individual.

Being a learned person, Confucius knew about the virtues of the past, and what qualities people and leaders had exhibited. Confucius probably said something like:

Let's research the past, and take all of the most useful concepts and behaviors, and reconstruct a tradition that will bring out the best in Chinese culture. Instead of useless, counterproductive, spontaneous actions, let's create a deliberate tradition that can be emphasized through education and government leadership. Once we lay this out, and people learn what is expected, the whole society will reinforce this set of values. Actions will no longer be spontaneous, but will always reflect our deliberate cultural decisions, grounded in the best qualities from Chinese history. Because these values will now be passed on, this will create a country like back in the good old days with efficient, benevolent, government and hardworking, virtuous, people.

The focus of this philosophy is about the individual, and how the individual acts in all of his relationships. It's not that the main idea doesn't stress the importance and happiness of the larger group, but there is a realization that society will best be served by individuals who act in a certain way, and that all individuals will best be served by a harmonious, well-functioning society. Confucius believed that by nature, all people are basically good, though they can be led astray. Obviously, if people are starving to death, they might do things they would not otherwise do, but if you give people a decent government, fair opportunities, and a reasonable situation, they will naturally do the right thing.

So, what were the qualities Confucius was trying to inculcate? Some of the more important ones are outlined below.

Ren- Kindness, benevolence and human heartedness- the ideal and correct relationship between people. This includes the right sort of love for your spouse, and a different sort of love for your children or your parents, the right sort of love for all your friends and acquaintances, and a general compassion for all human beings, even those you will never see or meet. Confucius felt love had to be appropriate and the "love everyone" views of the Mohists, discussed later, were wildly out of touch with human nature.

Junzi- Personification of the qualities of Ren. This is an educated gentleman or lady, in the best traditional sense of the word, who demonstrates superior character and behavior. Such a person always knows the right thing to do or say and is virtuous and kind, so everyone feels at ease and comfortable with him/her. This is a person of wisdom, intelligence, and compassion, never brusque or violent, and not into "politics," but sides with the right. This is the kind of person you most want to be, and the sort of person you most want to hang out with.

Li- Propriety- Rites, rituals, ceremonies. Doing the right thing, at the right time, in the right way. Understanding the reciprocal nature of the five relationships (ruler to subject, father to son, husband to wife, oldest son to younger brothers, elder friend to junior friend) and the correct way for these relationships to work in a hierarchical system. This includes the appropriate rituals for the correct occasions, whether involving heaven or earth. Especially important was filial piety, the idea of obedience and devotion to your parents and your family. One story tells of two brothers who slept outside their parent's window so the mosquitos would eat them, not the parents. That is devotion.

As hierarchical and one-way as this bottom up system may seem, it is not meant to be totalitarian. The dominant person in any situation, for example, the husband in the husband-wife relationship, is clearly in charge, but should be following the benevolent principles of a Junzi. The obligations in this relationship are a two way street. He is owed love and obedience from his wife, but he is also supposed to give her love, affection, and make decisions in the best interests of her and the family. Likewise, you owe the emperor your obedience if he wants to send you off to war, or to build a Great Wall, but ultimately his decisions must be in the best interests of the people. If the husband or the emperor do not fulfill their part of the relationship through their benevolence, the family or the country will fall apart. Then, in the chaos, someone else will have the opportunity to start a dynasty.

Te- Correct use of moral force, the correct use of political power. Using this power wisely for the good of the people by, for instance, selecting officials based on quality. This led to the earliest civil service tests and includes the idea of the leader as a moral exemplar. In this society, everyone looks to the higher-level person for cues on how to act. If the emperor is not moral and ethical, how can his advisers be? This continues down through society to the family. If the village leader is not virtuous, how can the men of the village be? And, if the men of the village are not virtuous how can their families be? It all starts at the top.

Wen- Appreciation and development of the arts and culture. Ultimately, great culture is the reflection of a great society. The arts can enrich us and help us to be better individuals.

Confucius's ethical views are summarized in his "Golden Rule." "Do not impose on others what you do not wish for yourself."

Saying all of this is one thing, but how do we attain these lofty goals of personal excellence? While Confucius was idolized by his students, he stated he had not yet reached these goals himself. In the *Analects*, a collection of his sayings and conversations written by his students after his death, Confucius discusses in meticulous detail both the personal and formal ritual qualities a person should try to develop. Gods, ancestors and parents should be revered appropriately, and, if possible, one should strive to acquire education. In the West, most people see education as a way to gain knowledge to get a better job. However, in China the process of education was seen as a way to develop personal virtue. An educated person in China was considered a moral person, and an exemplar of what it meant to be Chinese. All in all, Confucius was recommending massive personal and societal change. All of this change, however, was based on the traditional qualities of ancient China, so there was nothing alien or unusual involved, just an editing of the old ways and a reemphasis of what was most important.

22

THE MAN WITH A PLAN FOR TODAY

"The Master said, The ancients were loath to speak because they would be ashamed if they personally did not live up to what they said."
- Confucius (The Analects, 4.22)

When individuals in society are only interested in what benefits them, and people are looking for and finding enemies around every corner, it's hard to get anything done for the common good. If all arguments boil down to good (our side) versus evil (their side), how can we get to win/win?

Confucius said a lot of things, but let's focus on his primary solution to the problems of his day, which sound a lot like the problems of our day. First of all, Confucius might advise us that if we want to solve societal problems by looking for the answer "out there," we are looking in the wrong direction. He would agree with Pogo's (Walt Kelly's) famous observation, "We have met the enemy and he is us." We have forgotten that all people, including those we most blame, are people too.

What do we do? There is relatively little an individual can do to move the massive mountain of complex societal, political issues, and history that brought us to our bad place. As the Stoics taught, almost all events are beyond our control, but what we can control is how we react. Confucius would agree, but might also add that the problem is ultimately not between us and an amorphous, demonized "them," it is with all of us, and how we relate to and treat each other as human beings. The most important question to focus on is, "How am I living my life on a day-to-day basis?"

Confucius tells us society's ills can only be solved if we turn our focus to what we can best control: ourselves. To solve this he recommended, as did Socrates and Plato, we each strive to be paragons of virtue. We do this individually through a three-pronged approach. First, we develop qualities of humaneness, nurturing respect, regard and consideration for all other beings. This is not a "yeah I like people but they all suck," moment. This a deep, serious, and sincere effort to appreciate, and share, the humanity that I feel for those close to me, with all people, even those I disagree with. As I have the human right to receive this compassion from others, I also owe it to them. I can't control how others act. I can only control me.

Second, this appreciation of humanity should show itself in our actions. We should think deeply about our social relationships and only act in ways consistent with this humane view. We should work on our reactions to others, so we only respond with a sincere attitude, and appropriate actions that demonstrate our humaneness. This includes re-inculcating proper social conduct in everyday situations, such as a smile, a kind word, please and thank you, and other actions of courtesy that demonstrate our respect for everyone. We want to show the respect we expect to be shown, even if it is not reciprocated.

Third, at the same time we should engage in continuous critical ethical reflection of ourselves and our actions. We must relearn what ethics mean, and use critical reflection to examine our motives and responses, until we develop a sense of what is right. This will allow us to come to the correct action in any situation. We have to keep our emotions under control. If we make a mistake, we should fix it, and we can look to examples from history, literature, and philosophy to help us. The key is to develop a personal ethic not subject to compromise. Sure, I can be an honest person, but what if someone hands me a bag of cash to look the other way? Sure, I love my wife, but baby don't you look good. Nope. No good. These rationales can't work anymore. We will all make mistakes and have failures but we have to be able to get back on that horse, with a stronger resolve to hang on tight because that is what is right, what will work best for each of us, and what is best for society.

This combination of changing our attitudes to put humaneness, proper actions, and critical ethical self-evaluation first, is a tremendously difficult task requiring both diligence and patience. Confucius focused on filial piety, originally meaning our relationship with our parents, but, in application, our relationship with our whole family. He recommended we first use our family relationships in developing these qualities. Once that is successful, we can bring this to more people in different situations, in expanding concentric circles, until this way of approaching people becomes habitual.

Those who become accomplished at developing themselves in this way are Junzi- as mentioned earlier, the perfection of the ideal lady or gentleman, in the best sense of the word. These are the virtuous people you want to elect to government positions because they will propose solutions that do not reflect ideology, party, or interest groups, but only what is best for the people. They may seem wishy washy to some, but the Junzi realizes situations change. We are looking for the best answer today, not a warmed over one from the past. They are practical and pragmatic, while still focusing on humaneness, correct actions, and ethical self-reflection. Making virtuous actions common and admired again will, Confucius believed, create a harmonious society that will serve the best interests of both humans and heaven.

23

CONFUCIUS' LEGACY

"Real knowledge is to know the extent of one's ignorance."
- Confucius

While Confucius seems to have been a great teacher, his quest to change society was a failure during his lifetime. No leaders would buy his program, and the Warring States period continued unabated. However, his students learned their lessons well, and continued to teach his ideas to their pupils, and they to their pupils. His influence continued to spread until his ideas were picked up during the Han dynasty.

Now you might ask, all of this is very interesting but where is the religious aspect in Confucius' philosophy? Good question. Remember back a bit when we talked about Yin and Yang, the harmony and balance of complementary opposites? From a Chinese point of view, there is no difference between a philosophical discussion and a religious one. Both are dealing with how we are to best maintain harmony and balance for the individual and for society. Every action in our lives is tied into the cosmos, heaven, the world, and our relationship to them all. Nothing is exempt. Call it religion, or call it philosophy, this is the way, it was believed, reality is structured. Chinese actions may not look or seem religious from a Western point of view, where the world is clearly divided between that which is sacred and that which is profane. But remember, in Chinese thinking, sacred or profane is not an important distinction, since all things are part of the cosmic whole.

In a way, the Chinese considered every aspect of life sacred, since every aspect of life has to do with relationships, harmony, and balance. Traditional medicine and cooking, flower arranging and art are all based on the balance of different factors and forces, tastes, sights and objects. Besides, while Confucius thought straightening out society was of the highest importance for people, he instinctively knew you couldn't ignore the gods and ancestors if you wanted to maintain harmony and balance. If you want to get picky and insist on a direct, Western style religious connection, Confucius was eventually declared to be a god after his death, temples were built to him, and people prayed to and venerated him (looking for benefits of course). That must qualify as "religious" from anyone's point of view.

Legalism, Mohism and the Han Dynasty

Bad times, like those during the Warring States period, bring forth a hothouse of philosophical ideas as solutions. In addition to Confucianism, there were two major (and several minor) philosophies of government and society, competing in ancient China, during and after this time period. Legalism, the first of these, was based on the premise that people are not basically good or bad, but are always looking out for themselves. If the Emperor decides to build a Great Wall down the street to protect the whole country, suppose the local people sneak out at night and steal the building materials. Just asking them to stop, and do the right thing, will not work. Some people respond to rewards, but everyone responds to punishment, the tougher the better. Want to stop theft? Cut off a few hands, or a few heads, and that will keep everyone in line. Once they understand it is in their best interests not to steal from you (because of punishment), they will stop. There is no "better nature" to appeal to, just self-interest. This is real tough love.

The poster boy of Legalism was the Qin emperor Shi Huangdi (260 BCE-210 BCE). Legalism had been around since the time of Confucius, but the Qin drank the Kool-Aid. Laws were written and enforced enthusiastically and the rights of individuals, whether of high or low station, were not important. Qin armies did not pay attention to the chivalrous rules of warfare widely followed at the time. They looked for weaknesses, were sneaky, and fought only to win. When China was consolidated under the Qin in 221 BCE, the government made great progress with reforms and created huge construction projects, but ran roughshod over everyone. When the emperor died and his son was his successor, there were massive revolts all over China. The Qin were kicked out and the Han dynasty came to power. Even though the Han were saying, "Oh those bad Qin," they kept a lot of centralized authority, but also adopted some of Confucius' ideas. They kept the powers of the Qin, but were more restrained and smiled more.

The Han made Confucianism the state ideology, but molded it to what they wanted by adding other ideas, and a dash of Legalism, to the mix. However, Confucius did have quite an impact. His ethical ideas and his views on education were embraced. He was all about respect for those above you, whether they be parents, elders, rulers, or ancestors, and the Han liked that. Confucius' high regard for the arts led to a revival of literary and artistic culture. His editing of great works, and views on education, led to appointments made to government positions, based on merit through written examinations. The theory here was that the country would most benefit from government leaders who were the best examples of what it meant to be Chinese. How better to determine that than to find the people who had memorized the most from Confucius, or the books he had edited? You could always hire engineers or other technical workers, but how else could you find enlightened leadership that "embodied" the Chinese essence?

The second rival philosophy originating in the Warring States period was Mohism. It was based on the writings of Mo Tzu, who thought what people responded to most effectively was love, and the more the better. The Mohists believed everyone was best served by a state that improved the quality of life for everyone equally. They weren't crazy about religion or the arts, since those are big-time wasters, but were very interested in math and science. Believing war was also a waste, they later influenced many pacifists. Ironically, to deter attacks, Mohists became experts on defensive siege warfare and were therefore in big demand, by many cities, in times of war. However, once the Qin took over, and war temporarily ended, others absorbed their best ideas, and they essentially died out.

Confucius is the single person, who has had the most profound effect on China and, consequently, all of East Asia. I read a historian who was convinced because of the influence of Confucius, that over the last two thousand years the Chinese people have enjoyed, overall, the best government of any people in the world.

Not bad for a teacher.

24

TAOISM (DAOISM)

Tao Te Ching,
Ch. 1
If you can talk about it, it ain't the Tao.
If it has a name,
it's just another thing.
From *Getting Right with Tao*, by Ron Hogan

I often take a copy of the *Tao Te Ching* with me when I go camping or backpacking. To have a translation that "speaks" to me and to sit on a rock, under a tree on top of a mountain, or by a stream, to read and ponder, is a sublime experience. When asked by students to recommend a version of the *Tao Te Ching*, I first gave them a handout that has chapter one, from ten different translations, including a set of Chinese characters. Each English translation is different from the others even though you can tell they are pretty much talking about the same general idea. Students do not understand why there are such obvious discrepancies in each translation.

Translating Chinese to English must be a rough business. Chinese writing is made up of characters that each represent a word or phrase. English is based on a phonetic alphabet and they just don't easily convert into each other. The *Tao Te Ching*, originally written in classical Chinese, is considered poetry. Because of this difficulty, each translator derives his own best version of the meaning and puts that into the English words they feel are most congruent. This is why the translations can differ. So, I tell students to go to a good bookstore that has several translations, and then pick out several chapters they like. Read each translation for each chapter and decide which one "speaks to you" or at least, makes the most sense.

Ron Hogan's version, *Getting Right with Tao* is interesting because it is not a translation. Since he doesn't know Chinese, he has taken a number of English translations and synthesized them into very accessible English, while trying to stay close to what he believes is Lao Tzu's meaning. While scholars may poo-poo this methodology, I like it for what it is.

By the way, as I showed in the heading for this section there are two ways to spell the word, with either a T or a D. The new is Dao, the traditional, Tao. If you are really into phonology (study of organizing the sounds of languages), there are many scholarly arguments to be made for both sides, but most people just pick one. As far as I know, both are pronounced the same (like Dow). I learned it as Tao, so that is what I use. If you like Dao better, good for you.

In talking about all of this, I am avoiding talking about the Tao, which, of course, is the point here. But, if you read Chapter 1 of the *Tao Te Ching* you will see if you can talk about it, it is not the Tao. We want to talk about the Tao, but realize as we talk about it and think we understand it, we don't. Basically, trying to understand the Tao is like trying to understand God, Nirvana, or Brahman. We can give names to particular things, and definitions to limited objects, because we can pretty well grasp them. But those other words are forced to apply to what is just too big to accurately name, define, or comprehend. Trying makes our poor little heads hurt. The Tao has no name, but we call it the Tao because we are compelled to call it something, even if the label is meaningless and erroneously leads us to think we understand it. I don't know what else we can do, except accept these limitations and soldier on.

The traditional story is that Taoist thinking was codified in the *Tao Te Ching* by a court official called Lao Tzu. When he decided to retire, he climbed onto his water buffalo and headed for the hills. A border guard implored him not to leave until he had written down his wisdom. It took him all of two days, and he left behind the *Tao Te Ching* as he ambled off into the sunset. Another story has a young Confucius meeting an old Lao Tzu and being impressed by the older man's inscrutable wisdom. Did they really meet? Did Lao Tzu actually exist? Was he one guy or a compilation of several authors? No one knows, and it probably doesn't matter outside of history professor circles. It's the thought that counts.

To help grasp the ungraspable, we will pretend we can slice the Tao into understandable chunks. One way to think about the Tao is that it is the ultimate *something* of the universe. Why does existence consist of *something* rather than *nothing*? Because of the Tao. Everything comes from the Tao and goes back to the Tao. It is the womb from which all things spring. It is transcendent and a mystery we cannot perceive or process. Next, think about the Tao as the way the universe works. Think of it as the driving and ordering force behind all of nature. Stars are formed, flowers bloom, babies cry, old folks die. The Tao is a flowing force, which impels all things in nature to perform their processes to do what they do. It keeps all things moving and flowing and going. Last, think of the Tao as the way of a human life. The Tao is the force animating all things, fueling processes, and keeping everything going in the way they are supposed to. This works for human beings too. Following the Tao for us as individual human beings means we will live our lives in the best, most natural way.

Unlike animals who live their best way pretty much by instinct, we have some degree of free will and intelligence. We have developed very complex societies, so it is possible for us to make choices, as we often do, that do not follow the Tao, and are actually not in our best interest. We find ways, it seems, to distract ourselves from the Tao. Each of us, as a part of nature, is a unique blend of millions of different factors, most of which are beyond our control. But, as humans, there is a way of being and doing that is the best and most natural for who we are, as individuals and as members of our species. This is reflected in the lives we live, the choices we make, the careers we have, and our natural inclinations.

One way to determine whether our life decisions are in accordance with the Tao is to decide how happy we are. Do we enjoy our jobs? Is work fun? Do we dread certain people and situations? Is life hard for us or easy? Do we intuitively feel our lives are heading in the "right" direction? In thinking about this, I am reminded of a character in the movie *Dead Poets Society*. A young man who is intelligent, personable, and a leader among his peers, is in an exclusive prep school on his way to a successful law career, as has been determined by his father. The young man goes along with this for want of any strong personal goal of his own. When he discovers theater, however, he is enraptured and knows acting is what he most wants to do with his life. When his father categorically refuses to support this passion, considering only law school for his son, the young man feels trapped and the results are tragic. This young man had discovered his flow, his direction, his path. Every molecule in his body knew he was "made" for theatre. He was listening to the Tao.

Have you ever been tubing on a warm summer day? You float down the river with your friends on big inner tubes just going with the flow of the stream, wherever the current takes you, while you look at the beautiful, ever-changing scenery. You are happy. If you decide to go upstream, to see what's there, you would begin to paddle backwards furiously against the current. You might make some headway, but eventually you would begin to tire. As you paddle, you might look at the bank and see how little progress you are making for all your effort, feel frustrated and eventually unhappy. Finally, you grow a brain cell and realize it is easier, and more fun to go with the current than against it. If you can find the job, lifestyle, society, and people that are most aligned to your "current" or "flow," your life will work out well (or at least better than it otherwise would), and you will be happier. Go with the flow; things work out. Fight your natural direction; be unhappy.

25

THE WU WEI WAY

"When there is no desire, all things are at peace."
- Lao Tzu, *Tao Te Ching*

Different Applications of the Tao

There are three primary ways to understand the actions of the Tao in our lives, philosophical, physical, and religious Taoism. To follow the Tao philosophically, one must live in accordance with Wu Wei, which is to find the most natural way of moving through life effortlessly.

Read *The Tao of Pooh* by Benjamin Hoff. In a way that is very accessible to the Western mind, Hoff shows how Winnie the Pooh teaches us Wu Wei by example. Wu Wei literally means "without doing anything" but the real meaning is much more subtle. It really means "don't mess with what is natural" or "don't mess with what works". Sometimes doing nothing, or very little in a situation, is the best answer. Hoff suggests Wu Wei means to do things, but do them without "meddlesome, combative, or egotistical effort (68)." Actions reflecting Wu Wei follow the natural, efficient way to do things. The most efficient way is usually the best way.

Water runs down a mountain in the most efficient way. Over long periods of time, it patiently continues to flow, gradually carving into the rock as it improves its path. Water is persistent and never loses sight of its goal. At one level, all of the people who do hard or complicated actions with ease, have mastered Wu Wei, because they are accomplishing at the highest, most efficient level. Great athletes and dancers perform almost by instinct, with no wasted motions, seeming to be, almost effortlessly, in the zone.

It was very difficult when you first tried to ride a bicycle. Now, it is effortless. Whatever our work or effort, we should strive for greater efficiency, the natural way, Wu Wei. This is not a philosophy for slackers who don't want to do anything. It is really just the opposite, because those who are attuned are usually accomplishing a lot, even if their actions seem easy and effortless. They have found how to listen to the Tao.

One of my hobbies is splitting logs for the wood stove. I have learned, over the years, to read the grain of the wood, and when to use a wedge or the maul, and about how difficult a piece of wood will be to split. I am much more efficient than I used to be, though I wish I could consistently strike the same spot twice in a row. Once, a friend and I, on a wood gathering expedition, came across a young woodsman who, with just an axe, was able to take apart a large round of wood we had been trying to break for ten minutes. The young man was able to diagnose the grain and the knots in the wood so well, and was so skilled with the axe that he dissected each piece of wood quickly. We were in awe. Life, from a Taoist perspective, is taking the time to read the cracks in the wood correctly, and to apply just the correct amount of force to achieve the result. That is the natural way.

In our daily lives, we find we usually operate very inefficiently. Wu Wei suggests we do less interfering and follow our instincts, simplify our lives, and go with the flow. Take out the ego, the competition, and the compulsion to "do" something. However, it does take a lot of persistence and practice to become good. Many people have the potential to be great athletes, dancers, teachers, and computer systems engineers. Yet they do not apply themselves. They see their work as a negative experience, something to be avoided or done as quickly as possible. They do their work, take their money, go home, and forget about their day. It is very hard to become good at something you don't enjoy. Others consider every day at work to be a growth opportunity and are continuously learning the better, more efficient way to do their tasks. Work does not have to be a four-letter word. When everyone is gathered around the computer trying to debug code, the person who embodies Wu Wei will walk up, look at the situation, make a suggestion that solves the problem, and walk away. It looks so easy when they do it.

In Chinese philosophy and culture, everything is connected to, and influenced by, everything else. In light of this, there are a number of different ways to understand and practice Taoism. So far, we have discussed philosophical Taoism. This view of Taoism is very popular in the Western world because it is an alternative to prevailing "Western" ways of doing things. Some would suggest our society teaches us not to be introspective, but to be competitive, controlling, overly rational, and to put money and material goods above everything else. As a remedy, whether it is how you live life in the largest sense, or how you play tennis, there is a self-help author who will suggest the "Taoist" way to approach the subject. There have been a lot of books published that are titled, *The Tao of_____*. Seen as inspirational, the *Tao Te Ching* itself, in different translations, has been a big seller.

The other two applications of the Tao are physical and religious Taoism. To see the differences clearly, it is necessary to understand the Chinese view of energy flow. Traditionally, the Chinese believe, as part of the operating system of the cosmos, there is a type of energy, ch'i, that flows through all things and can be beneficial or not, depending on how the energy is utilized. Many believe if they can increase their flow of energy, they will be healthier, happier and live longer. In fact, throughout Chinese history, some people have used a variety of Taoist methods, including special diets, meditation, and many other formulas, actions, and combinations, to try to achieve immortality. This appears to be an interesting contradiction. While the Tao Te Ching encourages us to be "natural," some Taoists have searched for what seems to be a most unnatural result, eternal life. However, one could argue that if it is natural to eat right, and do other good things to lead a long healthy life, then, if you find the correct formula, there is nothing unnatural about immortality.

In physical Taoism, there is a belief that our well-being is affected, for better or worse, by how we interact with this energy flow in our everyday lives. In the art of placement, Feng Shui is utilized to find the best location for a house, the best floor plan, and the best way to arrange the furnishings in a room, always keeping in mind the patterns of energy flow. Put the house in the wrong spot, or your bed in the wrong location in your room, and you will not be happy with the results. By paying attention to the physical layout and the placement of things, energy will flow through the house, and through each room in the best possible way. In theory, if you have ever sat in a room in which you feel very comfortable and serene, the furniture may have been arranged, consciously or not, according to Feng Shui principles. As we push our couch around a room, looking for the location that "feels right," it might be we are subtly feeling the quality of the energy flow. The same principle works for acupuncture. Energy is flowing through our bodies at all times, and if there is a blockage, it manifests as illness or pain. The trained acupuncturist is able to use those little thin needles to break up the jam, and get the flow going again, so we feel better.

Different forms of Taoism focus on different ways to affect our personal energy. Philosophical Taoism, as exemplified by the *Tao Te Ching*, helps us conserve our energy and use it in our lives most efficiently. Physical Taoism encourages active ways to increase our energy. Feng Shui, acupuncture, Tai Chi, meditation, and eating certain foods, herbs, or combinations of foods are all ways to do this. In the movie *Remember the Titans*, there is a scene where quarterback Ronny Bass is exercising outside the school, ogled by a bevy of girls who think he is "so cute" and "so weird." The weird part is his Tai Chi exercises. After all, he is from California.

The third type of Taoism is religious Taoism. If ways of acquiring positive energy through philosophical or physical Taoism don't appeal to us, maybe we can get the spirit world to send us more. This involves priests, rituals, rites, magic, gods, spirits, etc. Taoist deities share space in temples with other deities, and their rituals lead us back to, and seem indistinguishable (at least to outsiders) from, traditional religious practices. It seems, in Chinese thinking, nothing stands alone. Sooner or later, everything comes back to align with everything else. It's all just different parts of the same interconnected whole.

As mentioned earlier, traditional Chinese thinking is syncretistic and religious beliefs are not compartmentalized into either/or groupings as we do in the West. Except for limits warranted by one's place in society, belief and practice are more like a buffet where you can create the combination of selections to make the plate that looks the yummiest to you. While there were intellectuals and government officials who were primarily Confucian, monks in monasteries who were focused on Buddhist ideals, and nature loving hermits living in caves trying to be pure Taoists, the overwhelming majority of Chinese people didn't have the time or inclination for such exclusivity. They had crops to plant and children to raise, so their focus was with the gods, the ancestors, and maybe a little bit more of this or that. However, even the busiest Confucian government bureaucrat probably had a quiet spot in the garden, with a stream flowing by, where he could sit, de-stress from the day, and get in touch with his Taoist side.

26

RELIGION IN CHINA TODAY

"Chinese culture has a lot of virtues that are tremendously valuable to not only us as Asian-Americans, but also the world in general."
- Martin Yan

In 1949 when the Communist Party took control of mainland China, religion was "de-emphasized" and the government officially became atheistic. Religious practices were discouraged in every possible way. Traditional Marxist ideology identifies religion as a false belief. The ruling class uses religion to control the people. Religion is an "opiate" to make people feel better in a capitalist society that exploits them. The Chinese communist government was not gentle in closing temples, churches and monasteries and jailing religious leaders.

Even though the government continued this policy for many years, it remains to be seen how these actions affected what it means to be Chinese. The problem is traditional Chinese religious beliefs and practices cannot be separated from Chinese culture and daily life. When a person lived with their family in their community, every day-to-day act reflected both the Chinese belief systems, and what it meant to be Chinese. Chinese syncretistic thinking, which, as mentioned earlier, does not differentiate between philosophical and religious thought, has an ancient lineage. It has imbued religion into Chinese culture in ways that make it hard for outsiders to understand in a "Western" way. Maybe it is more accurate to say Chinese religion is a product of Chinese thinking, and Chinese thinking demonstrates, in the activities of daily life, what it means to be Chinese. However, in recent decades, due to economic growth, the Chinese people have been strongly encouraged by the government to move from their small farming villages, to new urban high-rises, and work in factories. There is now concern that the decline of villages, where the vast majority of people lived in a traditional manner, is also killing the source of much that is unique in Chinese culture. Traditional music and dance, tied to temple worship, is being lost as village families are scattered across a developing urban landscape.

In the last twenty years or so, the Chinese government has mellowed somewhat and religion seems to be moving, slowly and carefully, back into the picture. As social stability and the economy of China continues to improve, there is a growing official tolerance of some religions, especially traditional Chinese ones. In fact, China has repaired and reopened many Taoist and Buddhist temples and monasteries, citing their historical value as examples of traditional Chinese culture.

Recently the government has broadened religious rights for the five officially approved religions: Buddhism, Taoism, Islam, Catholicism, and Protestantism. However, the practices of other faiths are illegal, and even some of these "approved" religions have been part of hard-line crackdowns. For example, the second largest ethnic group of Muslims in China, the Uighurs, are a Turkic people. They have friends and relatives extending from Western China, where many live, to Turkey. Even though Islam is an approved religion, the Chinese are concerned about Islamic terrorism and keep a very tight rein on Uighur religious practice, recently moving a million of them into internment camps in the far west. Also, while Buddhism is widely accepted throughout China, Tibetan Buddhists have a much harder time because Tibet was taken over by China in 1950, and not all Tibetans seem to appreciate that. It's not the Tibetans' Buddhism, per se, but their loyalty to the Dali Lama and other political issues that attract unfriendly government attention.

In order to organize congregations, Catholics and Protestants have to register with the government. There are not enough officially approved slots to cover the number applying, so many people worship in quasi-illegal groups at each other's houses. While the government has harassed some of these people in the past, there are mixed feelings about whether or not this will gradually lighten up. Some Protestant groups are having a harder time, but Catholics are more optimistic, since the Vatican seems interested in working out a deal with the government, regarding the appointment of bishops. Historically, this was a big problem for the pope and European monarchs. Should the bishops, who run the local church, be appointed by the pope or the kings? To whom are the bishops beholden? Other religious groups are forbidden and some, like Falun Dafa (Falun Gong) are persecuted.

Most "religious" Chinese folks, especially those in the country, have always quietly followed traditional folk practices. There are reports that these beliefs are returning, and not just to the villages. In a *New York Times* article, Dan Levin[1] noted, "As Marxist ideology has faded in China, ancient mystical beliefs once banned by the communist party are gaining ground. Guides to geomancy now fill bookstores, fortunetellers are busily offering costly sessions in astrology and numerology, and tycoons consult Feng Shui masters for financial guidance." Levin reports many government officials are using public funds to pay for these services in order to bolster their own careers, not for the public good. While there is a law forbidding "belief in feudal superstitions," a 2007 survey showed 52% of the nation's county level civil servants believed in divination, face reading, astrology or dream interpretation, all attributes of traditional Chinese religion.

Since traditional religious expression in China is syncretistic, it is very hard to be sure of the accuracy of current numbers regarding religious affiliation. Belief patterns do not fall into easily countable groupings. In addition, Chinese government statistics are thought by some to drastically underestimate religious belief. The Chinese government says there are about 100 million religious folks in China (about 10% of the population, while other sources suggest there may be over 200 million Buddhists alone, or over 20%). Perhaps 60+% of the population is atheistic, agnostic, or non-religious, though some of those probably follow traditional beliefs that don't show up in a neat category. I know several second or third generation Chinese-Americans who say their parents or grandparents still follow some of the traditional ways.

Best estimates suggest 3-4% of Chinese people are Christian, and 1-2% are Muslim. While there are probably many who could be described as "pure Buddhists," almost every person with religious leanings, except Muslims and Christians, would probably claim Buddhist ideas as part of their belief system. However, everyone seems to agree that the overall number of religious adherents is going up, as the government grows less concerned religion is going to cause trouble, and people keep looking for something to believe in.

All is not sweetness and light however. As Ian Johnson reported in *The New York Times*[2], the Chinese government has cut the crosses from the steeples of as many as 1700 Christian churches in Zhejiang province, citing building code violations. Locals are pressured to take them down or have them cut down. One observer suggests this is happening because the crosses look "foreign," i.e., not Chinese. If the churches look foreign, officials may be concerned the people worshiping there will begin to think like foreigners, and, perhaps, forget their government approved, core values. It seems those religions least harassed are either "traditional" ones, or those that can keep their practice quiet and out of sight.

Most recently, the government has instituted a crackdown on Christian churches who have tried to resist government control. Dissidents who have tried to become socially engaged are arrested and charged with publishing books and CDs without government approval[3]. However, the severity of this seems to fluctuate as some dissidents have not been touched.

There has also been a revival of Confucianism, first among intellectuals and now, somewhat unexpectedly, among high government officials. In "Why China Is Turning Back to Confucius," Jeremy Page of *The Wall Street Journal*[4] describes how the teachings of Confucius and other ancient Chinese philosophers, once labeled as medieval superstitions, are brought back into the limelight after years consigned to the dustbin of Chinese history. As it turns out, while the Chinese government still cheers for Marx and Lenin, nobody cares much about them anymore. The modern Chinese brand of capitalism is creating lots of prosperity and, despite occasional economic slow-downs, more people in China are not only better off than ever before, but also more open to the rest of the world. Since the government had already bad mouthed traditional Chinese culture, and hardly anyone believes in the old communist tropes, there is deep concern, at high levels, that without any cultural moorings the Chinese people are becoming cynical, corrupt, materialistic Worst of all, they might be attracted, by default, to Western values of democracy and individual freedom.

To plug the hole in this dike, the ancients are being rehabilitated and trotted back out to help everyone remember China has a deep, rich, 5000 year old culture of its own. The Education Ministry has mandated more Confucius at all grade levels. President Xi Xinping has been leading a public push to appreciate Confucius and the other ancients, so the Chinese people will realize they are already part of an important historical/cultural movement. Maybe the qualities Confucius tried to teach 2500 years ago will get another chance.

It will be fascinating to watch this scenario play out over the next several decades, as China tries to reinvent itself, by combining the very ancient with the very modern. If you take traditional Communist economic and social ideology out of the current Chinese government, which has already happened for all practical purposes, and you keep self-perpetuating one party rule, you have…I don't know…a dynasty? How the leadership of this current dynasty reacts to China's many opportunities and challenges, and how the Chinese people react to those policies, will determine whether the current regime will continue to enjoy the Mandate of Heaven.

27

ABRAHAMIC FAITHS
THE ABRAHAMIC RELIGIONS

"All religions are true. I just want to love God."
- *Life of Pi* by Yann Martel

Judaism, Christianity and Islam have a lot in common. Not everything, by any means, but they all claim the same Abrahamic/Mosaic religious origin, though their interpretation of what that means is different. If we want differences, we can find differences, but that riles folks up, and then they overlook the similarities in ethical and moral teachings. All three faiths base their ethics on the scriptures originating in the Hebrew Bible. While there are differences about meaning, and there are those who take passages out of context for their own political/religious purposes, the ethics taught in both the New Testament and the Qur'an are not far apart. Ethically speaking, taken as a whole, all three faiths are in sync. Based on that, you would think good Jews, good Muslims and good Christians should all be able to live together harmoniously. That record is spotty.

Talking about Christianity or Islam can sometimes get a person in trouble. In a recent poll, 56% of Americans said kids in public schools should not have to learn "Arabic" numerals in math[1]. Please. There are a lot of confused people out there. There are also many different points of view within each religion, so it is difficult to determine what everyone believes. In the upcoming chapters, I will discuss my understanding of these faiths, and what they have, more or less, in common.

Bible Stories

Kids in all Abrahamic faiths learn about religious stories, from the Hebrew Bible (Old Testament) in Church, Temple, or Synagogue and from the Qur'an in Mosque. Back in the old days, before the Supreme Court cases, they also came across Bible stories in public schools. However, even though I went to Catholic school, I have absolutely no memory of learning about them there. My recollection is that we were very New Testament oriented. So, most of my early understanding of Bible stories comes from movies such as *David and Bathsheba*, *Solomon and Sheba*, *Samson and Delilah*, and my favorite, *The Ten Commandments*. Only later did I read them in the Bible. Curiously, Bible stories are often studied in literature classes, not for religious purposes, and only sometimes to understand the Bible as literature, but because of the prevalence of biblical allusions in many classic literary works. A working knowledge of the basic events surrounding Abraham, Isaac, Joseph, Jonah, Noah, Moses, David, Solomon, Adam and Eve, Cain and Able, Sodom and Gomorrah, and a few more, is essential to both serious literary navigation, and a basic understanding of many metaphors and references in aspects of Western culture. In the 2003 movie *Master and Commander* one of the officers is called a "Jonah" by the crew. If you don't know, you won't get it.

Sabbath and Sunday

All Abrahamic faiths have a Sabbath or equivalent. While Muslims have prayers on Friday, different countries are split on whether there is a full day, half day, or no day of rest involved. Shabbat, as a Jewish day of prayer and rest (from Friday night to Saturday night), will be discussed later. The early Christian Church thought it would be a good idea to move the day of rest and worship to Sunday, though the Orthodox Christian churches still keep to Saturday. Whereas Orthodox Jews define work on Sabbath as doing "anything" including turning on a light switch, or driving to synagogue (you have to walk which does keep the community compact), Christians have always had a much more liberal interpretation. As a kid, if I didn't do it on Saturday, I had to mow the lawn on Sunday, despite my protests about a day of rest. We used to have "Blue laws" in Virginia that kept most stores closed on Sunday. I suspect legislators had a religious intent, to encourage us to go to church rather than go shopping. But since "religion" was not in the legislation, the courts upheld these laws until they eventually faded away, under the crushing demands of a new faith, modern seven days a week consumerism.

Monotheism

Monotheism in the modern sense means just one thing, there is one, and only one, God. If there are other spiritual creatures of some type, like devils, angels, saints or jinn, they have been created by God for God's purposes and they only have the powers God allows them. I think most Muslims, Christians, and Jews would attest this to be generally true. This same definition would probably also allow room for those Hindus who believe the many Hindu gods are actually creations of the "one" God, Brahman.

While Muslims and Jews might make a few comments, under their breath, that the Christian concept of the Trinity doesn't rise to an absolute monotheistic standard, we will note it, and let it go for now. I had originally thought monotheism began with Abraham and the early Hebrews, but I have since found I was incorrect. In fact, pure, modern, monotheism takes a long time to show up. When Abraham made the original covenant with God, it was to certify his allegiance to only this one God, not others. This point of view did not deny there were other gods around, worshipped by other peoples, but this God was to be THE God of Abraham and his descendants. God was a jealous God and didn't want these people messing with those other gods. Later, according to scripture (Exodus 7:8-12), when Moses faced Pharaoh, he told Aaron to throw down his staff and it became a snake. Pharaoh's priests and magicians also changed their staffs into snakes. However, Moses' snake devoured theirs, which showed his God was the most powerful. But, it does say those priests changed their staffs into snakes, which seems to imply a belief that their deities also had some sort of power. Versions of the Ten Commandments have God saying, "You shall have no other gods before me." That implication seems clear.

Over time, views shifted in different places, moving people closer to the idea there was only one God. During the Axial Age, very roughly 800 BCE to 300 BCE, in diverse locations around the world, the old idea of many gods who had to be placated, began to adjust to the more elegant notion of one God. It went from this is our God (and I recognize you have yours), to ours is the most powerful god; to ours is the only God. The timeline and location of these changes is controversial, but it does seem like, in most places, there has been a long-term trend toward moving from many gods to one. Zoro-astrianism lays a claim to the first monotheism, as does Judaism. Hinduism lost its polytheism early on, and has found other explanations and functions for its many gods. Maybe the brief Egyptian worship of Aten, led by Pharaoh Akhenaten in the 1300's BCE, gets the earliest pure monotheism prize.

While both Christianity and Islam claim monotheism, their adherents have also believed other forces exist in the world, and have to be taken into consideration, and sometimes placated. Common people believed in Jinn in Islam and little people, fairies, demons and other magical powers and forces in Christianity, for a long time. I am not entirely sure that period has ended. Today is Friday the thirteenth, and the comics in the newspaper have several mentions of good/bad luck, carrying rabbit's feet, and skipping over the cracks in the sidewalk. I have ridden in cars with "good luck" St. Christopher (the patron saint of travelers) medals and suction cup statues. If you believe in the power of all of those things, are you truly monotheistic? Some religious folk I know believe that the spiritual battle between our guardian angels and Satan's devil minions over our souls, is not metaphorical but very real, with demons fighting angels for our souls at this moment.

The earliest Greek philosophers noticed every cultural group they were aware of seemed to have their own pantheon of Gods and Goddesses and collections of mythological stories (my story is true; the other guy's is a myth). All of these had some unique features, or at least were significantly different from each other. For instance, every group seemed to have a different creation account. The philosophers asked, how could all of these be true? Shouldn't one be correct and not the others? How can we tell? Maybe none of them are true? The beginning of philosophy dates from this quest, cutting through contradictory stories, to discover what actually happened. Later, Plato's theory of forms pointed Greek thinking toward the idea of the ultimate source of all objects and concepts, the form of the Good. This led to Neo-Platonism, with its emphasis on this ultimate source being God, which helped to inform Christian doctrines.

The idea of God as "One" eliminated the problem of contradictory stories. If you believed in one God, then those who believed in many gods were simply either wrong, or if viewed generously, were discussing the same God as yours but, in their telling, God was dressed in different cultural clothing. Throughout this process, most people began to feel there was something intellectually and emotionally satisfying in identifying God as One. However, as the Scottish philosopher David Hume pointed out centuries later, just because the idea of one God has gained widespread acceptance, this does not prove in any way there is only one God, not two, or a committee of 16 or none at all. Thanks David.

28

JUDAISM
THERE IS NOT ONE JUDAISM

"I know, I know. We are Your chosen people. But, once in a while, can't You choose someone else?"
- Tevye, *Fiddler on the Roof*

Once upon a time in the nostalgic suburban world of a 1950's kid, everything made sense. If you had asked me about religion then, I had that covered. We had three religions in my world. Catholics were people who believed in Jesus and the pope; Protestants believed in Jesus but not the pope; and Jews did not believe in Jesus or the pope. While theoretically I should have thought Jewish lack of proper Jesus belief was a bad thing, it didn't register that way. I had a Jewish friend, David, who was a regular guy. In Catholic school, while Sister Bernadette let us know how Protestants and other non-Catholics were going to go to hell, she never said that about Jews. I don't remember Jews ever being criticized in church sermons either. Thinking back, I wonder if she may have had a soft spot for Judaism from her New Testament point of view. The Jews were different, and, of course, as we were taught, wrong to deny Jesus, but somehow they were important enough in God's overall plan and the whole "story of Jesus" scenario to have earned a pass from her, and she was tough. I never quite understood how that worked.

Whether or not you agree on points of belief or scripture, it's abundantly clear Judaism has had a massive impact on the world over the last several thousand years and is probably at the top of the list for most influential religion, per capita, of all time. Jews are believed by many to be, through the actions of Abraham and Moses, the "Chosen People" of God. They developed a system of beliefs and practices, some of which were later prominent in the establishment of both Christianity and Islam. The stories of the Hebrew Bible (Old Testament) have not only affected religious belief and action throughout the world but have had a tremendous impact on the arts. The contributions of individual Jews throughout history in literature, science, philosophy, the development of the bagel, and every other serious area of thought and study is unmatched. For the less serious aspects of life, which group can put up a better record of contributions to humor and entertainment? Jewish humor is always clean and always funny. For example- Short summary of every Jewish holiday, "They tried to kill us. We won. Let's eat" (Alan King). For a deeper, more considered examination of this topic, I recommend *The Gifts of the Jews*, by Thomas Cahill.

This is only a small part of the legacy of the Jewish people. In trying to explain how and why these enormous contributions came to be, one's mouth is left to hang open. The fact that Jews, as a people, were not extinguished a dozen times by the vagaries of history is amazing. While thousands of other tribal groups lost their identities by being scattered or absorbed into larger populations, the Jews maintained their unique cultural and religious beliefs and practices. Recently, it was suggested to me that when other peoples in the ancient world were conquered, they switched to the conqueror's gods because gods they were clearly more powerful. Jews on the other hand, when they were conquered, decided their God was angry with them for some reason and they were being punished.

Wanting to get back on God's good side, they doubled down on being good Jews and following the rules.

While on one hand we have this massive amount of contributions to world culture, there has often been, ironically, for at least the last 2000 years, a deep and bitter current of anti-Semitism in many places. Any serious discussion of this ugly state of affairs, either historically or currently, is far beyond my abilities. There are always, it seems, twisted people in every country, who blame others for their misfortunes. They revel in the hatred of a vulnerable group. In the United States, there has recently been a sad resurgence of white supremacy, neo-Nazis, racism, and religious hatred, sometimes aimed at Jews.

While anti-Semitism today is seen sometimes in Muslim countries, students are often surprised to find Islam and Judaism share many similar ethics and beliefs. Think of them as cousin religions. Historically, Jews have been treated extremely well in Muslim lands, certainly better than they were in most Christian countries. The change in attitude over the last seventy years is tied to the formation of the state of Israel, and how that was accomplished. Until that issue is settled to everyone's satisfaction, this relationship will most likely continue to be contentious.

What Does it mean to be Jewish?

Judaism is not a religion of fixed dogmas. In Jewish thinking, trying to understand God, God's place in history, the meaning of scripture, and what God expects of each of us, is a challenge. While some religions might be noted for their docile acceptance of what they have been told is God's will, Jews, as communities and as individuals, have been struggling for centuries to figure out just what it is God wants from us. And, as the world has changed, Judaism has changed. Reliance on thought and reason has brought about a continuing evolution and diversity of Jewish positions on the sacred writings of the Hebrew Bible, and the place of this in Jewish lives. At one time, it was very important that Jews sacrifice animals at the

Temple in Jerusalem, often traveling long distances. This doesn't happen anymore, and there is only one wall left of the Temple, yet Jews are still Jews.

Understanding Judaism was a hard nut to crack for me. With most religions I can list a set of beliefs and, if anyone wants to know if someone is of that faith, we can check off the beliefs until we figure it out. But Judaism doesn't seem to work that way. While there are, potentially, a lot of things to believe and do, there doesn't seem to be any absolute requirement, other than belonging. One of the texts I consulted said there are atheists who consider themselves to be Jews. What's up with that? I'm pretty sure no one can legitimately call themselves a Christian if they don't believe in God, not to mention Jesus.

So, one day I am a teacher and somehow have developed sufficient hubris to think I can teach about world religions. In my second year of the class, I am confronted with the question I cannot yet answer, "What does it mean to be Jewish?" As I did the first year, we went through readings and class discussions, and talked about a lot of Jewish ideas and beliefs, but I am not much closer to a real sense of understanding. I feel I know the facts, but not the guts. Fortunately, that year, I had three very vocal Jewish students in one class. I don't remember how the discussion got around to it, but I remember saying to them, "OK, why don't you tell us it means to be Jewish." With the whole class watching in fascination, they argued amongst themselves for over twenty minutes before announcing that what it means to be Jewish. is to argue about what it means to be Jewish. Almost at once I felt the fog lifting.

To be Jewish is to be a member of this ethno/religious quasi-tribal group, usually with a family connection. If one belongs, then exactly how membership is demonstrated, or should be demonstrated, is up for individual consideration and debate (except, of course, as limited by what your momma thinks which, frankly, seems to be a factor in every religion). Since membership is inherited through birth, Judaism does not actively seek outside converts but does provide a method for conversion (though some Orthodox Jews do not believe certain conversions are legitimate).

As far as I can tell, everything in Judaism is up for discussion. God gave us intelligence, a rational mind, and a set of incomplete or vague instructions, subject to interpretation, that don't always seem to apply to the circumstances of our daily lives. It is OK to disagree. We have to take the questions we have, and figure out the answers. But, and I think this is key to separating a Jew from any random philosopher, that discussion has to be within the parameters of Jewish history, theology, Torah, customs, and God.

Not all of this argument and discussion is seen as a bad thing, it's a good thing. It is considered worthy, and by many, intellectually satisfying, to spend time arguing over law and interpretations. In some religions, adherents are encouraged to agree to, or at least go along with, some aspect of belief or worship because that is the "right" answer, as determined by scripture, or tradition, or the leader. If you don't like it, there's always the highway for you. In Judaism, the point of view is we have God given abilities to figure out what God expects from us, so use those abilities. Each person decides how he or she will or will not practice Judaism as a religion. They might follow the ways of their parents, or they might not, and not everybody's momma will be happy with their decision, but God wants us to use our noodle.

29

PRACTICING JUDAISM

"If you are not a better person tomorrow than you are today, what need have you for a tomorrow?"
- Rebbe Nachman of Breslov

"A Jewish woman had two chickens. One got sick, so the woman made chicken soup out of the other one to help the sick one get well."
- Henny Youngman

All of the deep thinking and arguments over thousands of years has yielded a Judaism, which exists across a wide field of practice and belief. There is truly not one Judaism.

At one end are the ultra-Orthodox who live their lives adhering closely to the most specific, numerous and precise interpretations and practices. You cannot watch a documentary about New York City without catching street scenes of Orthodox or Hasidic Jewish men, with their distinctive clothing, beards and sideburns. At the other end of the spectrum are those who are Jews through family relations and ethnic heritage, but don't practice or even believe. These folks may still consider themselves Jews, but ethnic Jews, not religious ones. They celebrate holidays, eat the food, maybe dance the dances, and participate culturally, just not religiously.

Eric Weiner, in his book *Man Seeks God*, describes his upbringing as a "gastronomical Jew." "If we could eat it, then it was Jewish, and by extension, had something to do with God." "We believed in an edible deity, and that was about the extent of our spiritual life." Further out are those who are slowly fading away from Judaism because they just don't have the interest, or easy opportunities, to stay active. Their parents or grandparents might have been Jewish, but maybe someone married outside the faith, or they are living separated from the cloud of relatives and so have been sliding slowly, year after year, away from the family religion.

A survey I saw some years ago said over half of American Jews were marrying outside their faith. One of my wife's best friends, who is Jewish, married a Catholic man. When I spoke to her about this, 25 or so years ago, she said the plan was to raise their children in both faiths. In other words, to do both Hanukah and Christmas. Several years later when a Conservative Rabbi spoke in my class, I asked him what he thought this couple should do. First, he was opposed to them marrying across lines of faith. His concern was this is a sure way to have fewer Jews in the world because, in his experience, Jews in religiously mixed marriages tend to fall away from active practice. Then, he said if they are going to get married anyway, they should just raise the kids in one religion, not both, because they will either become confused or drop both. When I later spoke to our friend, I asked her how her daughters, then 21 and 18 were doing religiously. Were they Jewish or Catholic? The Rabbi was correct; they do not practice either religion. However, she reported they are spiritual, but not religious. Like a growing number of young people, they reflect to her, the Jewish belief in "Tikun Olam," to make the world a better place. Since Judaism focuses very closely on how one's life is lived, developing yourself, your community, and your world to be better can be seen as a religious function that might be more important to some than theological beliefs and practices. In this regard, Jews are well known for philanthropy and championing the oppressed. Neither our friend, nor her husband, practice their birth faiths either. She is sad there is no one around to share Yiddish expressions with her.

Being Jewish

"Being Jewish is just one part of their lives, for us being Jewish is everything."[1] Gitty Wolf, then 17, summarized the differences in lifestyle and attitude between her Orthodox family in Boro Park, Brooklyn, and the two teenage girls from a Conservative congregation who were visiting from suburban Maryland. While the families of the suburban girls try to fit their religion in with the other typical suburban teenage activities, such as sports, music lessons, and friends, the Boro Park family's daily life is only about their religion. To them, the covenant with God is the center of life, and obedience to the laws is taken for granted. There is Jewish and then there is Jewish.

When someone accidentally turned off a light during Shabbat preparations, no one could turn it back on because that was forbidden. Families in Boro Park sometimes have as many as a dozen children, each with an Old Testament or old country name. The kids go to sex segregated religious schools that don't teach anything that might contradict the Bible. In this neighborhood, where almost everyone is Orthodox, there is little assimilation with the modern world. Sexes are segregated in the synagogue, where men are the only ones involved with the service; girls will become housewives and mothers. All activities are governed by the many rules and interpretations derived from the Torah. Individual autonomy is important, but it must be realized within the rules. Marriage and children, optional in the larger society, are required within the orthodox community. As David Brooks pointed out in the *New York Times*, 21% of non-orthodox Jews between 18 and 29 are married, compared to 71% of orthodox Jews. With families of four, five, or more children, the Orthodox make up 32% of Jews but have 61% of Jewish children.[2]

The suburban Conservative Jewish girls visiting Boro Park, go to public school with boys, and students of many different religions and backgrounds. They are taught a secular curriculum, which includes evolution and other topics that contradict literal religious interpretations. In their synagogue, a male and female rabbi are at the pulpit and all the families, usually with one or two children, sit together. Women are as involved in the service as are men, and there is probably not a family that doesn't want their daughter to get into a top ranked college so she can get a good job when she graduates. The idea of using a matchmaker to have their daughter married soon after high school would not go over well here. Reform Jews probably would not have sent their children on the Boro Park field trip.

The degree of assimilation of traditional beliefs and practices, to the modern world and the larger culture, is the question at the heart of the differences between Jewish denominations. Should the traditions of the past remain unchanged (Orthodox)? Should the traditions be recognized as the ways of an ancient people, and discarded or adapted to life in the 21st century (Reform)? Or, should we maintain a connection to the traditions of the Torah, while still incorporating the modern world (Conservative)? In a very small nutshell, these are the differences between the three groups. Of course, just because I said three groups, I don't mean there are only three opinions within Judaism. That would be laughable. Not only are there a number of smaller groups not discussed here, but there are also, within each grouping and each individual congregation, many different points of view on both ancient theological questions, and the issues of the day. Jewish thought is a very broad continuum. While almost everyone within any religious community feels an inclination to go along with the group, Judaism, by its nature, demands each of us use our reasoning and intelligence to find the answers, given our religious and ethical beliefs that make sense to us.

30

WHO IS A JEW, ETC.?

"There is a famous story in which the Kaiser asks Bismarck, Can you prove the existence of God? Bismarck replies, "The Jews, your majesty. The Jews."
- Unattributed

There are a number of topics in and around Judaism that have always fascinated me. These comments are not exhaustive on the subjects, or definitive, but really just lay out how I make sense of them. Topics are in no particular order.

Bar and Bat Mitzvah

Two Jewish rituals widely known outside of Judaism are the Bar Mitzvah for 13-year-old Jewish boys, and the Bat Mitzvah for 12-year-old girls. This is a coming of age ceremony, which makes young people responsible for their own religious decisions, and their participation in the religious community. However, you still can't drive the car and you still have to do your chores. When my kids were younger, our family was invited to, and attended, one of each.

The Bat Mitzvah was held in a firehouse party hall, and I think the major theme was dolphins, because that is what the young lady liked the most. It was quite a blow out and everyone had a great time. I don't recall anything overtly religious happening, but maybe that occurred earlier. Bat Mitzvahs are held by Reform and Conservative congregations, because Orthodox groups do not believe women should preach to the congregation during services. I have been told some Orthodox groups will do this, but if the girl only speaks to a gathering of female members.

The Bar Mitzvah we attended was at a conservative synagogue, and did have a service where the young man read in Hebrew. Then there was a great party, which seemed much more "Jewish," since we did a lot of dancing in circles singing "Hava Nagila," even though I did not know any other words. It seemed many guests didn't know the words either.

If you have a Bat Mitzvah for girls and a Bar Mitzvah for boys, what do you do for young Jewish people who claim a fluid gender identification?[1] As it has with other aspects of society, this question confounds many, and does not yield an easy obvious answer. Recently, progressive synagogues have worked with young people to develop alternatives such as a neutral "b mitzvah" or a "they mitzvah" (using a non-gendered pronoun). To the best of my knowledge, Orthodox communities are not on board with this.

Who is a Jew?

The tradition is a Jew is a person born of a Jewish mother. In a Reform congregation, that can also be from a Jewish father and a non-Jewish mother. A Jew is considered a Jew even if they convert to another religion. Ironically, while Jews do not beat the bushes for gentile converts, converts are often pursued between the various branches of Judaism. For outsiders, converting to Judaism is not as easy as it is to join a denomination of Christianity or Islam. To become a Jew, from the outside, one has to really want it and work for it. It is more like, back in the old days, wanting to join a different tribe. Those who are serious about conversion, go through a complete psychological and lifestyle change. I don't think you can convert to Judaism and wake up the next day with your life as usual. This is a profound decision, and those who make it, are welcomed with open arms. However, all Reform and most Conservative conversions are not recognized by Orthodox congregations. A friend of ours toyed with the idea of converting to Reform Judaism some years ago. She had been raised as a Christian, but she said she "could never quite get the whole Jesus thing." I was looking forward to following the conversion process with her, but she got divorced instead. Probably a better decision. I have told students, when they go to college, sometime during their four years, someone will knock on their dorm door or come up to them in the cafeteria and say, "Have you found Jesus?" No one will ever come up to them and say, "Have you found Moses?"

As I mentioned, the only time I have heard of Jewish proselytizing is among other Jews. My friend David (not the same David I knew as a kid), a reform Jew who wears a yarmulke, told me that, while visiting in New York City, he was enthusiastically greeted by Lubavitch Hasidic Jews, and encouraged to join them. In Orthodox circles, some hold the belief that Conservative and Reform Jews are really not Jews, since they do not adhere sufficiently to traditional Jewish law. Naturally, the Orthodox want to encourage them back into the fold. Understandably, this causes the American Conservative and Reform Jews to be upset, since they consider themselves totally dedicated to their religion, and totally Jewish. Gabrielle Glaser, who converted to Reform Judaism, commented on a meeting with her Rabbi, and his feelings about Glaser's conversion: "The rabbi said he wished all Jews had to convert. He understands that we converted because we wanted to make a commitment to Judaism. And that the commitment of converts, often goes beyond that of born Jews . . . It is particularly painful to me that many Orthodox rabbis both here and in Israel don't understand that. Am I a 'real' Jew? Am I authentic? I think I know and I suspect God does too."[2]

The question over who is a Jew, and who is not, and who defines the difference, is sometimes very complex. There have been many books written about Jewish identity and continuity. I am neither Jewish, nor scholar enough to comment intelligently on these issues, but it does seem Judaism is struggling to understand its place and future in the world. Issues having to do with the Holocaust, the importance and survival of Israel, the disappearance of Jews into the larger culture, and continuing anti-Semitism are of greatest concern. News stories from Israel tell of splits and divisions there. A large part of the Israeli population are secular Jews.

Beliefs

There is no central authority in Judaism to decide what religious beliefs a Jew should have, so while there are some views generally held in common by most, other views are widely divergent. Unlike other Abrahamic religions, Judaism does not hold that belief in a particular creed or savior is necessary to be right with God. Many Muslims believe salvation depends on believing there is one God, and Muhammad is his prophet. Many Christians say belief in the salvation, provided by the death and resurrection of Jesus, is absolutely required. In Judaism, which is primarily focused on life here on earth, there is not even much speculation about what happens after life, since it is thought God has room in heaven for all good people, and whatever the setup is, that's how it will be. Trust God.

The history of Judaism consists of God, and the Covenant between God and the Jewish people. The job of each Jew is to decide how to respond to that contract. According to tradition, Abraham, by accepting God as his God (a choice from all of the many gods available during that time period), became the first convert to what is now Judaism. The relationship of Abraham's descendants to God, the renewal of the Covenant by Moses, and the rules and instructions laid down in the Hebrew Bible, provide the basis for understanding what God wants of his people. But what does this understanding mean today? That is a central question. Essentially, God said his people are to worship and love him, and to reflect his love for them by loving each other. This appears to be a very enlightened point of view, compared to the other Gods of the ancient world. With the exception of the generally friendly Egyptian Gods, who provided the Nile floods, ancient gods were not particularly caring, and used and abused humans at will.

Orthodox Jews try to follow the 613 rules, or mitzvah, found in the Torah. In trying to understand what this would mean in a person's life, I found the book, *The Year of Living Biblically* by A.J. Jacobs, to be both entertaining and informative. The author, who describes his level of Jewishness as similar to the level of real Italian food to an Olive Garden restaurant, tries, over the course of a year, to obey every single mitzvah. This includes the most well-known ones like following the Ten Commandments, loving his neighbor, and being fruitful and multiplying (his wife had opinions about that), but also lesser known laws, like not wearing clothes with mixed fibers, never shaving his beard, and stoning adulterers. Highly recommended (not stoning, the book).

31

RULES AND SCRIPTURE

"In Jewish history there are no coincidences."
- Elie Wiesel

Keeping Kosher/ Dietary Laws

If a person on the street knows anything about Judaism, beyond Moses and the Holocaust, it is something about Jewish dietary restrictions. Laid out in the Torah, restrictions have to do with not eating pork or shellfish and various impure foods, or combinations of foods. Also covered is the correct method to slaughter animals. These restrictions are followed very scrupulously by Orthodox Jews, generally followed, but with different degrees of intensity, by Conservative Jews, and rarely, only if they really want to, by Reform Jews. While some Christians believe the literal words in other parts of the Hebrew Bible, I have never heard of them following these restrictions.

Some historians and anthropologists have speculated that in the ancient world, certain animals were literally unclean, or full of disease, and therefore dangerous to eat. Perhaps under-cooked pork led to widespread outbreaks of trichinosis, or something like that, so these rules were developed and followed for practical reasons. I asked the Rabbi why pork and other foods were out, even in modern times, when meat packing is so much safer. He said it was because "God told us to do this." His point was, if there were health benefits from eating Kosher in the old days that was just a coincidental, secondary benefit. The only reason people did, and still do, follow kosher rules is because "God told us to follow them."

Since eating is seen as a religious ritual, there are special rules, such as all blood must be drained from slaughtered animals (similar to Muslim Halal rules), and only from animals with cloven hooves can be eaten. No mixing of meat with any milk products is allowed, and the more observant will have separate sets of cooking utensils, dishes, and sometimes dishwashers, so what touches meat, never touches what touched dairy.

The Ten Commandments

Everyone has heard of the Ten Commandments, believed to be the set of rules given to Moses by God, and followed by Abrahamic adherents, with various degrees of interpretation and intensity. In the U.S., religious Christian conservatives have often tried to put them up in courtrooms and classrooms, because they felt just seeing the Commandments is good for us. The courts, citing separation of church and state, usually take them down. As a world religions teacher, who had many decorations in my classroom representing all of the major religions, I put the Ten Commandments on the wall because they were part of my curriculum. I told the class, if the proponents of the Ten Commandments posting were right, and viewing the Commandments made you a better person, then my students would be ahead of everyone else in the school.

The Ten Commandments is probably one of the most well-known and popular religious icons in the world, since it is approved of and appreciated by Muslims, Christians and Jews. I know the religious story of how we got the Commandments, because I have seen the movie *The Ten Commandments*, with Charlton Heston as Moses, many times. If this event was real (scholars disagree), and did not happen the way it did in the movie, it should have. I would hate to think Cecil B. DeMille was a better director than God. Despite Indiana Jones, no one really knows what became of Moses' tablets of commandments and their container, the Ark of the Covenant, if they actually existed. However, there are conspiracy theorists, UFO enthusiasts, and others, who will be glad to pass on their pet theories.

A problem with the Ten Commandments, is there is not one set of Ten Commandments listed in the Torah, but several. Different religions focus on either Exodus or Deuteronomy as their source, and those sources appear, in the original, as blocks of text without paragraph breaks or numbers. Everyone is sure there are supposed to be ten, because the number of commandments is referred to elsewhere, but the exact translation and numbering is a matter of interpretation. There are four versions I know of: a Catholic/Lutheran version, a Protestant version, an Orthodox Christian version, and a Jewish version. If you are a Protestant committing adultery, you are violating Commandment 7, but if you are Catholic caught in the same sin, you are violating Commandment 6. One year, on the first day of class, a student came into the room, looked at my Ten Commandments on the wall and said, "That's not correct." I later found out he was Catholic, but my wall poster came straight from the King James Bible.

Torah

The Torah consists of the first five books of the Hebrew Bible- Genesis, Exodus, Leviticus, Numbers, and Deuteronomy plus the Oral Torah, as written in the Talmud (the rest of the Hebrew Bible consists of the Prophets and the Writings). This contains the story of creation, the lives of the patriarchs and all of the rules, including the Ten Commandments, that God wants Jews (and the rest of us) to follow. The tradition is that God gave the content of Torah to Moses, who wrote it all out, except for the last part about his own death and burial. Tradition says it was Joshua who filled that in. Not everybody buys into the tradition, however. Most scholars believe critical analysis shows at least four distinct story lines in the Torah, written by different authors. They believe the Torah information was passed on orally for many years. Then it was gathered and compiled by scribes, over several hundred years around the 6th and 5th centuries BCE. Many scholars also hold those various scribal authors each had their own political and religious agenda. Belief in the validity of Torah content ranges from, "This is the word of God," to "These are a bunch of stories, told by a wandering people, that may or may not have any deep lessons or meaning," to "these were stories hijacked from Mesopotamian mythology." Take your pick. I guess that is what faith is all about.

For those who believe, there is no question that studying the Torah is essential. Studying the Torah is one of the 613 mitzvah. This extends to the Oral Torah as well. Tradition says the Oral Torah was also given to Moses and passed down, well, orally, until it was written. Once written, it became the Talmud, a record of rabbinic discussions pertaining to Jewish law, ethics, philosophy, customs, and history.

Talmud

If you have decided it is important to live your life the way you believe God wants you to, but you find God's scripture to be somewhat vague on the finer details, you need a solution. If you are into total obedience, you could find someone to be in charge of making all your religious decisions, so you just obey, which, in a way, takes the heat off you. Unless, of course, she is wrong. However, if you have been raised to believe God gave you a brain to think about things like this, you might do as the Jews have done, and argue it out. However, most people do not have the time for a lot of weighty religious arguments. There are children to feed, cows to milk, and computers to be programmed. Luckily for Judaism, there have always been learned men (and now women) who study the scriptures as a full time job, and have the intense interest to discuss and argue about the meaning of every line. At first their arguments were memorized, but after the destruction of the Temple in Jerusalem in 70 CE, they were written down and collected in the Talmud. Almost two thousand years, and many thousands of words, have been spent trying to understand God's meaning, and the resulting collection is a monument to human thought. For an argument in the Talmud to be accepted, the logic has to be sound, the evidence has to be good, and the reasoning must be right. The arguments of the Rabbis are studied as a sound basis for further thinking.

32

RULES AND HOLIDAYS

"Let me tell you the one thing I have against Moses. He took us forty years into the desert in order to bring us to the one place in the Middle East that has no oil."
- Golda Meir

Noahide Laws

It is rare among religions to find something like the Jewish idea that you don't have to believe our beliefs, or follow our laws, to be right with God. While some Christians and some Muslims, among others, insist X, Y, or Z belief must be held, in order to not become toast after you die, that is not the case in Judaism. The general Jewish feeling, as I understand it, is Judaism is the correct religion for Jews, but there is not one right faith for everyone. Jews respect devout people of any faith, and believe good people, even those without a faith, are going to be OK with God. It is our actions that count.

While the Orthodox believe there are 613 mitzvah or rules Jews might follow, there are only seven listed in the Torah that must be followed by everyone else, to have God's approval. These are the Noahide Laws given to all of the children of Noah, which is all of us, if you believe all of humanity, except Noah's family, was wiped out in the big biblical flood. That would make all of us his descendants.

Here are the seven Noahide laws listed by the Talmud[1]. My comments follow.

1. Prohibition of Idolatry- No worshiping idols. Since most religions with idols are worshiping or praying "through" the object to the spiritual source, that may be OK here. Worshiping the idol itself, as if it was a deity, might be what this means.
2. Prohibition of Murder- unlawful, premeditated killing of a person. You can have a big discussion about the criteria for deciding lawful v. unlawful killing.
3. Prohibition of Theft- No one likes thieves.
4. Prohibition of Sexual immorality- What is immoral sexuality and what is not? The Torah will tell you, though you may not agree.
5. Prohibition of Blasphemy- speaking evil of religion, God, or religious things. Very vague, and hard to reconcile with free speech.
6. Prohibition of eating flesh taken from an animal while it is still alive. Yuck. Very cruel.
7. Establishment of Courts of Law- makes sense.

Jews do not get a special pass to heaven by following more rules.

Being Chosen

If easy is what you are looking for in your religious faith, you don't want to be an observant Jew. The option of seven laws for gentiles to follow, as opposed to up to 613 for Jews, and you are still good with God, is a no brainer for the slacker mentality. It is said the Jews were chosen, or perhaps allowed to volunteer, for the task of being an example of how God wants people to act and behave. Having such a close, important relationship with God is not easy, as history sadly demonstrates. Yet, Jews are still here. Tevye in *Fiddler on the Roof* was really tired of every bad thing dumping on him and his people when he asked God to choose someone else for a while. Christians and Muslims recognize this "closeness," and the roots of their own faiths in Judaism, but both believe the Jews have missed out on an important change of direction. For Christians, that is the coming of the prophesied Messiah, Jesus, whom they believe modernized the covenant with God. For Muslims, it is the updated revelations given to Mohammad. Despite the worldwide popularity of both those faiths, Jews abide. It's not a popularity contest.

The Messiah Question

One of the questions my students usually asked the Rabbi, when he came to speak to the class was, "Why don't Jews accept Jesus as the Messiah?" They asked this question a little tentatively; embarrassed that this might be seen as a "Gotcha" question for a guest to our class. The Rabbi's answer was always the same, as he explained Jesus did not meet the criteria the Hebrew Bible set up for the Messiah. Basically, the Messiah was supposed to be a charismatic warrior king from King David's lineage, who would defeat Israel's enemies and overthrow evil, and be a great judge. He would also be a human being who would not die until his task was complete. Jesus, from a Jewish point of view, did not do any of the things the Bible calls for, so he could not be the Messiah. Jews For Judaism, a group countering Christian missionary work focused on Jews, goes into more detail analyzing Christian claims, and providing alternative points of view on their website.

Jewish Holidays

"And on the seventh day, He rested." One could argue the Sabbath is the most important holy day in the Jewish calendar, since it happens every week. Officially Sabbath begins at sunset on Friday, and ends at star rise (dark enough to see three stars) on Saturday. For many Jewish families, this is a deeply meaningful time to focus on rest, family, familiar rituals and God, and be to be separated from the day-to-day concerns of the world. And especially, to do no work. Reform Jews generally believe what a person does on Sabbath is an individual decision.

The most holy days are Rosh Hashanah (New Year's Day in the Jewish calendar), Yom Kippur (Day of Atonement and Repentance), and the days between them in September and October. These are the days where individuals ask God for forgiveness for whatever wrongs they have done, and try to set their minds not to do those things again. It is something like Roman Catholic confession but directly to God, instead of to the priest. If a person who thinks they are Jewish only does one religious activity, it is probably participating in these holy days. There are many other holidays where, God did something in history and everyone is glad about it.

Kabbalah

One of the ways some people study the Torah, is to find hidden, mysterious, esoteric meanings, through Kabbalah. That is, if you believe the Torah has a hidden, esoteric meaning. As I understand it, the Kabbalah theory says the Torah was written in a way to conceal its true meaning until we, or at least certain people, were able to figure it out and understand it. Using metaphor and numerology (in this case the number value of a word based on the number in the alphabet of each letter in a word, I think), these secrets were hidden away, with everyone thinking the Torah meant what it said, until the middle ages, when Kabbalistic books were written. Kabbalah is not a straight forward look at Judaism, but a way of approaching it more mystically, and, from what I understand, it takes a little daring and tenacity, because it is not an easy read. Somewhat like Gnosticism in Christianity, the belief is the deeper truths have been hidden within the material, and one has to learn how to pry them out. By delving into Kabbalistic material, one is trying to discover the hidden relationship between the creator and human beings. Why are we here? What is the purpose of life? Kabbalah is not a sect or particular group, just those who choose to study the Torah in this manner. It is based on spiritual writings from the 11th to 13th centuries, and while some believe it is the way to understand the truth of everything, others believe it goes against the basic tenets of Judaism. It has become trendy in the last few years to study Kabbalah, attracting movie stars, entertainers, etc. When I have asked Jewish friends about this, their answer is it is very hard to explain or understand.

Curiously, during the time I was first researching this, I heard an ad on the radio for the Kabbalah Center. I went to the web page where they advertised "The Power of Kabbalah," which said "No matter what your religion, race, or background, regardless of your current level of understanding, education or skill, Kabbalah: The Power of Kabbalah, can give your life new meaning and fulfillment." Looks like someone thinks they have cracked a way to make Kabbalah easy and popular. I was curious and tempted to click on the "Register Now" button, but thought better of it. Maybe later.

Today and Tomorrow

The contributions of Jews to civilization, throughout the ages, have given Western culture a degree of "Jewish flavor," far in excess of their numbers. Christians and Muslims have a historical and theological connection with Judaism, and through that, with each other. In the past, when peoples were separated, and tolerance was less widely practiced, Jews demonstrated their mettle and individuality, by resisting and surviving the forces that wanted to stamp them out of existence. Even though today's world might be more benevolent than in the past, a lot of anti-Semitism still exists. A recent study has found the number of Jews in European countries has been falling over the past few decades[2]. It seems the fall of the Soviet Union, leading to the opening of borders, is a contributing factor. As it faces continuing stresses, will Judaism, despite its historical contributions to the world, survive intact, or fade into the larger population?

33

CHRISTIANITY
THERE IS NOT ONE CHRISTIANITY

"Christianity, if false, is of no importance, and if true, of infinite importance. The only thing it cannot be is moderately important."
- C. S. Lewis

The History in a Nutshell

There never has been, and probably never will be, one Christianity. Going back to the very beginning, Jesus and his earliest followers were Jews. Today there are a host of Christian denominations, who all disagree with other denominations about something, and a few who think some others who say they are Christian, aren't.

After Jesus' death, and what believers say was his resurrection, his Jewish followers met in local synagogues, if allowed, or in each other's homes. A few years later, after claiming to have had a vision of Jesus, Paul preached an expanded view of Jesus' purpose, and established predominantly gentile congregations outside of Palestine. Disagreements between Paul's groups, and the Jewish followers in Jerusalem, were essentially ended with the 67-70AD revolt against Rome. This horrific event pretty much rubbed out or scattered Jesus' Jewish followers. Paul's views, as reflected by the gentile groups he had established, became the official dogma and Jesus' followers became known as Christians. This word is from the Greek word Christos, a title, which meant "anointed one," and was used in place of the Hebrew word Messiah. Christians believe Jesus is the Christ or Messiah.

As Christianity grew during its first several centuries, it began to organize and regulate itself. It developed a hierarchy, and began to sort through differences in belief and practice, to determine what was correct. Over time, the gospels, letters, beliefs, and practices, preserved by different congregations, were examined and debated until a canon of scripture and theology was approved. Once an occasionally persecuted minority, Christianity, through the intervention of the Roman emperor Constantine, eventually became the favored, and later, the official religion of the Roman Empire. Constantine, wanting to end all divisions within the Church, called a council at Nicea in 325 CE to finalize the process of standardizing Church doctrine. Later, with the end of the Roman Empire in the west, the Roman Catholic Church became the major surviving institution, dominating religious, social and political life in Europe for centuries. The Eastern part of the Roman Empire continued until the 15th century as the Byzantine Empire.

Of the five patriarchs designated to oversee the Church, one was in Rome, while the others were in the east. Eventually the Eastern Churches agreed on theology, but defined and organized themselves along cultural and language lines, such as Greek, Russian, Romanian, and other congregations. Each ethnicity was then operating under its own bishop or patriarch. Generally in agreement about most issues, there was no central authority like the papacy in the Roman Catholic Church. The Orthodox Church, as these groups became known collectively, had the problems of dealing with both the domination of the Byzantine emperors, and later, wars with Islam. Cultural and religious differences, including some that had long existed between Eastern and Western Mediterranean congregations, brought about the eventual split between the Roman Catholic and Eastern Orthodox churches in 1054 CE. Despite the crusades ostensibly coming to the rescue of the East, this bad blood between Western and Eastern Christians led to Constantinople's capture by the Fourth Crusade in 1204. Recovered in 1261, this marked the beginning of the end for the Byzantines. Constantinople was finally taken by the Turks in 1453.

Therefore, in Europe during the Middle Ages, the Roman Catholic Church was the only game in town, when it came to the interpretation and definition of religious beliefs and practices. The sacraments of the Church, which provided the grace needed for salvation, were the most important aspects of religion in believers' lives.

Since literacy was low, and there were few copies of the Bible available, it was not important for individuals to read the scriptures. If there was anything you needed to know, the Church would tell you. However, the invention of the printing press changed everything. What was the first thing Gutenberg printed? Bibles! When books were scarce, there was not much point in learning to read, but within a few generations after printing became established, books, pamphlets, and especially Bibles, were everywhere. Now a person could read the words of Holy Scripture himself. Martin Luther, John Calvin, Huldrych Zwingli, and others, disappointed with the corruption of the Roman Church, encouraged each person to read and find meaning in scripture on their own. They said there was no longer a need for the heavy-handed rules of the Church, and they denied the Church's exclusive role in salvation. People, they believed, could now be their own priests, and responsible for their own religious decisions.

Unfortunately, this openness did not prevent them or their followers from being intolerant toward each other. With more interpreting going on, Christian denominations were formed, split apart, and reformed. The Catholic Church launched a counter-reformation, kings took sides, religiously themed wars broke out, and disparate groups left Europe for the new world, to practice their brand of religion without fear of persecution. The Protestant search for individual religious meaning was full speed ahead.

Today

This great diaspora of Christian religious thought has given us forty or fifty major denominations, and thousands of minor ones, depending on how you define a denomination. Most people in the U.S. claim to be Christian, and many of those also claim to know something about their religion, but do they really? As mentioned earlier, Steven Prothero, in his book *Religious Literacy: What every American Needs to Know and Doesn't*, has pointed out that only half of all Americans can name one of the four gospels, and only one-third know it was Jesus who delivered the Sermon on the Mount. Prothero says the reason for this lack of knowledge is the victory of "piety over learning" in Christian thinking. In the past, American Christians were known for their Bible quoting, verse memorizing, religious lifestyle. Prothero believes, however, since modern Christianity emphasizes believing in loving, and having a personal relationship, with Jesus, it is less concerned about knowing scripture or much of anything else about the faith. If you believe Jesus loves you, what else do you need?

Since Christianity is the majority religion in the U.S., but made up of many different denominations, it is hard for most of us to distinguish one group from another, without doing some research. This diversity raises an important question: Is there a way to determine who is a Christian, and who is not? If you claim it, is it so? As a system of religion based on faith, are there beliefs which define absolutely who is a Christian, and other beliefs which are extra, optional or incorrect? This is not a trivial question. Given the prevalent (but far from unanimous) Christian belief in an afterlife, knowing what one must believe to qualify for that, is crucial. While many, often called progressive Christians, disparage the existence of hell and are open to salvation for all good people, even non-Christian ones, there are large numbers of Christians who still have faith that the correct beliefs are absolutely essential to salvation, and that is that. So, we have Christians who support LBGTQ folk, and those who oppose them, Christians who oppose abortion, and those who support choice, those who believe scripture is literally true, and those who believe it is not. It can be confusing.

One question that came up a few years ago in class, and in the media, was, "Are Mormons (Latter-day Saints) really Christians?" Given that a presidential primary contender for the 2012 election was Mormon, this was an interesting and timely question, especially since a politician's religious beliefs can affect voting preferences for a sizable number of Americans. Issues like this, as they pop up in the news, provide a great opportunity to examine a religion in a real-life setting. My answer to the Mormon question is, "I don't know." Every Mormon I have known, considers him or herself to be a Christian. However, from news reports, there are some Christians, primarily evangelical ones, who disagree, and say Mormons are definitely not Christians. One of my evangelical friends told me that as much as she admires Mormon family and ethical values, they twist the meaning of the gospels, so they are a cult. I have a paperback book I picked up at a yard sale, written by a Protestant minister, in which he explains why they are not. However, I have also checked out reader responses to articles on-line where people, who seem to be mainstream Protestants, accept the Mormon's Christian credentials.

I have used the word "Mormon" here to identify this group of believers, since it has been used forever, both within and outside the religion[1]. However, in August 2018, the president of the Church of Jesus Christ of Latter-day Saints announced God had impressed on him the need to use the full name of the Church or "Latter Day Saints". Using Mormon or L.D.S. is now unacceptable. Since then, Church members have been wrestling with this directive. Web sites and Instagram accounts have been, or will be, adjusted. The group previously known as the Mormon Tabernacle Choir is now the Tabernacle Choir at Temple Square. The members of the Mormon History Association decided to keep their name because, "You can't scrub 'Mormon' out of Mormon history," said W. Paul Reeves, the group's president.[2] While the Church will undoubtedly come to accommodate this change, I am not as sure the general public will be quite as easy to persuade.

Tomorrow

While Islam is the fastest growing major religion in the world, Christianity is still the largest. It is maintaining its size because of growth in Africa, Asia, and Latin America. Church membership in the U.S. and Europe has been declining, although still somewhat bolstered in the U.S. by immigrants. According to Wesley Granberg-Michaelson writing in *Religious News Service* (Jan. 10, 2019), Africa is now the continent with most Christians, about 631 million. He writes, "Globally, thanks to dramatic geographic and demographic changes, Christianity is re-centering its footprint, and becoming a non-Western religion." He also believes the "Trump affect" has damaged American Christianity's reputation abroad, since so many support the President, even while he uses bad language to describe many of the countries where Christianity is growing fastest, and trumpets American superiority. As Granberg-Michaelson summarizes:

"If there is a theme in what lies ahead for the church as we enter a new year, it is that the white Western Christian bubble that has powerfully shaped Christianity for the past four centuries is now beginning to burst."

34

WHAT CHRISTIANS BELIEVE

"Jesus did not spend a great deal of time discoursing about the trinity or original sin or the incarnation, which have preoccupied later Christians. He went around doing good and being compassionate."
- Karen Armstrong

Ensuring salvation is the goal at the heart of what most Christians believe. If a detailed, specific, belief system is required to achieve that, then, because of the diversity within Christianity, is one group correct (or mostly correct), while the others are wrong, to some degree? However, if more general beliefs are all you need, then would most, if not all, Christian denominations fit? But, if only the most general "be a good person" definition works, that would save most people, including atheists.

What makes sense is to find a common definition almost all Christians share that is relatively short and simple. The other differences separating Christian groups might be a matter of taste and style, or additions that adherents believe might make them better Christians, assisting in getting them into heaven. Christianity rests its foundation on its beliefs about the life, teachings, and ultimate purpose of Jesus of Nazareth, called the Christ.

Our definition should be like a salad. The basis of a salad is lettuce or other leafy greens. If you don't have that, you don't have a salad (I know there is potato salad, but stay with me here). However, almost no one, except rabbits, just takes the lettuce. Everyone goes through the salad bar, adding the ingredients they like best, in the quantities they want, resulting in a lot of variety, like Christian denominations. You might not like other people's results, but you still recognize they are salads. Then someone might come through with a plate of ice cream and add salad fixings to it, but when you see what they have done, all you can say is, "Man, that is not a salad," and just about everyone will agree with you. Someone might say, "Well, it's sort of a salad," and you just look at him with disgust because, you think, "Aren't there standards anymore?"

So, this is my take on the Christian salad, based on the Nicene Creed. This is the minimal "lettuce" and fixings someone needs to have on their plate, before they can accurately call themselves a Christian. First, they must believe Jesus is the son of God. This does not mean in a metaphorical way like "we are all the children of God," but in a very unique and real way. Jesus, is believed to be the incarnation of God on earth, living life as a man, but in reality, also being God. He is not a servant of God, or a man selected by God, or a special creation for a purpose of God, but pre-existing God, transformed into a man. He was not just God, and not just a man, but both simultaneously, in the same being, the precise understanding of which is a mystery since it just can't be explained. Furthermore, it is believed Jesus came to earth for a purpose, which was to save humans from our sinful nature, by opening the doors of everlasting life in heaven. Old Testament literalists believe Jesus also saved us from the original sin of Adam and Eve against God. In order to achieve this, Jesus, as the perfect sacrifice to atone for humanity's sins, so loved us that he gave up his life, to suffer and die in torment, crucified. He did this, but on the third day after his death, it is said he came back from death and his body again lived. He was reportedly seen by many, and gave his followers blessings, counsel, and advice before he rose into heaven to be reunited with/as God. In that position, he will judge those who die to determine their place in the afterlife.

Most Christians, I think, will deem anyone who believes this definition to be a Christian. However, I have spoken to a number of self-identified, committed Christians, who say it is the model of compassion Jesus provides that is most important, not whether or not he is God. Their belief is that loving God, and loving people, is what God most wants from us, and is all we need to act on. My follow-up question, about why someone should become a Christian if there is no belief requirement, elicits the response that no one needs to, and missionary activity is a waste of time and money. Their view is that Christianity is a cultural expression of a relationship with God that they are comfortable with and which works for them spiritually. If they had been born elsewhere, they could have been a Muslim or Hindu, and still be spiritually successful. They believe all good people, who show love for God and other people, will be saved. Particular beliefs are not required. The big question is, are they right, is this enough for salvation? Many other Christians disagree with this point of view, and would contend these people's beliefs are not Christian and are all wrong.

There are other fine points of theology and practice Christians will disagree about. Is belief in the divine nature of Jesus, and his plan for salvation, the main deal? Yes, of course, they would say, but other important points of dogma might also be essential. Roman Catholics might insist on the primacy of the pope, and the importance of the Church's sacraments. Other differences of opinion might include the importance of the Trinity (involving the correct understanding of the relationship of the Father, Son, and Holy Spirit), original sin, what determines salvation (faith alone, good works alone, or both), and the status of Mary, the mother of Jesus. Mary is believed, by most Christians, to have conceived Jesus while in a virginal state through an act of God, and by some, to have remained a virgin for her entire life. There are obviously many more differences that could be listed, especially those involving current issues such as gay marriage or abortion, but we cannot be exhaustive here. Let's just poke around with these traditional issues.

The Trinity

Many Christians would say, you have to add the belief in the Trinity to a definition of who is a Christian. In the concept of the Trinity, Christians believe God operates through three divine forms, God the Father, Jesus (the Son), and the Holy Spirit (the power of God in human lives). Exactly how this works, and the relationship of each of these facets of God to the other, was debated vigorously during the first few hundred years of Christianity's existence. For instance, is Jesus equal to God the Father, is he subservient, is he separate, or in some way, the same? It boils down to a question of faith because this is another mystery. While it is easy to understand the idea of the Trinity, if you don't think too deeply about it, it is tough to work out a rational, logical explanation. For instance, how does the Trinity square with the purest idea of monotheism? I have always liked the comparison of the Trinity to different states of water- solid, liquid, and gas. They are each very different at different times but they are all still water. Or try "three in one and one in three" if that helps. However, there are substantial minorities, such as Latter Day Saints, Jehovah's Witnesses, Christian Science and a number of other smaller groups that either do not believe in the Trinity, or have a sufficiently different interpretation, to make them substantially divergent from the mainstream. If a belief in the trinity is essential to our definition of Christianity, then these groups would be outside of it.

JAY LAMB

Original sin

As the saying goes, "With Adam's fall, we sinned all" (1784 New England reading primer). Original sin is the sin committed by Adam and Eve (the first two human beings, according to the book of Genesis in the Hebrew Bible) against God, in the Garden of Eden. They ate the fruit from the Tree of the Knowledge of Good and Evil after that had been forbidden by God. A fascinating idea, first discussed in the early Church by Paul to explain why Jesus had to be crucified, the concept of original sin was developed further by other Church writers, including St. Augustine, whose ideas were eventually incorporated by the Western Church. Original sin, courtesy of Adam and Eve, is one of the major reasons human beings are in need of the salvation brought by Jesus. Gallup polls show 40% of Americans believe in Creationism, and that Adam and Eve were real historical people.[1] This belief is strong. "Without Adam, the work of Christ makes no sense whatsoever in Paul's description of the Gospel, which is the classic description of the Gospel we have in the New Testament," says Albert Mohler, president of Southern Baptist Theological Seminary in Louisville.[2]

Sinning is one thing, but to sin after a direct, specific, in your face admonition by God must be really bad. Some believe the sin of Adam corrupted human nature from a good, natural, God fearing, pristine state, to the way we are today, always living with the inclination to sin. Now you might be thinking, "Well thanks a lot Adam and Eve for ruining a good set-up. Why should we revere these people if they messed up so badly?" It was explained to me that Adam and Eve were just first, and any of us put in that position would have eventually sinned too. Just be glad God picked them instead of you.

Augustine believed the taint of the original sin is a corruption passed on to all of us, during the act of our conception. Though Catholics and most Protestant denominations believe in original sin, there are many definitions of exactly what it is, and how it might impact human beings. Catholics believe baptism washes away its effect, and so are baptized shortly after birth, like receiving an inoculation, and being returned to a state of grace. Protestants generally believe original sin cannot be washed away, but when a person is baptized, usually when they are older and request it, the sin is hidden and forgiven. Notably, Latter Day Saints, and the Orthodox Church, do not believe in original sin, as it is defined by most other Christian denominations.

35

MORE BELIEFS

"How did the beatnik refer to the Trinity? Daddio, Laddio, and the Spook."
- Art Lamb (circa 1961)

Blessed Virgin Mary

Christians have differing views about Mary, the mother of Jesus, who is held in high esteem by almost everyone. Even though Protestants reject the veneration of saints prevalent in the Catholic and Orthodox Churches, most of them seem to have a soft spot for Mary. Every Christian denomination I know of agrees, whatever else she might have done or been, Mary was still a virgin at the time of Jesus' birth, which would, considering human biology, be a miracle. The precise explanation of how that came about, as opposed to the usual way humans are conceived, is a mystery. However, if you find a web chat room as I did several times, it is clear not all Christians believe this is important. Some commented that the virgin birth was absolutely essential, and everything about believing in the unique status of Jesus follows from it. Others said, since it was the actions and teachings of Jesus that were really important, it did not matter whether the virgin birth was true or not, and therefore, it is not important to the definition of being a Christian. However, the Catholic and Orthodox position is Mary was a virgin before, during and after the birth of Jesus.

In order to explain why the New Testament mentions the brothers and sisters of Jesus, most Protestants figure Mary was a virgin before Jesus, but had more kids later with Joseph, conceived and delivered in the usual way, as a good, traditional, Jewish wife would. Catholics have said these were children of Joseph, from an earlier marriage (Mary's stepchildren), but not her birth children. I have also read a suggestion that "brothers and sisters" in the New Testament is not literal, but metaphorical as in "we are all brothers and sisters as children of God." The argument goes on.

There is also a split within Christianity over the concept of the Immaculate Conception: the idea that Mary, as the future mother of Jesus, was herself conceived without sin. This has been a very controversial idea, generally rejected by Protestants and only accepted by the Catholic Church in 1854. Orthodox Churches do not believe in original sin, so they believe Mary was born sinless just like the rest of us. There have been groups within the Roman Catholic Church who have tried to elevate the status of Mary. They give her part credit for helping with the process of redemption, brought on by Jesus, and some also see her as the heavenly being who dispenses the grace obtained by the sacrifice of Jesus. Many people also pray for her to intercede with God on their behalf, sort of like a good lawyer. For Catholics, saints are venerated and prayed to for help, while God/Jesus is both prayed to and worshipped. Mary is somewhere in between. Where she is, exactly, depends on your point of view.

Importance of Faith versus Good Works

Traditionally, based primarily on Paul's teaching, and later supported by Luther and Calvin, most Protestants have believed the only way a person can be saved is through belief in Jesus Christ, and acceptance of Him as a personal savior and redeemer. It is through Him alone that we can reach atonement with God. In the Catholic Church, such belief was considered important, but insufficient. What was also needed, the Church said, was the grace, guidance and sacraments supplied by the Church, plus each individual's good deeds. Catholics point out that Jesus, in the gospel of Matthew (25:32-46), said treating other people humanely and caring for the poor, sick, and downtrodden was the only way into heaven. As mentioned earlier, some Christians don't think such specific beliefs are required.

The most influential religious authority in my early life was Sister Bernadette, my 6th grade teacher in Catholic school. Sister Bernadette, who was very old school, told us Protestants could not be saved because they were not Catholics, and therefore could not receive the Church's sacraments. After all, they didn't even believe in the authority of the pope. Today, Catholics I know do not believe Protestants are automatically doomed. Most seem to believe being Catholic is better suited to certain religious personality types (similar to music, fashion, culture or food taste differences), or being Catholic is just a better way, with better odds, of getting into heaven. I do not know any Catholics who still follow Sister B's philosophy, but there could be some out there.

Even though many Protestants insist belief in Jesus, as the Son of God and your personal savior, is the one absolute essential for salvation, surveys by the Pew Charitable Trusts show more American Christians are finding that view to be untenable[1]. The idea that everyone who does not accept Jesus is sent to hell for all eternity is rejected by growing numbers of people, especially young folks. For example, a student told me it didn't make any sense to her that Gandhi, a spiritually devout humanitarian, would have been sent to hell because, even though he was a great guy and a world historical figure, he was not a Christian. "It's not fair," she said. I wonder what Sister Bernadette would have thought about that.

The Bible: Literal or Metaphorical?

Traditionally, Christians have believed the information and miracles described in the Old and New Testaments are factually correct. Until Darwin, there was no good reason for most believers to doubt the earth had been created in six days, and was a few thousand years old. After all, Bishop Usher had gone through all of the biblical "begats" to calculate that creation took place on October 22, 4004 BC. That seemed reasonable at the time. Then, not only did science begin to contradict this, but modern biblical scholarship also challenged accepted facts, interpretations, and translations.

Today, while some folks are still very literal in their beliefs, there are many Christians who are comfortable with the science based geological and Darwinian views, about the evolutionary development of the earth, and of human beings. They see biblical creation accounts, which contradict science, as more or less metaphorical. For instance, one modern interpretation of scripture is that the names Adam and Eve, in the original language, are plural words, referring to a lot of individual men and women, not just those two. This could explain how their son Cain finds a wife. Further, it has also been suggested that Cain and Able are not two literal brothers, but representatives of herders (and hunter-gatherers) v. agriculturalists. Then the story becomes a metaphor for the dominance of agriculture and advancing technology, over the old ways of hunting and herding.

Those however, such as Evangelicals, who believe strongly in a literal reading of the Bible, think these metaphorical suggestions are nonsense, and science is wrong. They believe the Bible to be infallible. For instance, if the Bible says it took six days for creation, then it took six days. Each day was a 24-hour day, not an epoch, or an eon, or a billion years. If it took a billion years, it would have said, a billion years. In the view of one spokesperson, if the Bible is wrong about this, it could be wrong about anything, which it is not. To demonstrate this, literalists have opened a "creationist" oriented museum of the history of the earth, in Kentucky, with explanations accounting for dinosaurs and Noah's flood.

The Second Coming

Christians, Muslims, Zoroastrians, and Jews have had, or still have, beliefs that one day God is going to say, enough is enough, and will close the show on the whole human experiment. Both Jesus and John the Baptist sound, at times, that they are saying something like this, "Better get right with God, because the end is coming soon and God wants to know who his friends are. Wheat and chaff, my friends, wheat and chaff." I have read that even when the Romans were battering down the doors of the temple in Jerusalem, during the revolt, there were Jews inside who were sure God would appear at the last second to blast the Romans. He didn't. Many of Jesus' followers expected him to return within a generation of his death. He didn't.

Today there are many different points of view on this, too many to discuss here. As usual, there are literal and metaphorical believers. Some are vague, while others are very specific. Among literalists, there are those who believe a certain set number and type of events will take place, including the reign of an anti-Christ, raising the dead, and a time of judgement. Much of this is based on interpretations from the Book of Revelation. In recent years the idea of the rapture, when all believers will be raised to heaven so they will not have to suffer a time of tribulation, has become popular with some Christian groups. The one image that stuck with me about this, is your airplane falling out of the sky because your pilot was raptured to heaven. And you weren't. Ouch.

36

JESUS AND PAUL

"But I say unto you, Love your enemies, bless them that curse you, do good to them that hate you, and pray for them which despitefully use you, and persecute you."
- Jesus, Matthew 5:44

"Do not repay anyone evil for evil."
- Paul, Romans 12:17

Jesus of Nazareth

While there are several contemporary authors who suggest the story of Jesus was just made up, it seems almost every historian has given his existence the benefit of the doubt. Besides, it is extremely difficult to prove any particular person actually existed 2000 years ago, if they weren't born as an emperor, or some other significant citizen, or wrote something that somehow survived the ages. As far as we know, Jesus didn't write a thing. However, it is Jesus who is the central figure in Christian worship and the raison d'être of Christianity. My Christian friends tell me Jesus' most important teaching was reported in the Gospel of Matthew, "Thou shalt love the Lord thy God with all thy heart, and with all thy soul, and with all thy mind" and "Thou shalt love thy neighbor as thyself."

The information we have about Jesus comes primarily from the four gospels of the New Testament, which are accepted by the vast majority of Christians, even though scholars believe they were written from three to eight decades after his death. While it is clear they are talking about the same person, the gospels occasionally disagree, or are vague, so for instance, we are not sure if the time of Jesus' ministry was one year or three years. We also don't know when Jesus was born or when he died. The most common dates I have seen are 4-8 BCE to 30-36 CE. The gospels say Jesus was born during the reign of Herod I, who died in 4 BCE, so it had to be then or earlier. No scholar thinks it was 0-33 CE the way I was taught.

It is worth noting that the exact status of Jesus' divine nature was controversial in the early Church until, with imperial Roman backing, it was finally decided, during the Church councils of the 4th century. Some groups had believed Jesus was a man, selected by God, some that he was a special creation of God, and others that he was God, in the form of a man. The third view won out in the end.

Trying to discern Jesus' real human personality and operating style depends on which scholars you read or how tightly your view of him comes from a faith-based upbringing. He has been portrayed as a tough minded, reformer Rabbi, speaking out for the poor and downtrodden, and against the rich and powerful, a calm and gentle guy surrounded by little lambs and children. In another recent book, he is a revolutionary who wanted to boot the Romans out of Palestine. Maybe Jesus was some combination of all of those personality types. Some modern writers have tried to link him romantically with Mary Magdalene. Despite the popularity of *The DaVinci Code*, any circumstantial evidence implying this assertion seems very conjectural to me.

Jesus is said to have performed miracles such as healing people, raising the dead, walking on water, feeding thousands with a few loaves and fishes, and my personal favorite, changing water into wine. He preached a love your neighbor and get your act together theology, with a dash of the end of times is coming. He enjoyed a good parable, hung out with all sorts of people who were not on the Jerusalem "A" list, and was eventually crucified by the Romans. He is definitely the number one person in history I would like to talk to if I had access to Dr. Who's TARDIS.

Importance of Paul

In *The 100: A Ranking of the most Influential Persons in History*, Michael Hart places Jesus as #3 and Paul as #6, splitting the credit for Christianity between them. Incidentally, Mohammed is ranked #1. This surprises most students because they assume Christianity, having been around longer, and having more adherents, has had a greater impact on history than Islam, and Jesus should get the credit. Hart has an interesting rationale for his judgement. If Jesus had a role in the development of Christianity, like Mohammad did for Islam, he would have clearly been ranked #1. Mohammad was both the prophet of Islam theologically, and the early guiding force of Islam organizationally. He got the faith up and he got it running. Jesus, on the other hand, while clearly the progenitor of what became Christianity, died, is believed to have ascended into heaven, and left a small number of followers, huddling in fear and hiding from the authorities. The gospels do say Jesus appeared to his disciples and told them to spread the word, but he did not leave any organizational instructions or theological details. Someone else was needed to get the religion running.

Since Jesus and his followers were Jewish, most of them seemed to feel that convincing other Jews to follow the teachings of Jesus was the assignment. Scholars assert Jesus' brother James, not the Apostle Peter, as I was taught, was the real leader after Jesus. These early followers of Jesus could be considered a sect of Judaism, as their evangelizing focused on convincing other Jews to join up. Except for Paul. Paul, who began his career named Saul, was a Jew, a follower of the Pharisees, and spent his spare time beating up on Jesus' followers. After a reported conversion experience on the Damascus road, where he said he received a divine revelation directly from Jesus, he did a religious 180. He changed his name to Paul, and began to work for Jesus' followers, focusing his conversion efforts almost exclusively on gentiles outside of Palestine. As a Jewish citizen of the Roman Empire who had grown up outside Palestine, he had a great understanding of Greek and Roman culture.

In spreading the word to the gentiles, Paul's point of view became an important part of Christian theology. It was Paul who insisted, Jesus was the promised Messiah, and therefore divine. The old biblical rules had now changed, and strict obedience to Jewish law, such as observing the Torah, was no longer needed. In fact, Judaism itself was no longer needed, since Christianity, as part of God's new covenant, had now replaced it. He said gentiles who believed in Jesus no longer have to become Jews first (including adult male circumcision required!), to be followers. Many gentiles who were interested in Judaism, but balked at that membership requirement, found Paul's brand of "Judaism" refreshing and inviting. Congregations were started at many locations around the eastern Mediterranean.

Paul's interpretation of the meaning of the life and death of Jesus, and his assertion that this belief guaranteed salvation, eventually became the gold standard for the faith. He wrote that the main point of Jesus' mission was to rescue us from Adam's sin. The Jewish revolt against Rome (66-70 CE) ended disastrously, for both "regular" Jews and Jews who were followers of Jesus living in Palestine. The non-Jewish congregations Paul established outside of Palestine ("Hey Romans, we are not Jews!") survived, flourished and dominated the development of the early Christian church. Those surviving followers of Jesus, who still operated within Judaism, were marginalized and eventually died out. I've often wondered how Christianity would have turned out if the Jewish followers of Jesus had remained in control, rather than Paul's primarily gentile congregations.

Paul's other great contribution to Christianity comes from his letters to the various congregations he established. With no easy system of communication, and no early hierarchy in place, each scattered Christian congregation could only rely upon themselves to interpret the meaning of questions that arose about what beliefs, actions, and writings were correct. If a member of the congregation came in one day saying Jesus had spoken to him in a dream, who could say whether this was true, and if the message received was valid? Paul would say. Paul's epistles have become an important part of the New Testament, and a guide for many Christians who find deep value and meaning in his point of view. Certainly, his ideas on the divinity of Jesus and the importance of faith for salvation, have influenced all Christian theologians since.

Many scholars believe some of Paul's letters were not written by Paul, but by others after his death, who wanted to use his name and influence to advance their own point of view. One of these, Dr. Bart Ehrman in *Jesus, Interrupted*, has written that both 1 Timothy and the Letter to the Ephesians were clearly not written by Paul. Not every person of faith agrees.

Ironically, as far as anyone knows, Paul never met Jesus when he was alive. Paul is among those major early Christian religious figures who never read the gospels, since it is believed he died (sometime in the mid 60's CE, as a prisoner in Rome) before the first gospel was written. He also preached, as Jesus and Peter did, that the end of times was coming soon. It didn't. Were they wrong in saying this? Or were they speaking in a metaphorical way, not a literal one?

So, would Christianity have survived and developed as it did without Paul? You are welcome to argue this with Dr. Hart.

37

BIBLICAL SCHOLARSHIP

"Alcohol may be man's worst enemy, but the bible says love your enemy."
- Frank Sinatra

When I was growing up as a Catholic kid, I often thought if all the divided parts of modern Christianity (Roman Catholic, Protestant, Orthodox, etc.) could just get back to the original Christianity of the early Church, everyone would be happy and in agreement. After all, they had written down the words of Jesus in the gospels, as they heard them, I believed, so their understanding of what Jesus was saying was pure, and only heretics (and later, Protestants- see Sister Bernadette) had tried to mess this up. Of course, I was a kid and didn't know anything.

About 30 years ago my mother introduced me to a magazine she, a devout Catholic, had been receiving for years. I dissed it at first as another "Catholic" magazine until, for some reason, I read a few of the letters to the editor. In one issue, someone was saying the author of an article was going to burn in hell for what he had written in an earlier issue, and to please cancel her subscription immediately. What could possibly have been said in one of my mother's magazines that would send someone to hell? I began to read some of the articles, written primarily by university professors, or ministers at theological colleges, and I was hooked. This was not the religious propaganda I had feared, but a journal of serious religious scholarship, based on evidence and reasoning. These articles were written for ordinary people, who have just a little background knowledge. It was *Bible Review* magazine (1985-2005), published by the Biblical Archaeology Society, and my introduction to biblical scholarship.

There is a whole world of scholarship having to do with the New Testament, the Hebrew Bible, the works and acts of prophets and apostles, and the life of Jesus. What we know, or don't know, about the early Church doesn't seem to be discussed much in Christian churches, at least not in the one I grew up in. Yet, this seems to be an important topic. If your faith is based partly or completely on scriptures, wouldn't you want to be certain your bible had been translated correctly, and your preacher had his facts straight? This type of scholarship, which often challenges traditional views, gives some people of faith fits.

As in any other intellectual field of endeavor, scholars, in pursuit of the answers to historical biblical questions, use the methodology of scientists, historians, and other researchers to write articles supporting their point of view. Scholars use their reasoning and knowledge of the subject to follow the evidence, and develop hypotheses. The first article I read in Bible Review, the one being responded to by the letter writer mentioned above, was by an author who suggested that Paul, after he had been arrested and imprisoned in Rome, had committed suicide.[1] Paul, the author pointed out, though he was Jewish, was raised in a Roman culture, which approved of suicide in hopeless situations. By the way, the letter writer had justified her position by saying Paul would never have done that, since suicide is a sin. Ironically, it seems suicide was not determined by the Church to be a sin until after Paul's time. As with scholarly writing in science or history designed to be read by us mortals (not just for other experts in the field), you, the reader, get to weigh the evidence, and judge how correct you believe the author's book or article to be.

My next biblical shock was to find that scholars do not believe the Gospels were written until decades after Jesus' death. Mark is thought to have been written first (65 or 70 CE), followed by Luke and Matthew (around 85 CE) and later, John (around 90 or 100 CE). Curiously, it seems most scholars believe none of these were written by their named authors, and none of them were first-hand accounts. From what I understand, these gospel writers were probably sitting at their desks, with some miscellaneous written accounts about Jesus, perhaps supplemented by oral stories passed down from person to person, and wrote their gospel out fresh, in a way that made sense to them. In fact, this is just how Luke opens his gospel, which he is writing for his good friend, "...most excellent Theophilus..." It is interesting to note the gospel writers wrote in Greek. If they were focusing on a Jewish audience, they would have written in Hebrew or Aramaic, but Greek was the most common language for gentiles in the eastern Mediterranean. Some scholars have suggested, in light of the disastrous Jewish revolt against Rome, the gospel writers wrote for a particular audience. They were trying to make nice with Rome, at the expense of the Jews, and to show they were not the same religion.

As examples of biblical scholarship, I offer two articles, both from issues of the extinct *Bible Review*. The first is "The 34 Gospels," by Charles W. Hedrick (*Bible Review*, Vol. XVIII, #3, June 2002), which is about the 34 existing gospels, in whole, part, or by reference, that we know about. This is a lot more than the four I was raised with (that number having been justified in the early Church, because there were believed to be four winds, and four corners to the earth). Most Christians only accept Matthew, Mark, Luke and John, but it is fascinating to read about the others.

It turns out, these gospels were written in the time of the early church, and include the Gospel of Mary, the Gospel of Thomas, the Gospel of Judas, and the Q Gospel, none of which made it into the

New Testament. As gospels, and fragments of gospels, have been discovered over the last seventy years, each raises questions about their authenticity, the value they might have had to some group in the early church, and their relationship to the canon of accepted New Testament gospels. For example, as far as anyone knows, no copies of the Q Gospel exist. However, some scholars suggest it did exist at one time and has an interesting relationship in the chronology of the three synoptic Gospels, Mark, Matthew and Luke. They are called synoptic, since they share parallel content and style. The fourth gospel, John, is noticeably different in both areas.

Scholars have long noticed Matthew and Luke seem to have cribbed a lot of their text from the earlier Mark. They have also noticed Matthew and Luke have a lot of text in common, which does not come from Mark, or any other known source. From this they hypothesized there must have been another document, that both Luke and Matthew accessed, which seems to have been a collection of the sayings of Jesus. Called Q for quelle, in German, meaning "source," scholars have reconstructed it, based on those common sayings in Luke and Matthew. Other scholars believe different explanations could suffice for this anomaly, but they are in the minority, as far as I can tell.

The "Gospel of John" is believed to have been written much later than these (I have seen articles proposing dates from 85 to 120 CE, with most scholars around 90-100 CE). While Jesus is still the main subject, it has a distinctly different writing style, and does not share the common themes of the other three. Any ambiguity in the earlier gospels, about whether Jesus is really God, is taken care of in John. Unless the scholars are way off, it looks like my early notion of verbatim copying of Jesus' sermons for the gospels was wrong.

Another example is "All in the Family: Identifying Jesus' Relatives" by Richard J. Bauckman in *Bible Review*, about those people who, a few hundred years after Jesus, claimed to be related to him. It makes sense, if Jesus had brothers and sisters, he might have had a lot of nieces and nephews. Some Christians, as mentioned earlier, believe Jesus' siblings were either half-siblings, or step-siblings, depending on whether Mary had more children by Joseph after Jesus, or whether these were Joseph's children from an earlier marriage. Some believe there were no siblings. As far as I know, all Christians agree that since Mary was pregnant when she married Joseph, he was not the biological father of Jesus. This, of course, raises the question of how Jesus can be descended from King David's lineage (as, it is said, was Joseph), which is apparently one of the biblical requirements for being the Messiah. This discrepancy bothered me when I was a kid, but since no one else seemed to notice, I let it slide.

38

THE ROMAN CATHOLIC CHURCH

"I must not take this or that doctrine by itself; but I must make up my mind whether or not it is the one only Catholic Church, and then I shall believe all that she teaches, because she teaches it, and not because I understand it."
- Robert Hugh Benson, *By What Authority?*

The Roman Catholic Church has one thing no other Christian religion has, the pope. As the undisputed leader of the Catholic Church, he traces his lineage back to the first Bishop of Rome, Peter, believed to be the top apostle for Jesus. In any discussion comparing religious hierarchies, the pope and the Catholic Church are at one end, and almost every other religion, Christian or otherwise, is at the other end. The pope is believed to be infallible in any matter involving faith and morals. It was the insistence on papal authority that was the most controversial issue in the first Christian schism, between Western Christians (Catholics) and eastern Christians (the Orthodox Churches). The Orthodox Bishops felt that, as

Bishop of Rome, the pope had no more authority than any other big city bishop.

The Church hierarchy from the pope through the cardinals, archbishops, and bishops, to parish priests is one of top down, unimpeachable authority. There is always room to think and have an opinion, but on the issues that matter, there is no popular vote. It is believed the Church, being the instrument of Christ on earth, has a unique position and knows best. I do know Catholics who disagree with the Church on one issue or another, especially on birth control. They are also concerned, since the Church has taken quite a black eye from a decade of revelations about sexual assault cases, but these Catholics are still very loyal. I also know a couple who recently changed parishes, which are generally attended geographically, when they felt their pastor was becoming too "political," but they never considered leaving the faith.

Recently, some elements of the Church have taken aim at LGBTQ folks. Liam Stack, in the July 24, 2019 *New York Times* ("Indianapolis Catholic School Fires Gay Teacher at Archbishop's Request") informs us that the Archbishop of Indianapolis fired a teacher in a Catholic school because she was married to another woman, in a legal same sex marriage. Since gay marriage is against Church teaching, the Archbishop maintains she can no longer be a good role model for children in a Catholic school. Teachers must "abide by all Church teachings, including the nature of marriage." Critics complain this is blatant discrimination, since he has not taken similar action against teachers who use birth control, engage in premarital sex, or divorce without a church approved annulment. It is not clear yet how popular the Archbishop's position will be with most Catholics.

This seems to run counter to the very exciting, or concerning, depending on your point of view, changes in direction, initiated by Pope Francis (Jorge Mario Bergoglio), who was elected by the College of Cardinals to the job in 2013. Naming himself after St Francis of Assisi seemed to send a strong message to the Church that the recent lineup of conservative and traditional popes was coming to an end. Certainly, Francis' personal qualities have endeared him to many people, but it remains to be seen, depending how long he is in office, to what degree he will shake up Catholic theology and practice.

The factor that sets Catholics apart from other Christians, besides papal authority, is the importance of the Church's seven sacraments. The Orthodox also count seven, but have traditionally believed everything within the church is "sacramental." From the earliest years to today, it has been a Catholic article of belief that faith in Jesus as the Savior and Redeemer is essential, but not sufficient for salvation. The Church, through its interpretations of doctrine, and the benefit of its sacraments, is believed to provide the advice and grace that are essential for salvation.

Going to confession (called reconciliation now) and mass every week (unless you qualified for a limited list of exemptions), receiving communion, being married within the church, baptizing your kids, seeing them through their sacramental development, and receiving last rites when you die, are pretty essential. If you want to become a priest (still guys only), there is the sacrament of Holy Orders, which is believed to give the power to perform the miracle of the Eucharist during mass, and other sacraments. In addition, each believer should demonstrate their living faith by regularly engaging in good works and deeds. Belief, without actions rooted in Christian ethics, is barren and does not enhance the odds of salvation.

Transubstantiation

Catholics believe a miracle occurs in the mass when the substance of the bread and the wine that the priest is praying over, is transformed into the actual body and blood of Jesus. This miracle is called transubstantiation, and can only be brought about through the actions of an ordained priest. If you looked closely at the wine and wafer after the transformation, using all of your senses, and even subjecting them to chemical analysis, it would still show up as wine and wafer. But the belief is the appearance belies what it actually has become - the real body and blood of Jesus. While the appearance is the same, the substance of the bread and wine, in a sense, departs to make room for the substance of the body and blood. I do not know, and so cannot explain how, in a scientific sense, this transformation takes place, but fortunately I don't have to, because it is a miracle. If you believe God has intervened in the past, and continues to intervene in the present, in the workings of the laws of science to make miraculous things happen, this is not necessarily much of a stretch. After all, if God created the whole universe out of nothing, most other miracles are small potatoes.

The Orthodox Churches agree substantially with the Roman Catholic Church on transubstantiation. They don't use the "T" word, and they don't really try to explain it, but even though they have minor differences, the Catholic Church seems to accept the Orthodox point of view. Some Anglicans (Episcopalians) also accept the notion of transubstantiation, while other Anglicans and almost all other Protestants, do not. Most Protestants see the 'communion experience' as a symbolic remembrance of Jesus' sacrifice, while some groups have other, diverse explanations, for what is going on.

Other Catholic Churches

Despite this description, and the seemingly monolithic nature of Roman Catholic theology, there are a number of other "Catholic" churches who are "at one" with the pope, but have different traditions and, by agreement, don't have to follow all of the Roman Catholic rules. They share the basic beliefs, but are allowed to exercise their practices differently. My friend Nick told me his family has always family belonged to the Ukrainian Catholic Church. He was fuzzy on some of the details, but told me they recognized the pope, did the sign of the cross right to left (instead of left to right) and that their priests could marry. Apparently, at various times, from about the 4th century CE on, different churches have broken with the Roman Catholic Church, the most memorable being the Orthodox schism of 1054. Some groups never formally broke with Rome but wanted to maintain their own traditions, and others that broke away, later split again, and then wanted back in. In all such cases, these churches were allowed to continue their traditions, as long as they recognized the pope as supreme, for ultimate theological purposes. While most of these groups come from Eastern Europe, the Middle East and other "eastern" places, many of them now have congregations in the U.S., like the one Nick's family attends. I asked Nick if his church was on the boundary line, theologically and traditionally, between the Eastern Orthodox Churches and the Roman Catholic Church. He said, "Uh, yes, maybe." So, there you have it.

Back in the Day

There are a number of unique experiences and deep concerns a kid (like me) had growing up Catholic, back in the day. Whenever I meet anyone who went to a Catholic elementary school, we almost always have to compare notes. Two items that still interest me from my Catholic childhood are, the concept of Limbo, and indulgences on holy cards. I was always fascinated by Limbo because I couldn't quite figure it out. The reason for Limbo is obvious. If everyone is born with original sin, and a Catholic baptism is required to make it go away, what happens to babies who die before they are baptized? Well, we were told they go to Limbo, which is not a bad place, since after all, the babies have committed no sin. They have died, as all people die, because God decided it was their time. My mental image was room after room of shelves with babies, attended by angel-nurses. This did not seem to be much of an existence, but I figured it was better than going to hell. Apparently, Limbo was never a certified belief of the Church, but was widely taught. However, the Church did away with the concept in 1992. I'm not sure what happened to the babies.

The nuns in Catholic elementary school gave holy cards to us as rewards, the way smiley-face stickers and gold stars were used in public school. These cards have a picture of Jesus or Mary or a saint on one side, and a prayer on the back. It also had the number of days of remission from purgatory you would get for saying the prayer. Although I never got very many cards, I did have two or three once, and remember trying to add up the total number of days I could get out of purgatory, while wondering if it still counted if I said the shortest prayer over and over. I was sure I would end up in purgatory when I died, and wanted to make my stay as brief as possible. As far as I know, no other religion has a purgatory-like way station to clean out your soul on your way to heaven. At first, I thought purgatory was a mini-hell with some suffering, but not really bad and not forever. Later Sister Gertrude (the pretty, young, nun) told me it was only considered suffering since we would be kept from the presence of God. This made me feel a lot better, because as far as I could tell, I was not in the presence of God now, so purgatory could not be much worse than here.

On occasion, I did suffer some guilt and fear about possibly committing a mortal sin, but that got explained away for me too. Apparently, for a sin to be mortal you have to realize it is a mortal sin before you do it, and then you do it anyway. Heck, none of my sins were ever premeditated, they just happened sort of spontaneously. It took a weight off my shoulders to realize I had never committed an actual mortal sin, and probably never would.

In second or third grade, I was drafted to be an altar boy. I don't remember how this happened, but I do remember feeling I had better say yes and "volunteer" if I knew what was good for me. I was never an enthusiastic student in elementary school, so I never learned much of the Latin altar boys were supposed to be saying when responding to the priest during mass. Early on, I found if I just kept my head down and mumbled, that seemed to make everyone happy.

39

PROTESTANTS

"The three great elements of modern civilization, Gun powder, Printing, and the Protestant religion."
- Thomas Carlyle

There are many Protestant denominations, too many for me to keep track. If there is a particular denomination you are interested in, do what I do, and find it online.

To be a Protestant is almost, by definition, to be a person who doesn't see the absolute need for a church. That's not to say Protestants don't find great value in the church community for religious support, community togetherness, brotherhood, attacking social problems, etc. Everything else aside, most people prefer to get together with other people, whenever they can, for shared purposes. Restaurants provide that for dining, and churches provide it for worship and social activities. However, from the Protestant point of view, while extremely helpful, it is not essential to have a church to run interference between you and God, as the Catholic Church insists is necessary. For Protestants, there is God and there is you.

That is the relationship that counts. Each person is essentially their own priest before God, and can interpret scripture as seems right to them. As a Protestant, everything has to do with your understanding of scripture, your beliefs, and, to some degree, your actions in life. Traditionally, most Protestants have believed God has provided only one way to obtain salvation, through belief in the life, death and resurrection of Jesus. To achieve salvation, one must believe in salvation. It is believed God has also given us the scriptures of both the Hebrew Bible (Old Testament) and the New Testament as sources of divine information to help us understand our faith and guide our lives.

As to what degree all of this is essential or optional, to be a proper God-fearing Protestant, Protestants, again, sort of by definition, are all over the map. It seems programmed in the Protestant DNA if too many people agree on too much for too long, there has to be an eventual split, which is why there are so many Protestant denominations and many schools of thought. Some Protestants have believed only certain people are going to be saved by God, since God is omniscient and has, in fact, pre-destined those who will not suffer eternal damnation. This is the "Sinners in the Hands of an Angry God" school of thought, based on the teachings of John Calvin. Basically, we are all sinners, and we all deserve to go to hell, but for some undeserved reason, God will save a few of us, the elect, and don't you want to be one of them? I don't think this idea is held by many folks today, but in the time of Jonathan Edwards and the Puritans, it was a smash.

A more widespread belief now is the "You Must Believe" school of thought. This is based on Martin Luther's notion that the only way to be saved is by faith alone. It's up to you; belief in Jesus as your savior and redeemer will guarantee your salvation. This opportunity is thought to be offered to everyone, and for those who accept, there is heaven. For those who do not, there is only hell. What about good people who never heard of Jesus? One generous view is that at the moment of their death, God offers those people the choice of believing in Jesus or not, in a way that gives them a fair chance to decide. Therefore, even if there are hidden tribal groups somewhere in the world who missionaries have not yet reached, they are covered too.

In both of these views, the actions you take in your life don't really matter in determining your final outcome. In the "Hands of God" view however, believers knew intellectually they couldn't be certain they'd be saved. Psychologically desperate people calculated if they worked hard, lived right, were appropriately zealous and could demonstrate prosperity (i.e., God's favor) in their lives, which might be a hint that God had decided to save them. Maybe. In the "You must believe" situation, actions do not save anyone without faith, but if you truly believe in Jesus, this should show itself in your actions. Good deeds and actions will be a side benefit in the life of a true believer, but are not actually required for salvation. In both of these, it is thought everyone is a sinner, and all sins are equal, no matter what deeds we do. It is only good luck in one theory, and our faith and beliefs in the other, that can ultimately save us. The difference is your view of God's personality. Does God condemn most of us because that is what we deserve, or does God try to give us many opportunities, "throwing out the lifeline," for us to be saved?

Some Protestants have moderate or liberal beliefs, and are more likely to emphasize the loving Jesus over the angry God, in their understanding of Christianity. Most of these beliefs range from "only Christians will be saved (but not really, there's got to be room for good non-Christians)," to "every good person will be saved, there is no hell, and a loving and fair God will sort it all out." With these folks, there is a widespread belief that Protestant Christianity, if not the exclusive route to heaven, just might be the best route, improving your odds. Of course, there is always the most accepting point of view that all religions are aiming in the same direction, and Protestant Christianity offers one cultural expression of that fact, no better or worse, just different from other religions.

Literal beliefs

Back in the old days, no one had the slightest idea, in a scientific sense, how the world and human beings came to be. So in every tribe or culture, someone made up a story that explained how it all took place, usually with a God or gods involved. Believing one of these to be true, (especially if you had never heard of others, and all of your people agreed with you), was not an unreasonable position, and there was no scientific information to contradict it. If in Joshua 10:12-13, it said the sun had stopped in the sky, then you knew it had stopped; and who could prove it hadn't? However, beginning with Copernicus, then Galileo, then lots of other people, much of what was said in the Bible was contradicted by science. Could the Bible be wrong about some things?

As usual, Protestants are all over the map on this. There is a significant minority who believe the Bible is right, and science is wrong. There are those who attempt to show elements of the Bible (like Noah's flood) can be proven, by what they call Creation Science. Then there are those who are able to accommodate science, such as my friend who told me God created the process of evolution, to bring life to the earth. He sees the six days of creation as described in Genesis as metaphorical, not literal. So, if you are a Protestant, to what degree is the Bible true? Absolutely the literal word of God, without question, or a collection of ancient stories put together by people with their own agendas, which may or may not have relevance to today's world? Somewhere in-between? Just to be fair, we have to remember that there are literal fundamentalists in both Judaism and Islam too. While they each have different books, and would disagree with Protestants on the details and meaning of what God wants, they would agree that the modern world is wrong to have turned its back on what each would say are the literal words of God.

As mentioned in an earlier chapter with the Gandhi example, many Protestants have turned their backs on beliefs that require absolutes and dire consequences for those whose beliefs don't measure up. I can see why traditional believers would be dead set against so liberal a point of view, because it is suggesting a person does not have to be a Christian to be saved. They might say if a Hindu like Gandhi or a Buddhist like the Dali Lama can get to heaven without believing in Jesus as their savior, why would anyone need to be a Christian?

40

THE ORTHODOX CHURCHES

"To be Orthodox means to have the God-man Christ constantly in your soul, to live in Him, think in Him, feel in Him, act in Him. In other words, to be Orthodox means to be a Christ-bearer and a Spirit-bearer."
- St. Justin Popovich

When Christianity spread throughout the Roman Empire, it found its first home in the cities. In most of the empire, especially in the west, it took much longer to convert the countryside. However, the biggest, richest, and most powerful cities were in the eastern Mediterranean, so logically bishops, as the religious leaders of those cities, were also rich and powerful. After Constantine moved the capital of the empire to Constantinople, a wedge began to develop between eastern and western areas of Christianity. The patriarchs of the eastern cities had to contend first with the Roman emperor, and later with the Byzantine emperors. They spoke Greek and lived in a world derived from Greek culture. In the west there was only

Rome, and after the fall of the empire, an enormous power vacuum to fill.

The bishop of Rome, the pope, was the single source of religious authority in the west. He challenged the power of European kings and emperors for centuries, and claimed supreme authority in the Church. There were a number of cultural, geographical, and other theological differences added to the mix of disagreement between East and West, but the role of papal authority was the biggest issue. If East and West had been able to work that out, they probably could have compromised, or tolerated, their other differences, instead of formally splitting in 1054.

As far as day-to-day beliefs and practices, the Orthodox churches and the Roman Catholics are not so far apart. While Catholics look to the pope for infallibility and decisions, the fifteen self-governing Orthodox churches (such as Greek Orthodox, Russian Orthodox, Serbian Orthodox, etc.) are free to adjust their practices to suit the preferences of the cultures they represent, though they agree on important theological points. Since there is no ultimate papal-like authority, the Orthodox churches meet in synods, or church councils, to come to agreement. In these meetings, there is an effort to craft decisions that reflect the views of the various congregations, sort of a bottom up approach. In a sense, every person in the church is thought to be part of a synergistic relationship between God and the people, and participates through the Holy Spirit to find the truth. The thinking here is, if everyone sees an issue a certain way, that is a better guarantee their answer is closer to right than just getting a proclamation from the top.

While the Catholic Church is seen as more legalistic, (answers of theology are either right or wrong), the Eastern churches are understood to be more philosophical, working out the best answer they can, but recognizing there could be other, not unreasonable, points of view. Since they are struggling with complex and deep religious questions, for which they may not find a unanimous answer, absolute agreement or obedience is not required on every issue. Essentially, you should think about the issues, consider the answers of the church, and understand the truth of the issue in the way that makes sense to you. There are not many doctrines that have to be believed absolutely and literally. There is wiggle room.

There is an American Orthodox Church descended from Russian Orthodox churches in Alaska. Separated from Russian Orthodoxy, it became self-regulating in 1970. It exists throughout the US, Mexico and Canada. There are also three archdioceses, within the AOC, that serve American parishioners of Albanian, Bulgarian, and Romanian descent. As I understand it, after these countries fell behind the Iron Curtain after World War II, the Orthodox churches in those countries came to be controlled by the Soviet Union. Because of that, permission was given to set up supportive archdiocese in the US under the AOC.

ICONS

In 1995, I was fortunate enough to accompany a student group to Russia over spring break. While the students (ten boys and one girl) were supposed to be soaking up the culture and practicing their Russian, I was on the lookout for information about people's religious beliefs.

I knew from history that icons, statues or images of Jesus, the Holy Family, or Saints, had caused a lot of trouble during the time of the Byzantine Empire. Widely used as objects of devotion, their status changed several times in Byzantine history. One day Emperor Leo III woke up and decided (or was convinced) the use of icons was not good but evil. Most likely, someone read the Ten Commandments again and noticed the part about not making graven images. The government sent officials around to smash images. As people defended their images, some were killed, and it was a big mess. Later, after a lax period, they did it again. Apparently, the Orthodox Church is just fine with icons now, because I saw them in many places in Russia.

We visited a monastery and several very ancient Russian Orthodox churches. In one venerable church, the walls from floor to ceiling were covered with paintings showing various New Testament stories. Five hundred years ago, an illiterate peasant could just move from picture to picture, and receive an easy primer on the New Testament. Most imposing, as I looked up over my head to the dome of the church, was a massive Jesus painted with outstretched arms, as if enveloping the interior of the whole building. Standing in the middle of the church, moving around in a circle, looking up and down and all around me, with Jesus overlooking all, I had the very strange feeling of being inside the Bible. I could understand why icons and images can raise emotions and be so important to many Orthodox worshipers.

At the monastery, we saw old women kneeling and praying before paintings on a wall of Jesus or Mary or a saint, and moving from one to the next, sometimes lighting candles. The Catholic Church has traditionally been devoted to the statues, votive candles, and stained glass windows that decorate most churches, though after the Second Vatican Council, they are more restrained. However, the Orthodox are right there with the Catholics on the value of getting Mary, or your favorite saint, to pray for you, and advocate your cause.

In a way, watching those women in Russia reminded me of Hindu pujas, Tibetan Buddhist rituals, and Catholic midnight mass on Christmas Eve, where image and color, sound from a bell or chant, and incense, engaged all of the senses. I bet the same theory of sensual enhancement, ramping up our emotional involvement in the worship process, works in a similar way for each of these religions. Having an image to focus on, an image you are not praying to but through, seems to be compelling and effective. The old Russian Orthodox women were not worshiping Mary or the saints, but praying to them for help, and through them, to God. At least that's the theory. Whether the women knew this theory, I don't know. I would have had to ask them, but I didn't want to interrupt. I also don't speak Russian.

Speaking of icons, I remember when I was a kid, riding in cars with St. Christopher suction cup statues on the dashboard, which were supposed to keep us safe. How was that supposed to work? The best explanation I have is it was a good luck charm, or perhaps just looking at it triggered a subconscious prayer to St. C., like, "St. Christopher help protect us from crazy drivers." Well, I was never in a crash in a car that had a St. Christopher statue. However, you don't see those around much anymore. Even though St. C. was the patron saint of travelers, I believe the official word now is he may not have existed, and his commemoration has been downgraded in the Catholic Church. Did all of those suction cup statues do us any good or just make us feel better?

41

ISLAM

THERE IS NOT ONE ISLAM

"I challenge anyone to understand Islam, its spirit, and not to love it. It is a beautiful religion of brotherhood and devotion."
- *Life of Pi* by Yann Martel

There are many misunderstandings about Islam in the West, but the most important fact to know, in order to correct these misunderstandings, is that there is not one Islam. While the media, politicians, or bigots will speak of Islam as if it is a monolithic entity, this religion obeys the same laws of human nature and organization other religions do. Since Islam, in a few ways, is a very "Protestant-like" religion, there are many "Islams." There is no central authority and there are many points of view. Islam, like Protestant Christianity, believes each person is responsible for their relationship with God. Ultimately, there can be no church, grace, or intercessor between you and God. There is God, there is you, and you have to decide how to make the relationship work. If you decide to follow the direction of this Imam or that Ayatollah, and they turn out to be wrong, the blame is still on you.

There is no trinity, or son of God, or any other type of divine relatives, in Islamic thinking. Like Jews, Muslims are absolute monotheists. The universe consists of only two things- God and God's creation. God is one, and only one, in the most definite and absolute sense of the term. And you? You are the creation of God, and owe your existence, and everything that happens in your life, to God. There is nothing more important to you than your relationship with God. The word "Islam" means "voluntary submission to God," and a Muslim is one who has totally and absolutely done that. The main question Islam seeks to answer is, how does God want us to live our lives so we will spend the rest of eternity in heaven? Fortunately, God is loving, merciful, and fair, and has given us everything we need to know. Oh yes, God is also patient with us, because for a long time, we have been doing a great job of confusing God's instructions.

Let's look at the big picture, the way Muslims do. The Muslim word for God, Allah, represents, conceptually, the same God worshipped by Christians and Jews. Abraham, who, it is believed, first accepted this God as his only God, had a son, by Hagar the handmaid (slave) of his wife Sarah, since Sarah and Abraham had been unable to conceive. Hagar and her son Ishmael were driven into the wilderness (the Muslim view is they were resettled by Abraham), after Sarah unexpectedly became pregnant (the Bible says she was 90), and gave birth to Issac. Ishmael, the first son of Abraham, is considered to be the father of the Arab people, and through his lineage, of Muhammad.

While some in the West see Islam as a religion created by Muhammad, Muslims see their religion as a logical continuation of the information and revelations God has been delivering to human beings, as long as we have existed. Muslims believe in the list of prophets, from Adam on, mentioned throughout the Hebrew Bible (plus a few more mentioned exclusively in the Qur'an), and the prophecy of Jesus, all demonstrate the efforts God has made to help us stay on the straight path. Being goofy human beings, however, we seem to go out of our way to mess things up. We misinterpret, misremember, misquote, mistake, and miss the meaning of God's message.

The Muslim view is that even though the Hebrew Bible is filled with numerous prophets, and evidence of all of the help sent to them by God, the Jewish people seemed to lose their way. They became so locked up on the law and the rules, they forgot the point. So, God selected a man, Jesus, gave him a virgin birth, gave him the power to perform miracles, gave him the information he needed, and directed him to preach to the Jews. Jesus taught and preached, often using parables, and performing the occasional miracle. A group of people formed around him who seemed to understand what he was trying to say, but after Jesus was gone (Muslims do not believe Jesus was crucified, but brought by God to a spiritual realm to wait for his next assignment), his followers began to call him God. Once again, from the Muslim point of view, human beings messed up. One of God's primary and indisputable attributes, his oneness, was now compromised and confused by Christian belief in the "son of God" and the Trinity.

As Muslims, Jews and Christians all worship the God of Abraham; they revere a number of the same scriptures. They share similar ethical values such as peace, love, kindness, and compassion, and have similar ideas about how God wants us to live. Since they all claim the "Abrahamic" lineage, there is bound to be some degree of overlap. So, what is the Muslim view on the value of the other two religions, whose members, in the Qur'an, are called "the people of the book (the Hebrew Bible)?" Actually, Muslims are, as human beings tend to be in every religion, split on this. Like Christians who wrestle with these same sorts of questions, Muslim belief depends on each individual's understanding of the value God gives to faith, versus good works, as the most important criteria for salvation. Some who believe faith is the ultimate test, hold only those who believe in the prophecy of Muhammad, will get into heaven. No exceptions. Some believe good Christians and Jews, because they also believe in this God, have a chance to get in, but their odds would be better if they converted to Islam, since those religions, especially Christianity (with Jesus as the "son" of God, and the trinity), have views that might lead an otherwise sincere believer, down the wrong path. Traditionally, it was thought members of any religion outside these three were doomed, especially those who seem to be worshiping many gods or idols. However, some Muslims I know have a softer view on this belief, in the same way many Christians have softened their own "believe this, or you are doomed" tradition. That is, good people of whatever faith, or no faith, can still be saved. Again, it depends on who you ask.

At any rate, as Muslims see it, after Jesus' followers went the wrong way, God obviously needed another prophet to straighten things out again. For that purpose, they believe, He chose Muhammad to be His final prophet to mankind.

As mentioned in the last chapter relating to Jesus, it is extremely difficult to prove the actions, or even the existence, of most people from ancient times. As there are some people who say the traditional story of Jesus and his life is not true, some say the same things about the life of Muhammad. Both life stories, which are based on information from their own traditions and scriptures, are widely, but not universally, accepted by historians, since there is no evidence (I know of) to prove they are not true.

Muhammad

Muhammad, born in 570CE, must have been a great man. Whether or not you believe in the religious aspects, he did things that changed the world. In *The 100: A Ranking of the most Influential Persons in History*, Michael Hart rates Muhammad as #1. As mentioned when discussing Christianity, Hart does this because he divides the credit for Christianity between Jesus and Paul. Muhammad, however, was a one-man show. Hart argues there is no other single being in human history that we know of, whose actions have had such a profound influence. While it is fun to argue with Hart's point of view, I can't imagine any evidence that could knock Muhammad off, at least the top tier, of most influential human beings.

Critics of Islam, however, insist Muhammad, as influential as he might have been, was not a good man and, indeed, was a bad role model to base a religion upon. He was a war leader, caused directly or indirectly, the deaths of many people, and married young girls. His defenders say the context of his time and place must be considered, when evaluating his actions. They argue it is not fair to pull a leader out of 7th century Arabia, and judge him by modern standards. After all, to lead raiding parties against other tribes, or to kill traitorous opponents, were not only accepted aspects of Arabic culture at that time, but were also practiced by other ancient rulers throughout the world. This is a contentious issue.

42

MUHAMMAD'S LIFE

"You do not do evil to those who do evil to you, but you deal with them with forgiveness and kindness."

"He is not a true believer who eats his fill while his neighbor is hungry."

"However much the faith of a man increases, his regard for women increases."
- Prophet Muhammad (Peace Be Upon Him)

Overwhelmingly, Muslims believe Muhammad is the gold standard for human behavior. Certainly, to whip together a quarrelsome tribal people into a single political and religious unit, required both deft political skills, and the ability to apply force when needed. Sometimes he spoke as a prophet and sometimes as a political leader. Great historical empire builders and rulers generally must govern through realpolitik, and often leave a bloody record, even if they, like the Indian emperor Ashoka for instance, have the best of intentions.

It is difficult to try to judge Muhammed in the company of such peers. As much as we might not like the Machiavellian mindset required to protect and rule a realm in ancient times, it was undoubtedly required for all successful leaders. Muhammad used violence at times, but he also faced complex and volatile situations, and certainly felt obligated to use every means possible to protect his people.

We also have to keep in mind, after all, that Muhammed never claimed perfection. He was a man, in many ways, like any other man, and perhaps he made mistakes, as any man might. He only claimed to be the Messenger of God, not God himself. It seems clear, at the very least, Muhammed was a tremendous improvement in leadership on the Arabian Peninsula. To his people, he provided progressive and ethical social policies that displayed a humane approach, far in advance of his time period.

During Muhammed's early life, it was a tough time in the Arab world, where tribal loyalty was everything, and there was very little in the way of a social safety net. Vendettas and revenge killings were the order of the day, and life was hard for most. People worshipped many different gods, none of whom seemed to have any answers to make society better. Muhammad worried about this and often went off alone to think and meditate. According to tradition, the angel Gabriel brought God's words to Muhammad, ordering him to proclaim God's message. At first, Muhammad thought he was going nuts, and went home to talk to his wife, Khadija. Essentially she said, if God was going to pick any man in Mecca to be God's spokesman it would be Muhammad, because he was a good and honest man. Bolstered by his wife's opinion, which for any man is the most important one, he began to relate the messages he received to others. Some people were impressed by his revelations and began to memorize or write them down, while others, with vested interests, felt he was going to be a big problem for Mecca's economic and religious status quo. Tradition says Muhammed could not write down any of his revelations, since he was illiterate. One Muslim told me that was not true, Muhammad was literate. Others have said, "the tradition is true, he could not read or write."

It was not an easy task, but Muhammad was able to unite the Arab tribes of the Mecca-Medina area, and eventually all of Arabia, in alliances both political and religious. The organization he created, assisted by the weakness of the Byzantine and Persian empires, allowed Muhammed's successors to acquire a multi-national empire. In 632, he made a complete pilgrimage to Mecca (which had been a religious center long before Muhammad), teaching others what to do when they go on pilgrimage, and delivered his farewell sermon at Mt Arafat. Several months later, he died at age 62.

After Muhammad's death, there was a great void in Muslim leadership. For years, if any Muslim had a question no one else could answer, he could take it to the Prophet. That must have made everyone feel very secure having the acknowledged Prophet, chosen by God, readily available to settle disputes. But whom do you ask after he is dead? There is only one Prophet and, by his own prophecy, he is the last one. No one could be certain how to proceed. Shortly after Mohammed's death, different people, who had either written down the revelations, or who had memorized them by heart, began to write out and collect them. Later, variations in different versions lead the Caliph Uthman to have scholars work to develop what they thought was the most accurate, definitive copy. This document became the Qur'an (the Recitation).

The Qur'an and the Hadith

At its heart, Islam is a simple religion. One absolute God created you, me, and everything else. God selected Muhammad to be his messenger, after a long series of historical prophets, including Jesus, and through him, delivered the most complete and detailed revelation God had ever done.

The Qur'an is believed to not contain the words of the man, Muhammad, but the actual words of God, delivered to Muhammad, faithfully repeated, and memorized by others. Eventually, it was written down in a book of 114 chapters or surahs organized, except for the first chapter, in descending order by size. Muslims will tell you, if you want to know what God has to say, you don't have to meditate or go into a trance, just read the Qur'an. After this, it gets more complicated.

Even though the Qur'an is written in Arabic, the language of Muhammad, there are still scholarly disputes about the proper meaning of this term or that. Languages change over time, and trying to figure out the context for a term from the 7th century can create disagreement. And, as is true with most scriptures, translation to another language, especially a dissimilar one like English, can take the stuffing out of the meaning of the words. For that reason, the translated Qur'an is not considered to be "the word of God." The Qur'an is meant to be spoken aloud in Arabic, and is said to be poetry. It doesn't come across that way in English.

Fortunately, American Catholic scholar and intellectual Garry Wills, a Pulitzer Prize winning historian, has read the Qur'an for all of us. In *What the Qur'an Meant And Why It Matters*, he explains what the Qur'an actually says, as opposed to what both Muslim haters and radical Muslims say, about it. As it turns out, almost everyone who has something bad to say about the Qur'an, has not read it, and apparently those who use it to justify violence, haven't either.

For instance, there is no mention of the seventy-two virgins supposedly awaiting martyred terrorists in heaven. There is also nothing said about any duty to kill infidels. One of the things that gets Muslim haters going is any mention of Shari'ah law. However, the Qur'an uses the word only once, not as a legal term, but in the word's literal meaning, "clear path." Muslims worldwide are very conflicted by Shari'ah, since it is a man-made collection of rules, and subject to a variety of interpretations.

Wills tells us he could find nothing in the Qur'an to support the negative views of Islam so many critics insist are there. He could also find no foundation for the actions of Muslim terrorists, such as the killing of innocent people. It is clear the justifications terrorists often cite were devised by people, not found in the Qur'an.

The only ones who assert these subjects are in the Qur'an, have either never read it, have no knowledge about Islam, or believe it because someone told them it was so. Those most likely to make this error are radical Muslims, who don't know their own religion, those who hate Islam and pass on any lie they have been told without question, and those who just lie and know they are lying. As Wills states, "In such a climate our know-nothings cry out against foreign know-nothings, who reciprocate the anger."

Overall, Wills finds the tenor of the Qur'an to be one of mercy and forgiveness, and similar to the New Testament in "the nearly obsessive command to care for the poor, the weak, and the neglected." He believes appreciating the depths of Muslim religious devotion can help those of other faiths connect to their deepest spiritual selves. His last comment, "We believers (he is Roman Catholic) encourage each other over the barriers raised by people who do not wish any of us well."

As time and events moved on after Muhammad's death, and new situations and questions arose, both for the Islamic community and for individuals, believers were forced to use their own reason, intuition, and interpretations, along with the Qur'an, to decide how to lead a good religious life. Eventually such individualistic thinking led to a multiplicity of views, so decisions about how to proceed got more complicated. One clarifying source of information was the words of Muhammad, giving advice and interpretations on the Qur'an, speaking as himself, and not reciting revelations from God. It seemed reasonable, if Muhammad said it. His was a good point of view to consider and, over time, these sayings were gathered from memories or writings, and collected. Scholars then rigorously and scrupulously went through all of those sayings, called Hadith, to winnow out those that could be seriously doubted, were contradictory, or had little evidence for their authenticity.

The Qur'an is said to occasionally be vague and contradictory, and certain Arabic words have one meaning in one setting, but a different meaning in another. What if a Hadith seems to change or contradict the meaning of a passage from the Qur'an? Should reason have a role in understanding scripture? Are the words in the Qur'an meant for all eternity, or are they meant as guidance for a people in a particular place and situation, 1400 years ago? As the number of people who had known Muhammad decreased over time, a new industry of Islamic scholarship, based on the Qur'an and the Hadith, began to develop. In a story much too complex to consider here, a methodology was devised for scholarly work, and eventually, different schools of thought and vast quantities of written commentaries developed. In much the way Rabbinic Judaism brought about the Talmud, Muslim scholars, over hundreds of years, developed their own collections of discussions and debates which, studied by students today, have become much of the basis for Muslim beliefs and practices.

43

THE BIG SPLIT

SUNNI AND SHITTE ISLAM

"If I had an army like the 72 soldiers of Hussain, I would have won freedom for India in 24 hours."
- Mahatma Gandhi

The story of developments in Islam, after Muhammed, is a fascinating one. Imagine trying to fill the shoes of God's prophet. It was not going to be easy for anyone following Muhammad to be the leader of the Muslim people. At times, the succession process would get ugly and eventually lead to a major historical split within Islam, which reverberates to this day.

Muhammad's immediate successor was Abu Bakr, one of his earliest followers, selected to be Caliph while Muhammad's cousin and son-in-law, Ali, was making Muhammad's funeral preparations. Some people felt Muhammad had designated Ali to lead after him, but most did not agree. You might ask, how should a successor to the Prophet be chosen? The minority point of view of the Shi'ites, as the supporters and followers of Ali were known, was since God had selected Muhammad, this meant his family had been given a special divine leadership, a special understanding of the Qur'an, and what God wanted, which is unique to them. We might say this power was in the family DNA. Given this thinking, the logical choice for Caliph, they reasoned, was Ali, Muhammed's closest male relative. Then, at his death, Ali would be succeeded by his sons. The majority view however, by those who would be known as Sunnis, was that Ali was a great guy, but the successors of Muhammad should be selected by the community, whether they were related to Muhammad or not. They felt this method more accurately reflected how Muhammad would have preferred to select a leader.

When Abu Bakr died, a little over two years later, he was succeeded by a series of other early followers. First Umar, who was assassinated, then by Uthman, who was also assassinated, and finally followed by Ali, who moved the capital from Medina to Kufa in Iraq, and was also later assassinated. Each of these leadership changes was followed by a period of civil war. By the time of Ali's death in 661, Islam had expanded throughout the Middle East and North Africa, and the center of Muslim power had moved outside of Arabia. After Ali died, Muawiya, who had once been Governor of Syria and had fought against Ali, claimed the leadership. To avoid more civil war, Ali's oldest son, Hassan, signed a treaty with Muawiya which ceded the leadership to him. However, when Muawiya died, the Caliphate would be returned to Hassan, or if he was dead, to his younger brother Hussain. Muawiya agreed. By the way, some Sunni and Shi'ite historians disagree on exactly what the terms of the deal were, but we will go with the Shi'ite version here, as otherwise the story ends.

Muawiya moved the capital of the Caliphate to Damascus, Syria. Later, after the death of Hassan, Muawiya designated his son Yazid to follow him as Caliph, rather than Hussain, establishing what becomes known as the Umayyad Caliphate. This upset many people who believed that the earlier deal had been broken. What also upset them was that Yazid and his father did not even pretend to be religious leaders. The best that could be said was that they were protectors of the faith, but from this time on, the main interest of the rulers of the Caliphate was *power*. Islamic political leadership had been secularized.

In 680 when Muawiya died, Yazid took over. Shi'ites felt Yazid's actions to be an illegal usurpation of power, and still considered Hussain (in accordance to the treaty) to be the true leader of the Muslim world. To them, Hussain was their Imam. As the Shi'ites use the term, this is a divinely approved spiritual leader, and descendent of Muhammad, who God has given the ability to understand the hidden and deeper meanings of the Qur'an. In Sunni Islam, an Imam is a community's local religious official and teacher, something like a Rabbi. Unfortunately for the Shi'ites, they were in the minority. Even those in the majority, who disapproved of Yazid, were cowed by the power of Yazid's army.

Because of this, some Shi'ites living near Kufa in Iraq wanted to revolt, and asked Hussain to come to their city to lead the rebellion. Considering Yazid to be a tyrant, Hussain agreed. While he was traveling to Kufa, Yazid's Syrian army arrived first, and convinced the local tribal leaders who had promoted the revolt, that fighting was not a very good idea. The local leaders backed down. Meanwhile, Hussain and his seventy-two companions and their families arrived at a place called Karbala, and found the Syrian army waiting for them. To make a heroic tale very short, Hussain and his companions were killed, the men were beheaded, and the head of Hussain was sent to Damascus. This caused a tremendous uproar throughout the Muslim world. No matter what your dispute or your politics, this is not the way you treat the body of the grandson of the Prophet.

However, the people who were devastated were those Shi'ites who had encouraged Hussain to make this trip. They felt it was their fault he was dead. They had convinced him to come, and then backed out of the revolt idea, leaving Hussain high and dry. They grieved deeply for his death and felt terrible about the whole thing. Since then, Shi'ites mourn the death of Hussain during the month, and especially on the day, Ashura, that he died. It was later believed Hussain knew he was to be killed, and that his martyrdom had been predetermined to demonstrate how one must give one's life for God, in fighting for what is right. To Shi'ites, this became a holy event no less certain than the prophethood of Muhammad. On Ashura, there is still sincere and intense mourning for the death of Hussain, and many young men will whip themselves to draw blood in honor of his martyrdom. The Red Crescent is trying to get them to donate the blood instead.

The one thing the Battle of Karbala did settle was the political situation. Yazid and his heirs ruled the Islamic world as the Umayyad Caliphate for almost 100 years, and were then followed by the Abbasid Caliphate. Even though the Abbasid's were around from 750-1258, they soon lost most of their power, and served little more than a ceremonial function. Despite their loss, Shi'ites got something out of this also. A son of Hussain, being young and sick, had survived the battle and was installed by the Shi'ites as their religious leader, their Imam, since he was the great-grandson of Muhammad. As Imam, he and his descendants were believed to have those special spiritual abilities making them infallible in their religious pronouncements, and they ruled the spiritual lives of Shi'ite Muslims for many generations. Despite these political and religious disputes over the years, Muslims retained a high level of cultural unity. To make a long and complex story very short, the 12th Imam, in the genealogy beginning with Ali, then Hasan, Hussain, his son, and so on, was five years old when his father died. Then, the son disappeared. Historians have suggested he either never existed, or he was killed for political reasons, but that is not what most Shi'ites believe. They believe that to safeguard him, God took the 12th Imam to a spiritual hiding place, where he is waiting to return to earth as the Mahdi. When times on earth get really bad, and everything seems truly hopeless, the Mahdi will return to redeem the world, and convert everyone to Islam. The Mahdi will be joined by Jesus (who, according to Muslims was not crucified, but kept in special spiritual hiding by God), who will assist him in fighting the Dajjal (the Muslim version of the anti-Christ, a false messiah, evil being, deceiver) and they will straighten everything out. Muslims believe Jesus was God's prophet to the Jews, and this false Messiah, the Dajjal, will be killed in a final battle with forces led by Jesus and/or the Mahdi, depending on your belief. These events will lead to the actual end of times, involving the resurrection of everyone in their bodies, and the final judgement, which is another story.

Karen Armstrong, in *Fields of Blood: Religion and the History of Violence*, pointed out that Ayatollah Khomeini and the Iranian revolution made full use of the story of Hussain's martyrdom, and the importance of the hidden Imam, in rousing people against the Shah. Khomeini spoke about how Hussain had died struggling against tyranny, and likened the Shah to the Caliph Yazid. While many common folk did not understand the international ideologies and issues involved, "…everybody, especially the urban poor, understood the imagery of Karbala"[1].

Shi'ite Groups

Since there is not one Islam, there are many groups and divisions within both the Sunni and Shi'ite versions of Islam. As with Protestant Christianity, there are too many for me to keep track of, since I am more of a big picture guy.

While most Shi'ites are Twelvers (recognizing all 12 Imams), some are Fivers (believing the line ends after the 5th Imam), or Seveners (ending after the seventh Imam). Most Muslims believe in an end of times scenario of some sort, as many Christians also do, but there are significant differences, in group and individual beliefs, about the particulars. Many Sunni Muslims also believe in the Mahdi, but do not believe the Mahdi is a hidden Shi'ite Imam from 1200 years ago. They believe the Mahdi will be a descendant of Muhammad, who has not yet been born.

In some countries, Shi'ites are not considered by Sunnis to be true Muslims, and are discriminated against and occasionally persecuted. In *The Shia Revival*, Vali Nasr contends the ancient disagreements between Sunni's and Shi'ites inform the current split in Muslim countries, and the contention between Arab Saudi Arabia and Persian Iran. We can see this in Syria, Iraq, and Yemen, where contesting Sunni and Shi'ite groups align this way. Such divisions have become much more visible as civil wars and internal terrorism are tearing apart a number of Muslim majority countries. The accuracy of this prediction is foreshadowed in the news every day.

44

SUFI'S AND THE FIVE PILLARS OF ISLAM

"I searched for God and found only myself. I searched for myself and found only God."
- Sufi Proverb

Sufi Muslims

Sufi is not really a separate sect, but a tendency within both Sunni and Shi'ite communities. Sufi's are the mystical element within Islam. Their goal is to recreate the state of mind Muhammad had when receiving his revelations. They want to be open and ready if God wants to touch them, and desire their interaction with God to be in this world, in this lifetime, not just after death.

Mystics show up in every religion and have a different take on the whole religious experience. Most religions have places to meet, prayers, beliefs, rituals for adherents to perform, and sacred scriptures to read, and are pretty cut and dried. Mystics have nothing against this, but feel the others are missing the most meaningful part of having a relationship with the Divine. Mystics find different methods, usually in some form of meditation or trance, to generate a direct intuitive experience of God, becoming one with God, in a sense, or feeling some other sort of sublime connection. The experience is said to be breathtaking at the least. Institutional religions usually look down on these experiences as misguided, and occasionally mystical groups have been persecuted. Mainstream Muslims are somewhat embarrassed by their Sufi brethren, who don't seem to have gotten the point about how God wants us to behave. Sufi's, however, want to go beyond the day-to-day routine, and get to the heart of an internal relationship with God. Focused on love, Sufi's are best known in the West for their dancing (Whirling Dervishes) where they whirl around and around in place, until they achieve an intoxicated, trance like state.

The Five Pillars of Islam

If kids in public school learn nothing else about Islam, they learn about the Five Pillars, and how they are holding up Islam like pillars hold up a building. However, these pillars as religious practices, don't just belong to Islam. For each one, a comparable Christian action parallels it. Remember, both of these religions are brought to us by the Abrahamic stream of religious faith, so why wouldn't there be similarities?

Creed- To say this with meaning is all it takes to become a Muslim: "There is only one God and Muhammed is his Prophet." This is what a Muslim should hear first when he is born, and the last thing when he is about to die. While the Muslim creed is short and to the point, Christians have the Apostle's/Nicene Creed, which, while longer, also sums up the most important Christian beliefs.

Prayer- Muslim prayer facing Mecca five times a day at prescribed times, is well known, but my mother, a devout Catholic all of her life, told me Christians are supposed to pray five times a day too- when awakening, before each meal, and when going to bed. However, no washing up, as Muslims do before prayer, is required beyond normal mom enforced hygiene.

How did Muslims end up praying five times a day? Here is one widely known story. Muhammad goes on his famous night journey to Jerusalem, and is then transported to heaven, where he meets with Jesus, Moses, and Abraham. Muhammad appears before God and God tells him people should pray 50 times a day. On the way back down from God, Muhammad runs into Moses and tells him what God said. Moses says to go back to God, because the people will not be able to pray that many times. Muhammad goes back to God and explains 50 times is way too many, and can the number be reduced, please. God cuts it down to ten times a day. When Muhammad sees Moses again, Moses tells him ten times is still too many, and to go back to God. Muhammad does so, and God cuts the number of prayer times to five. Moses once again complains but Muhammad says he is too embarrassed to go back, and Moses can complain to God himself if he wants, so the number stays at five. Not everyone believes this story is literally true.

Charity- Muslims are expected to recirculate the wealth God has given them back through the community at about 3% of gross worth. Many Christian churches also ask members to tithe. When I was a kid, our church asked everyone to tithe 10% of their net income- 5% to the Church and 5% to other charities.

Fasting- Muslims fast each day during the month of Ramadan. This involves neither eating, drinking, nor having sex, during daylight hours. Since the Muslim calendar is based on the lunar cycle rather than solar, Ramadan, and the Eid feast days, travel backwards through the solar calendar, so at some time they fall in every season. Winter, with short days, can make Ramadan fasting easier while the long, hot summers can make it a trial. Fasting is voluntary and kids, old folks, pregnant women, and people with other difficult situations are excused. A Muslim at the north (or south) pole, where there is six months of daylight, must certainly qualify for an exemption. Ramadan fasting ends on the big feast day Eid-al-Fitr (feast of breaking the fast).

Fasting was a major part of the medieval Christian church, and is still practiced, on occasion, by many denominations. Roman Catholics used to fast from midnight Saturday until they received communion on Sunday, and many still fast from meat on Fridays, at least during Lent. The Campus Crusade for Christ recommends fasting as a way to intensify the power of prayer by disciplining and humbling the body.

Pilgrimage (Hajj) - Every Muslim, if financially able to do so, should go on a pilgrimage to Mecca, at least once in their lives. Those who can afford it, go many times. In a great display of equality and benevolence, Muslims emulate the worship process Muhammad taught. The experience of racial harmony and brotherhood on his pilgrimage, made Malcolm X realize it might be possible for white people and black people to live together in harmony. The end of the Hajj is celebrated at Eid-al Hada, feast of the sacrifice, referring to Abraham's situation when God asks him to sacrifice his son. Contrary to the beliefs of Christians and Jews, whose scripture say this was Isaac, Muslims believe Ishmael was the intended victim.

While many people these days have forgotten, Christians have traditionally been all about pilgrimage. Chaucer's *Canterbury Tales* is a series of stories told by a group of Christians on their way to the shrine of St. Thomas A'Becket at Canterbury, England. In Catholic school, the nuns used to tell us about Lourdes, France and all of the people who traveled there for miracle cures. After my father died, my mother went with a church group to the top dog of all Christian pilgrimages, the Holy Land. She walked where Jesus walked, went where Jesus went, and brought back slides and tons of souvenirs.

45

ISSUES WITH AND WITHIN ISLAM

"You and I are not Muslim because we were born in a Muslim family. You and I are not Muslim because you read a book about Islam, or saw a YouTube video and decided to become Muslim. We are Muslim because Allah chose us. Allah chose us."
- Nouman Ali Khan

Despite their common Abrahamic background, the values of Islam and the Western World often clash these days. By this, I don't mean terrorism, which almost everyone opposes, but differences in widespread cultural and religious points of view. I am not sure how much of this represents irreconcilable differences, and how much is about people getting more angry and excited than they really need to be. However, these topics have been on my mind when thinking of Western concerns about Islam, and Islamic concerns about the West. Hopefully, without offending anyone too much, I would like to both explain some misunderstandings about those differences, and question what I think are legitimate concerns.

Apostasy

Apostasy means to renounce a religious belief, or to embrace ideas opposed by one's original religion. However, one of the most quoted parts of the Qur'an is there should be no compulsion in religion. No Muslim can force anyone else to become a Muslim, and everyone should have the freedom to choose his/her religious faith. For a view out of the 7th century, this seems amazingly open-minded and humane. Unfortunately, at times in the past, and in some Muslim countries today, this has been interpreted into a violation of what seems to be its original intent. In these places, there are laws on the books about leaving the faith, or even challenging major beliefs that prescribe death or prison. In some Muslim countries there are punishments for this, and in others, no punishment at all. This is a very controversial question within Islam and has been argued by scholars for centuries. It boils down to a disagreement between what the Qur'an says, and what Mohammed said in one Hadith. Was he speaking as a religious leader or a political leader? Was he referring to religious belief or treason against the state? Scholars disagree. Muslims disagree. There is not one Islam.

Apostasy laws violate internationally accepted standards for human rights and freedoms, and condone discrimination based on faith. In the past, many Christian countries have discriminated against atheists, Jews, Muslims, and other brands of Christians, so neither religion has a clean record here. The two religions in the world recording the most incidents of harassment are Christianity and Islam, which are most often harassed by each other.

Family Issues

In traditional societies throughout the world, the husband has generally worked outside the house, to raise crops or earn money for the family, and the wife has stayed home in the role of mother and housekeeper. Only in the last several decades, and primarily in industrialized countries, has this scenario begun to slowly change for many women. Before, men were in charge of families, in most places, by both tradition and law. Women, while they had rights in different cultures, ranging from almost none to some, were often put on a pedestal socially, but were generally second-class citizens from an economic, legal, religious, and political point of view. Remember, women did not receive the right to vote in all of the U.S. until 1920. Their fathers were legally in charge of them first, and then after marriage, their husbands. Until modern times, for the vast majority of women everywhere, there was rarely an honorable career choice besides wife and mother.

When Muhammad took over, women had almost no rights in the Arab world. He gave them a large dose of equality in many areas of their lives, more rights in fact than European women would have for hundreds of years. Today, while some Muslim attitudes about women's rights have lagged behind the most liberal in the West, there are many traditional Christians and Jews who also believe the modern world has gone way too far in modernizing gender roles. Some socially conservative religious folks believe that, even though men and women are equal before God, there are basic biological differences and scriptural injunctions (be fruitful and multiply, for instance) that should determine how people must live. Most of these rules involve men being in charge, and women being subservient. These religions have been called patriarchal for a reason.

To gain insight into this point of view in today's world (if you don't already share it) watch the movie *Arranged* (2007). Two young women, one Muslim and one Orthodox Jew, both from traditional devout families, are elementary school teachers in New York City. They become friends and we watch as each family tries to arrange a suitable marriage for their daughter. What struck me was how similar the Muslim and Jewish families are. Both were led by kind and devout fathers. The mothers were intelligent and caring homemakers who were very influential with their husbands. Each girl had a sibling who annoyed her. Both families prayed to the same God. The only difference of significance in their lifestyle was the Muslim woman wore a hijab, and the Jewish woman will cover her hair, or wear a wig, once she marries. On any generic lifestyle question, both families would likely agree. Outside of their theological differences, and the political and social baggage their faiths carry, both would probably feel more comfortable with each other's lifestyle than with those of Reform Jews or more liberal Muslims.

While there is diversity within Islam, most traditional families, from whatever region, are patriarchal, with the fathers in charge of major decisions. Some Muslim countries allow husbands, for the "correct" reasons and following the "correct" procedure, to beat their wives. As we know, this type of crime exists in many places, regardless of religion. However, for most people, real married life is a complex give and take relationship and even in a patriarchy, the mother is usually extremely influential in the father's decisions. Happily married people, regardless of religious faith, have to work out a mutually acceptable family operating system, no matter who the religion or society says is supposed to be making decisions. Muslim men know, as do all men, the ancient truisms, regardless of society or religion, "if momma ain't happy, nobody is happy" and "happy wives, happy lives." This is not to deny the real problems many women face with abuse and unwanted or bad marriages in both the East and the West, but, given a choice, behind most family's closed doors, fair-minded people want things to work out. Nobody wants to live in an unhappy marriage.

I have been told the most important part of Islamic life is family, and the most important part of the family is raising the children. All of the decisions about how a family should function should be based on, "what is best for the kids?" Traditional Muslims, like people in many cultures, generally believe the best strategy for raising children successfully is to have them raised on a day-to-day basis by their mothers. Sending a kid out to Tiny Tots Day Care would be rejected by many Muslim families, if they had a choice. If the wife must work for economic reasons, then an aunt or grandmother or another female relative can provide the next best care. I don't know what Muslims would think if a loving, attentive, Muslim house-husband stayed home to care for the kids, while his hard-charging corporate wife went out to make big bucks.

Like everyone else, Muslim families want the opportunity for good satisfying work, a loving family, and a safe environment to raise kids and practice, or not be bothered by, a religion. Muslim students have told me the United States is a great place to be a Muslim because you have the freedom to practice your religion as you wish, not just according to local traditions or customs.

You can see this by looking at Muslims who live in the U.S. and, as we all do, enjoy the many social freedoms allowed both by the Bill of Rights, and whatever it is we have that passes for American culture. Muslim women are a most visible case in point. The Qur'an asks for modesty in women's attire. There are a few suggestions, but the wording is somewhat vague, and it seems like these passages might be open to some degree of interpretation. Since the Qur'an is not specific, this is exactly what happens as Muslim women, and Muslim countries, respond in a wide variety of ways to this injunction. In some countries Muslim women are punished if any male, besides family members, ever sees their faces.

In Northern Virginia, which is a very diverse ethnic and religious area, it is not unusual to see Muslim women wearing a hijab or, occasionally, a burka. But there are many Muslim women here who do not wear either. They simply dress modestly. The differences in how modesty is interpreted by Muslim women in the U.S. probably have to do with both personal choice, family influence, and some degree of left over cultural influence, if their family is originally from a Muslim country. The larger American culture has little or no direct impact on this beyond encouraging freedom of personal choice. However, there are some Americans who think Muslim women are coerced into religious garb by their families. While I have no data on this, it is not reflected by the Muslim women I have known. I also know that in the U.S. we give parents very wide latitude in deciding how their children will be raised, what they are taught, and how they dress. In contrast, for women in Muslim majority countries, a woman's decision on how to dress might have something to do with personal choice, but often more has to do with how strict the country or the local community is on this.

While non-Muslim Americans seem open to a headscarf (in my mother's day many women wore them much more frequently than today), they are not as accepting with the all-covering burka, a much more conservative dress option. For example, when my wife stayed in the hospital with one of our daughters, there was a Muslim mother, whose clothes covered everything but her eyes, staying with her daughter. When they crossed paths, they would nod. My wife developed a friendship with many other parents staying with their children. They would talk and laugh about all sorts of things while their children slept. One day, my wife saw the burka clad woman again, and she nodded. The woman spoke up and called my wife by name. It seems she was the same woman who had been laughing and chatting in the hall days earlier, but was back to wearing her burka now that men were on the floor again.

Why do women in burkas, which signify religious devotion and serious modesty, seem to rub many Americans and Europeans (the French have passed laws against wearing it and other face coverings) the wrong way? I am not sure, but it seems cultural background might have a lot to do with it. When I was a kid I watched a lot of TV, and the only people who hid their faces were bad guys. They pulled bandannas over their faces, except for their eyes, to rob the stagecoach or the bank. Honest people never covered their faces, except at Halloween parties. Perhaps, in traditional American culture, those who cover their faces, men or women, are seen as people who really do have something to hide, or are sneaky and can't be trusted. I was taught honest people look you straight in the face and expect you to do likewise. Even Catholic nuns who wore the traditional, extremely modest nun's habit and robes covering almost everything, showed their faces. The bottom line is that it is hard to trust people who do not match up with your cultural certainties, making it difficult to open up to their point of view.

The whole dressing modestly idea is supposed to apply to Muslim men also, but you don't hear very much about that. Men are supposed to dress in ways that cover them appropriately. The point of this is to insure against any possible arousal in the opposite sex by how one dresses or acts. So, a man working outdoors on a hot day can strip down a bit, but only if no women are present. He should lower his eyes when women walk by so it doesn't appear he is "checking them out." He would not touch a woman, even by shaking hands, that he was not related to, and would only speak with an unrelated woman if in public, and with appropriate space between them. Rules of modesty must always apply. Men must also not "dress like women," so no silks or jewelry. Anything that smacks of cross-dressing or homosexuality is strictly forbidden. As in all other areas, there are widespread differences in how all of these rules are interpreted and applied by both individuals, families, communities, and countries.

My feeling is that a little more voluntary modesty in society won't hurt anyone. If a Mosque wants to separate the sexes for services, that is what Orthodox Jews and some Buddhist, Hindu, and Christian groups also do. But it seems the rules for women in Islam go pretty far, while the impact of the rules on men is not noticeable. It doesn't seem equitable. As long as people can freely choose, it should not bother anyone if one decides to be totally covered, or chooses to just dress "modestly." In any house of worship, it does not seem just if only women are put in the back or the balcony. Why not put the women on one side and men on the other, and arrange a wall down the middle if you want. I wouldn't want my family broken up if we were there, but that's me. If there are segregated entrances, let the men come in the main entrance for a year while the women use the side door, and then swap it around the year after. No religion in this day and age should make it obvious they believe women are second class, even if their members are from a traditional culture. I have four daughters and they are not less entitled to spiritual equality than anyone's sons. If we are all equal before God, and modesty, not superiority, is what counts, then separate but really equal should work.

Polygyny (A man has more than one wife)

In trying to research current information about the practice of polygyny in Islam, I have been through a gamut of web sites. I have seen sites which have "proven" polygyny is not allowed in Islam, it is allowed, but under many heavy restrictions, and it is not only allowed, but is justified by God and the biblical patriarchs, good for society, good for women, and everyone should get on board. Those are just the Muslim sites. Maybe there is not a definitive answer. For example, a Muslim writer asserted that because many countries have a higher percentage of women than men, a little bit of polygyny will solve a lot of social ills. The author stated a man will be much less likely to step out on his wife if he has two or more loving women at home to attend to his needs. Also, with polygyny, all of those unmarried single girls won't be trying to tempt married men, because they will have a better chance of finding/sharing a husband. Everyone, he implied, will stay home with their enlarged family and we will all be better off.

I would have liked to talk to the person who put up that comment to see if his rationale could work the other way. While the policy has softened, China is still encouraging "One Child" or "Two Child" (in certain cases) family planning. Given traditional Chinese culture, if a family can only have one child, they will most often want a son. Right now, as I understand it, there are 119 men for every 100 women in China, and some provinces have imbalances as high as 130 men to 100 women. Would Muslims approve of a little polyandry, a wife with more than one husband? All of the same reasons would apply, allowing many more Chinese men to have/share a family. That is one question Muhammad probably never had to answer.

Although the vast majority of Muslims have one spouse, Islam has allowed a man to have up to four wives, which is common in some Muslim countries, primarily in Africa, where polygyny was culturally accepted long before Islam came along. However, there are reasons and rules associated with this. Muhammed was married to his wife Khadija for 24 years until she died. Later he had a number of wives, but tradition says most of those were widows and spinsters under his protection. Muhammad said, under normal circumstances, one wife is best.

Before Muhammad, tribal blood feuds were common and a woman had no rights or means of support beyond her father, when she was young, and her husband later. If her husband was killed in a raid or a battle, she could be in a very bad spot, given that there was no social safety net. Also, since women had no rights, a husband could just dump his wife if he wanted, and she had no recourse for support. There were always more women needing husbands than available men.

When Muhammed took over, he rearranged society to give women rights and set up a system to give widows more support. If a woman's husband died in battle, and there were no suitable single men, she could have support, affection, love, and children by marrying a man who already had a wife. Muhammad said a man could do this if he could be totally fair with both his economic support and his affections, otherwise don't bother, since being unfair to your wives would get you in trouble with Allah. In her book *Muhammed: A Biography of The Prophet*, Karen Armstrong comments on this requirement for a husband to be absolutely fair and equal with his wives: "It has been widely agreed in the Islamic world that mere human beings cannot fulfill this Quranic requirement: it is impossible to show such impartiality, and as a result Muhammad's qualification, which he need not have made, means no Muslim should really have more than one wife (191)."

When I think about the complexity of one spouse relationships, that makes a lot of sense. A 2009 NPR story, reported by Barbara Bradley Hagerty (*Some Muslims in U.S. Quietly Engage in Polygamy*), described the situations of a number of Muslim women being abused or mistreated in polygynous marriages. Some second wives were treated like servants. These do not seem to be the authentic marital relationships Muhammad spoke about and I cannot imagine he would approve.

For unofficial insight into the lives of "typical" Muslims, I highly recommend watching a few episodes of *Little Mosque on the Prairie* (a CBC show, available on YouTube and from Amazon). The show provides a humorous look into the lives of a tiny community of Muslims living in a small town in western Canada. Even though the show is plagued by exaggerated characters and typical TV sitcom silliness, there is a great humanity that comes through. On this show, Muslims are just people dealing with the same sorts of problems other people deal with, just with a funny Islamic slant. They are all trying to live a life of "true Islam."

46

TRUE ISLAM

"Islam is a mercy. If you see it's opposite, cruelty, then know that is not Islam. Islam is wisdom. If you see it going to foolishness and stupidity, then know that is not Islam. Islam is justice. If you see it going to oppression, then know that is not Islam."
- Ibn Qayyim al Jawziyya

When one of the Muslim speakers in my class was asked by a student to contrast Muslims in the U.S., who seem pretty much as peaceful as the rest of us, with those Muslims overseas, who commit or, at least, justify terrorism, the speaker answered, "Those Muslims overseas were not practicing true Islam."

In thinking about all of the different points of view in Islam, that phrase, "true Islam" has stuck with me because understanding it is key, I think, to understanding how Muslims practice their faith. All devout Muslims seek to do and believe what God wants us to do and believe. That is true Islam. Getting to true Islam, however, is, to some extent, both culturally determined, community influenced, and a process of individual decision-making. Since there is no universally accepted central authority, Muslims are expected by God to use their hearts and minds to determine, through the guidance of the Qur'an and Hadith, their community and family, how their faith should be practiced. In making these decisions, they are ultimately only responsible to God. However, does God want us to follow thousands of very precise and detailed rules, or does God just want us to be good people?

In some places, this yields many different points of view, while in others, that is not the case. Muslims, like everybody else, and especially in traditional societies, find it easy and comfortable to agree with the prevalent religious views of the larger community, reflecting their cultural upbringing. To what degree are our religious decisions truly independent, rational ones, and to what degree are they decided for us by our emotions, our family, and our culture? If we had been raised in a different culture, would we practice our current faith? Probably not. No matter how clear a religious teaching might be, there are many people who can only understand, or interpret its meaning and application, through their cultural point of view. In addition, as mentioned, Islam has a rich history of scholarship. Many Muslims look to scholars, or religious leaders they trust, to explain the right thing to do, but that still leaves a lot of possibilities.

Sometimes differences in religiously derived social practices are often dictated more by local custom than religion, though it is often hard to tell where one ends and the other begins. People in some cultures often do not distinguish between long standing traditions relating to ancient tribal customs, and the local practice of their religion. Even if those customs require actions which are very different from those practiced by others of their faith who live far away, they consider themselves to be true believers (remember all the dots on the graph). Those distant others, not doing these actions, also consider themselves to be true believers.

The degree to which culturally based customs are made and enforced by religious fiat varies widely throughout the world. Clothing, legal punishments, the roles of women and men, and rules about religious conversion and apostasy differ widely. Such practices as female genital mutilation, honor killings, forced and child marriage and other practices may strike many as abhorrent, but are historically endemic to particular cultures, and are often said by those folks to be required by their religion. Even though some of these actions happen in Muslim majority countries, American Muslims I know have pointed out to me there is nothing in the Qur'an justifying any of those practices. The interpretations of different practices by Muslims from different cultures might be very different. As mentioned earlier, Muslim students have said the United States is a great place to practice Islam because you are not required by custom or tradition to do things a certain way. It's totally up to you.

For instance, Ben Hubbard reports in the *New York Times* that one of the bureaucrats (Mr. Ahmed) who works for the Commission for the Promotion of Virtue and the Prevention of Vice (otherwise known as the "religion police") in Saudi Arabia, got in serious hot water for suggesting Saudi society lighten up a bit. Mr. Ahmed, doing his own research, discovered that the extremely restrictive Wahhabi based rules he was enforcing, do not reflect the society put together by Muhammad but are, instead, derived from earlier Arabian cultural practices. In this case, the culture co-opted the religion[1].

How Americans view Islam

Rudyard Kipling once said, "History doesn't repeat itself, but it often rhymes". Over the past 1000 years, Islamic and Christian countries have a bad history of occasionally not getting along with each other. I am not the expert on history who can engage in a Solomon-like apportionment of blame, but it seems to me that with the Crusades, the taking of Muslim lands by imperialistic European powers, and the occasional interference with present day Muslim countries by western governments, blame may lean more one way. The violent terrorism created by small numbers of radical Muslims cannot be justified despite this history. If the world is going to consist of groups getting back violently at those who wronged them in the past, we are all going to chew ourselves up and destroy any hope of peace.

Somewhere along the way, despite great difficulties, we are all going to have to declare "bygones."

In Pew surveys, non-Muslim Americans rate Islam as their least favorite of the major religions, about on par with their feelings about atheists. They are warmer towards Islam now than they were a few years ago. Republicans, and those who lean that way, are much more concerned about American Muslims than are the Democrats, with 64% of Republicans more worried about Islamic extremism at home, compared to Democrats at 30%. From a Feb. 2017 survey of Americans, "Overall, 40% say there is not much support for extremism among U.S. Muslims, while an additional 15% say there is none at all. About a quarter say there is a fair amount of support (24%) for extremism among U.S. Muslims; 11% say there is a great deal of support."[2]

American Muslims feel discriminated against by the larger society, are concerned about the castigating of Islam by Donald Trump, and feel most Americans see them as outside the mainstream. However, Muslims embrace traditional American values of hard work leading to success, are proud to be Americans, and are satisfied with the way things are going in their own lives.

Muslims around the world are concerned about terrorism and give little support to groups like ISIS. The highest level of support (14%) comes from Nigeria, where their home-grown terrorist group, Boko Haram, has pledged support to ISIS. Muslims, by large numbers in most countries, believe terrorism is rarely or never justified. However, differences in belief and practice beyond the basic tenets of Islam are widespread throughout Muslim countries.[3]

The search for true Islam is both an individual Muslim's responsibility, and one tied closely to day-to-day life in Muslim countries and communities. As Westerners try to understand Islam, they must understand there is not one answer to every question. There is not one Islam.

47

FEAR OF ISLAM

"If you fear Allah, no one will harm you, and if you fear other than Allah, no one will benefit you."
- Fudayl ibn Iyad

Like most people, I was shocked by the 2015 murders at *Charlie Hebdo* magazine in France in retaliation for satirical cartoons published about Mohammed, and the beheading of a French schoolteacher in 2020 who showed these cartoons to his class. There can be no excuse for these murders. Protests, boycotts, angry letters, or other civil actions have to be the strategies used to show objections, not killing. The freedom I have to print (or draw) in support of points of view you would fight against your whole life is widely accepted in the West. On the other hand, I can understand just a bit how some people might feel when their most important, cherished, beloved symbols are, ruthlessly attacked. Ironically, Muslims would never draw disrespectful cartoons of Jesus in revenge because Islam holds him in such high regard.

Perceptions of disrespect for religious icons work both ways. Some years ago, the photographer Andres Serrano exhibited a photograph of a small crucifix in a plastic bottle filled with his own urine. Called "Piss Christ" this picture was incredibly offensive to many Christians. Fox News went nuts, and many religious and political groups called on authorities to close the exhibit. There was vandalism, guards were posted, and eventually the exhibit shut down. No one was hurt, but the disgust and anger were palpable. Some conservative commentators said this was another example of the persecution of Christians in the U.S.

Christian or Muslim, can we put ourselves in the offended person's shoes? Imagine whatever you hold most dear in the world is being displayed by an artist in an exhibit in the most degrading, heinous and disgusting way you can imagine. Maybe a statue of the Blessed Virgin Mary, or your national flag, or perhaps a life sized, recognizable, model of your husband, wife, or mother posed in a horrible scene. Is this art? Is it protected free speech? How tolerant would you be?

This paints an ugly picture, but it is important to understand the impact of what has been called "aesthetic terrorism." If visual art is used to attack people, icons, or values, you would swear to uphold that give meaning to your life, and they are degraded and demeaned through this art, you would be very angry. You, of course, would not kill those responsible but you might wish someone would. You might pray for God to punish them. However, for people who are already angry and radicalized, the step from anger to violence might be a short one.

This is a conundrum. Free speech should not be limited, and people should not be afraid to speak out. Yet, I clearly do not want to make fun of the crazy person holding a gun to my head. How can we encourage free speech without it driving some people to violence? Maybe if we were all just more polite? Someone brighter than me will have to solve this one.

Jihad

Jihad has become a word often seen in Western media when describing Islam. Used with enough imagination, it can portray sword wielding Bedouins, racing across the desert to kill or convert you, or perhaps, in more modern terms, a wild eyed terrorist with bombs strapped to himself, eager to enter paradise. Both of those scenes have happened at some time and in some place, but, if we want accuracy, they should not be the model representing Islam in anyone's mind.

A hadith says that, when returning from a battle, Muhammed referred to the battle as the lesser jihad, and their return to society to improve themselves as the greater jihad. To most Muslims, the greater jihad is the struggle each person of faith encounters when trying to act as God wants us to act. This is obviously very hard to do for fallible human beings who continually focus on emotional responses and worldly needs. It might take a lifetime of conscious effort and dedication for an individual to make progress.

Sincere believers in all religions try to act this way. Hindus strive to better match their actions with Monist ethics, while devout Buddhists follow the Middle Way. Christians might call the same type of activity "trying to be Christ-like." As impossible as that would be to accomplish, motivated Christians believe it is a worthy goal to aim for. Likewise, the "What Would Jesus Do" movement is intended to remind Christians to make their day-to-day decisions based on what God wants them to do, and not on what the larger society dictates. This personal struggle is not very different from the great Jihad.

The second meaning of jihad is the struggle of a community toward a common goal, like building a new mosque. Since the Quran says it is wrong to take or pay interest on borrowed money, a community that wants its own mosque will try to raise as much cash as possible and really dedicate itself to the task. I read about a Protestant minister, who had given a Muslim group space to hold their services in his church, while they built a mosque nearby. He was somewhat jealous that their building was entirely paid off in short order, after a lot of community effort and sacrifice, while his church still had twenty years to go on its mortgage.

The third meaning of Jihad is war-like, but the overwhelming Muslim point of view is that this term has been overused, abused, and taken out of scriptural context by radical groups. There is no compulsion in religious belief allowed in Islam. The instructions and caveats for a just war, according to the Qur'an, are both conservative and very restrictive, both in allowing war, and in the conduct of a war. It is clear to most Muslims the radical version of Jihad is not what the Qur'an says. However, as has been done by extremists in other religions, there are those who interpret the Qur'an to justify the most violent actions. The frustration comes when people in the West persist in associating the overwhelmingly majority of peaceful Muslims with the radical message of violence from a small minority.

Similar to "jihad," the Western World has used an emotionally laden word, "crusade," which could be construed as violent. However, there are two distinct definitions for crusade. One is the military expeditions of the late Middle Ages waged by Christians against Muslims in the Holy Land. The second is "an enterprise undertaken with zeal and enthusiasm" such as the crusade for prohibition, or for civil rights. Like jihad, crusade has different meanings. You would think the military meaning that happened 900 or so years ago would qualify for "bygones," but this doesn't seem to be the case. Some easily riled people in the West get upset over "jihad" and some Muslims feel the same about "crusade."

There has been a public relations struggle going on in the U.S., between the American Freedom Defense Initiative (AFDI) and the Council on American-Islamic Relations (CAIR), over the meaning of jihad ("Killing Jews is Worship" posters will soon appear on NYC subways and buses," *Washington Post*, Michael Miller, April 22, 2015). CAIR claims the term jihad has been misused by both Muslim extremists and Muslim haters, and simply means "struggle," as in the personal struggle to follow God's will described earlier. The AFDI has paid for bus and billboard advertising, with pictures of noted Muslim terrorists quoting how it is their jihad to blow up or shoot Americans. They feel the true meaning of jihad for Muslims is the violent one, and CAIR is just trying to lull Americans into complacency.

Who is right? Both are right. Certainly, there are terrorists who are engaged in a violent "jihad" against America, the West and other Muslims. But, just as certainly, the vast majority of Muslims refute that meaning and insist Islam rejects such violence. In trying to decide the validity of the AFDI claim, can we definitively say violent jihad is the way Muslims see it? How do we decide? If one Muslim in the world sees jihad as violent, does that mean Islam is violent? If 10% of Muslims see it that way, does that make Islam violent? Do you need to hit 51% to decide? See the problem?

As we have seen, the real understanding of a religion is a scattergram of belief and practice, by individuals and communities, across time and space, not as a monolithic block. Every time a Muslim somewhere makes a decision about what they consider to be true Islam, the picture shifts. Every time a Hindu reconsiders his religion, the picture of the Hindu scattergram shifts too. To make an accurate, definitive, generalization about any large religion is almost impossible. AFDI may claim most Muslims see jihad as violent, but how can they say that? Both groups would agree terrorists see it that way, and both groups would condemn the beliefs and actions of the terrorists.

48

SHARI'AH AND SCRIPTURAL INTERPRETATION

"No one except God knows its interpretation."
- Qur'an 3:7

"People forget that they have a grave to go to and a God to answer to."
- Mufti Menk

Shari'ah

Shari'ah is the collection of Islamic law, ethics, and personal and private religious obligations that devout Muslims use as a guide for living their lives. It is an admittedly imperfect attempt to match their actions to God's will. God's will is said to be perfect, but human interpretation and application is flawed, so most Muslims either try to find a balance that feels right, or they go along with their local community. There are, however, people in the U.S. who want you (if you are not a Muslim) to believe this is an radical agenda, which extreme Muslims want to shove down your throat, and make the law of the land.

All religions try to help their members live their lives correctly, in agreement with their beliefs, by developing codes, rules, creeds and guidelines, so people can integrate their religious beliefs into the actions of their daily lives. Because there are many points of view in every religion, adherents often disagree about how seriously, or in what way, those rules should be followed. If faced with a serious issue many Christians might ask "What would Jesus Do?" Some might speak to their minister or consult scripture, while others might do what they wanted anyway. There are major differences within and between Jewish groups over almost every aspect of which rules, if any, must be followed, and they have been discussing this for a long time.

Many adherents of the Abrahamic faiths follow the advice of the Hebrew Bible (Old Testament) in a number of areas. Some use biblical verses to justify their opposition to homosexual activity and Harry Potter (witches). These selections, and others, are somewhat random as adherents seem to pick and choose some passages to focus on, while ignoring others. A Jewish friend suggested Jews should return to the concept of the Jubilee. As described in Leviticus, every fiftieth year, all leased or mortgaged lands were to be returned to their original owners, and all slaves and bonded laborers were to be freed to restore equality. According to various biblical verses, tattoos should not be allowed, there should be a lot more actions punished by stoning, and nobody should eat a cheeseburger. Because people can choose, most of these rules are not translated into action. Just some of them, by some people.

Many religious-based rules are not followed by numerous adherents since the number of ultra-literalists in each religion is relatively small. Most people just don't believe (or don't want to believe) they are supposed to follow every single rule written in that big book. Others rationalize that those were rules for the ancients, and just don't apply today. I know people who consider themselves to be observant Christians, whose only rule to follow is "be a good person."

Shari'ah is the rulebook for Islam, based on the Qur'an, the Hadith, and 1400 years of tradition, scholarship, and experience. The only thing that seems to be "one" in Islam is God, since Muslims are all over the map on scriptural meaning and interpretation. There is no universal understanding of what Shari'ah law is, or how it should be applied, and no central authority to make papal-like decrees. In some Islamic countries and cultures where there is little or no separation between mosque and state, various interpretations of Shari'ah are used. In Indonesia, the law for Muslims is based on Shari'ah and the law for non-Muslims is not. Even in Muslim dominant countries that say their law is based on Shari'ah, there are many different schools of thought about what should be included, and how it should be interpreted. I have been told even the most conservative Muslim countries are not able to use 100% pure Shari'ah.

This means that in Islam, as in all other religions, there are a wide variety of opinions on religious law, ranging from those pushing for total literal use, to those for whom the most casual observance is acceptable. Muslims with the most radical and fundamentalist interpretations of Shari'ah are on the fringe, as the great mass of moderate Muslims reject those views. Of course, being diverse, they are widely divided, and argue about what they reject, and why they do. As a result, I suspect there are many Muslims who, beyond the basics of their faith, base their actions on "be a good person," too.

There certainly are Muslims in traditional cultures who consider the existence of Western culture to be an affront to Islam. Perhaps they feel Western "decadence" and materialism is influencing the young, and pulling them away from the tried and true traditional values. Perhaps they are unable to get over imperialistic injustices from the past, or believe it is their religious duty to convert the world to Islam, one way or another. However, you don't have to be a traditional Muslim to be unhappy with modern culture.

There are conservative Christians who believe Christianity is under attack and want to return to the traditional American values (as they define them) of God and Country. Some support Israel politically only because they believe the Jerusalem Temple must be restored before the Second Coming of Christ can occur. There are also Orthodox Jews who decry the West's freewheeling secular society and believe the Godly way of life is being subverted. These are not isolated feelings. Religious history author Karen Armstrong said in a Bill Moyers' interview, "Every fundamentalist movement I've studied in Judaism, Christianity, and Islam is convinced at some gut, visceral level that secular liberal society wants to wipe out religion."

Scriptural interpretation

Many extreme positions in Christianity, Judaism, and Islam are justified by those who cherry pick passages from scriptures to support their views. However, even a casual reader of the Hebrew Bible, the New Testament, and the Qur'an, can see there are contradictions and inconsistencies within each book. In the Qur'an, there are passages that say essentially, "kill the unbelievers" and others that say, "there is no compulsion in religion." In Samuel from the Hebrew Bible, God tells the Hebrews to kill all of their enemies, even women and children, but other parts of the Bible overflow with God's love for all people. In Mark, Jesus ends his life crying out, "My God, my God, why have you forsaken me?" and in Luke he says calmly, "Father, into your hands I commend my spirit." If there are such wide differences in each scripture, how do people decide which parts they must follow and which they do not?

In *The Evolution of God*, Robert Wright suggests various scriptures were written at different times, by different people, and the version from any historical period fits what was needed by those people in whatever situation they faced. Each scripture should be seen as a collection of varied writings, not documents having one continuous thought on all issues. For instance, following Wright's line of thinking, contradictions in the Hebrew Bible would correlate to whether the Hebrews were conquering, or being conquered. Differences about Jesus' mission in the Christian gospels would reflect the different audiences, in time and place, for whom the gospel authors were writing. Finally, in the Qur'an, some surahs are recognized as having been spoken in Mecca, when Muhammad was a struggling prophet, others when he was organizing his base and involved in military operations from Medina. Still others were shared when Islam was a running religious and political concern, a growing empire containing many distinct cultural and religious groups. Each set of surahs would reflect the best direction for the community, for that particular time and place. While people of faith may be skeptical of this hypothesis, it would explain the contradictions.

In her recent book, *The Lost Art of Scripture*, Karen Armstrong contends that ancient scripture, from any religion, was never intended to be read as literally true. "Today we tend to regard a scriptural canon as irrevocably closed and its texts sacrosanct, but we shall find that in all cultures scripture was essentially a work in progress, constantly changing to meet new conditions (24)."

Did Elisha really curse that crowd of bad boys who made fun of his bald head and told him to go away (2Kings 2:23-24)? Did the Lord send those two she-bears to maul forty-two of them, as scripture states? Hard to believe. As with great art, scriptures were designed to provide a way for humans to step beyond the mundane world, to feel however briefly, connected with the mystical, indefinable spiritual world that lays just beyond our ability to grasp. For instance, the History Channel film I showed my classes (*Decoding the Past: Secrets of the Koran*, 2006), explains the Qur'an is best understood as poetry, not prose. It is written more like stream of consciousness, and is not a story, but God's message to humans. As always, interpretations of that message differ.

In every scripturally based religion, with very little work, dramatically different political positions can be justified by searching out appropriate selections, pulling them out of context, and presenting them as literally true. It is then just one more step to devise rationalizations for either violence or peace. The question is, why do some choose the violent, hateful interpretations and others, in the same religion, choose the peaceful way? Why do some few become terrorists and haters, while most others do not? The answer to this question is beyond my abilities, but I have a hunch it has more to do with human psychology than with any particular religion or scripture.

49

THE HEART OF ISLAM

"To some, Islam is nothing but a code of rules and regulations. But, to those who understand, it is a perfect vision of life."
- Yasmin Mogahed

In a democracy, despite whatever actions our faith might command, we cannot violate the secular laws of our country. We can try to change those laws to match our religious point of view, but we do not have the right to break the law for religious reasons, without expecting punishment. If our concern as citizens is that some extreme Mullah might decide what laws and rules we should live under, that makes sense, to a point. However, most of us also do not want zealous fundamentalist Christians, ultra-orthodox Jews, or any other religious group making those decisions. Two things keep us from having religiously determined laws. First we have a Constitution that keeps secular laws separate from religious beliefs. The state can't dictate faith to religions, and religions can't dictate government policy to the state. We seem to like it like that. It's not that our laws don't usually reflect an "Abrahamic" ethical point of view, but this view is so broad and widely acceptable, it generally does not violate the rules of any religion. When it does, we try to make accommodations, if we can.

For instance, Amish kids are allowed, after middle school, to engage in vocational education by learning to run the farm at home rather than spending time in high school, as required by state laws. The Santeria religion can sacrifice chickens if they want, and Jehovah's Witnesses' kids (and anyone else) do not have to pledge allegiance to the flag. However, the 19th century Mormon view on polygyny was not accepted by the U.S. Supreme Court (Reynolds v U.S.), and the court of American public opinion. Latter Day Saints were free to believe in polygyny, but could not practice it. In response, they adapted to the ruling by eliminating polygyny from their beliefs. There are a few break away L.D.S. groups who believe the church erred when making that decision, who currently live and practice polygyny in several "don't ask, don't tell" counties in Arizona, Utah, and probably other places.

Secondly, the other thing we have going for us here is a little bit of common sense. In Judaism, laws of the country where Jews live trump religious rules. That seems to be a good idea all around. When you think about it, we really don't want anyone's religious rules, not even our own, to dominate in society. What we want is for all religious groups to be able to do their thing, within the larger parameters of our secular laws, and we want to stick up for any religious group not getting a fair shake. It is much more important that everyone be free to practice their faith than that my religious point of view becomes the law of the land, even if I know I am right and all of you are wrong.

In the *Washington Post* one day, there were two articles about Islam. In one, reported by Michelle Faul ("Nigerian extremist says he approves of attacks on schools and teachers," July 13, 2013), Nigerian Islamist militants had burned schools and killed teachers who were teaching "Western education." Their leader said, "The Koran teaches that we must shun democracy, we must shun Western education, we must shun the constitution." He did not provide

Qur'anic verses to back that up. His is an ugly, violent, extreme, minority view within Islam.

The second article ("Recapturing the Arab Muslim world's golden age," July 12, 2013) spoke to the possibilities of Islam. David Ignatius reported on a column by a Muslim journalist from Lebanon, who visited the Grand Mosque in Cordoba, Spain. He noted that Muslim civilizations in the 9th century had been "characterized [by] confidence, courage, openness, tolerance and love of intellect, philosophy, arts, architecture and happiness on earth." Freedom of thought and tolerance for other religions had created a golden age. He wondered how modern Muslims had strayed so far into the chaos and repression, characteristic of some Muslim countries today.

The bottom line from these stories is to understand Islam is not fated by its scriptures to be one way or another. It is not the Qur'an or Hadith that dictates the action, but the minds and hearts of the people, and how they choose to interpret their faith. This is true of every religion.

PART 3

THE MAJOR MINORS

"I do benefits for all religions - I'd hate to blow the hereafter on a technicality."
- Bob Hope

It is estimated that over three quarters of the people in the world belong to the six previous religions discussed, and about 15% of the world's population is either non-religious, or so vaguely religious as to be almost unclassifiable. All of the many remaining religions comprise about 10% of world population. I have selected seven to mention because they have had a big impact on later religions, they are sufficiently spread geographically to truly be considered world religions, or because of some other unique factor that appeals to me.

50

JAINISM

"To kill any living being amounts to killing oneself. Compassion to others is compassion to one's own self."
- The Bhagavati Aradhana

Both Buddhism and Jainism were reform movements aimed at Hinduism, and both were started by spiritually enlightened men who lived at about the same time period. While there are only about 4.2 million Jains in the world, primarily in India, this religion has had a great historical impact, especially on Hinduism.

The historical founder of Jainism, Mahavira, lived in the 6th century BCE, just before and during the lifetime of the Buddha. There are many similarities in their stories, and followers of one or the other have been accused of copying some of the details. Mahavira was born to a rich, high caste ruling family and, like the Buddha, was not satisfied with the top down, fatalistic way Hinduism was being practiced at that time. When a group of wandering ascetics came to his village, he longed to follow them, and eventually did so, leaving his family and his wealth. But while the Buddha eventually felt asceticism was not the best path and opted for the Middle Way, Mahavira decided even more asceticism was what was needed.

He felt the universe was dualistic, consisting of soul, which was eternal and wonderful, and physical stuff. Physical stuff was bad, and the soul was trapped in it, until it could find a way to break through the cycle of karma and reincarnation that held it there. The trick we have to learn is to liberate the soul from the physical body, by picking up as little karma as possible, during our lives. After twelve years of asceticism, it is said Mahavira succeeded and achieved Moksha, the liberation of the soul from rebirth, though he continued to teach and preach for 30 more years.

The key to doing this, is to torture the body through extreme asceticism, to not harm any living thing (ahimsa), and to form no attachments to anything. This should keep your karma to an absolute minimum. Those who buy into this program totally become Jain monks, who lead lives of physical privation. To reduce negative karma, they sweeping the ground ahead of them to make sure they do not step on a bug. In addition, Jain monks are required to always tell the truth, not steal, to renounce sex and any other attachments. Conservative Jain's (men) figured, for obvious reasons, that women were the greatest temptation to be avoided, and did not believe any woman could reach liberation. I guess they thought it is hard to be unattached when you have babies, and they probably also thought good women would be reincarnated as men, if they were lucky. I don't know what Jain women thought about this. In another, more liberal branch of Jainism, women who renounce the world for the monastic life are on an equal footing with men and, in recent years, are more numerous. Despite an extremely ascetic life, monks are supported by the larger Jain community.

Obviously, this extreme regimen is not attractive to everyone. The Jain lay community continued to have families and jobs, while sticking to the truth, no stealing, and the "no harming" (ahimsa) part of the creed, and supporting the monks. Their hope was, if they could lead a good enough life, they would be reborn as someone who might become a monk. No Jain can have any profession where life is taken or harmed, which includes soldiers and ,butchers but also farmers, who might kill insects while plowing the fields. Forced by these limitations into commerce, and combined with their reputation for honesty, Jains, as a group, have prospered.

Like Buddhism, Jainism is an atheistic sort of religion. The universe is set up the way it is, and matter is eternal. There is no creator god, and since returning to pure spirit depends on our own actions, prayer or rituals don't do any good. Jains do revere Mahavira, and the twenty-three earlier founders of Jainism who preceded him, showing the way between this world and Nirvana. As it did with Buddhism, Hinduism absorbed many ideas from Jainism, most notably ahimsa, which had a profound impact on the beliefs and strategies of Gandhi, many Hindus today, and people throughout the world.

51

ZOROASTRIANISM

"One good deed is worth 1,000 prayers."
- Zoroaster

Even though there are not a lot of Zoroastrians in the world today, they were very influential in the ancient world and provided many religious ideas which are now essential parts of Judaism, Christianity, and Islam. Started by Zoroaster in Persia (Iran) around 1000 BCE give or take 500 years, Zoroastrianism was the first religion, as far as scholars can find, to develop the notions of personal ethical responsibility. These include decisions we make in our lives, spiritual judgement after we die, heaven, a hell with very individualized punishments designed for particular sins, resurrection at an end time, angels, devils, and Satan. Some scholars believe Zoroastrian monotheists were around before Jewish ones.

Back when the Persian Empire was the biggest boy on the block, Zoroastrianism dominated an area stretching from Greece to India, and Egypt to Russia. Even after the Empire fell to Alexander in 323 BCE, Zoroastrianism still influenced a large part of the population.

After Islam came to Persia, in the 7th century CE, however, conversions and persecutions eventually drove most Zoroastrians away.

The largest concentration of Zoroastrians is in Mumbai, India where, known as Parsees, they gained a reputation for hard work, education, and honesty. A modern diaspora has taken Zoroastrianism to the United States, Canada, Australia and England.

There are probably between 80,000 to 200,000 Zoroastrians in the world today, and there are concerns that in a few generations there will be none. Some sources suggest a population of 2 to 3 1/2 million, but that begs the question of defining who is a Zoroastrian. Some Zoroastrians do not recognize converts or mixed marriage families as truly Zoroastrian, so the real number depends on your criteria. In some areas with small Zoroastrian numbers, they have essentially disappeared into the local population. Since Zoroastrians encourage education and opportunities for women, many Zoroastrian women have professional lives, which, on average, lead to fewer children. Any way you slice it, the demographics are not good. The Guinness Book of World Records is said to have labeled Zoroastrianism as "the major religion nearest extinction."

Many scholars believe Judaism came into contact with Zoroastrianism after the Persians freed them from captivity in Babylon in 538 BCE. Jews took away a lot of Zoroastrian ideas that later influenced Christianity and Islam. Zoroaster said the universe is dualistic with a God of Good (Ahura Mazda) and a God of Evil (Angra Mainyu or sometimes, Satan) and we choose, through our actions, which side we want to join. Some folks believe the 'two Gods' idea literally, something like the Christian concept of God v Satan (Satan does have a lot of power it seems) and we choose sides through our life decisions. Of course, in both faiths the Satan side is eventually going to lose. Others believe the two God approach is more like the Yin and Yang concept in Chinese thinking, complementary opposing forces in the universe. Others believe this dualism is really a metaphor for the choices we face between good and evil as they battle for our allegiance in our own heads every day.

In Zoroastrianism, we find the first evidence for the importance of not just group, but of individual ethical decision-making. The belief is, when you die you are judged, as if you are brought to a great scale (ancient Egyptian religion used a scale for this sort of judging also), and all of your good deeds are piled on one side of the scale with all of your bad deeds on the other. If the scale tips ever so slightly one way or the other, you go to either heaven or to hell. So, in this life as you are deciding what to do every day, you know all of your deeds will be weighed, and your fate is entirely in your own hands.

While Zoroastrian heaven is wonderful and hell is gruesome, the evil person who is sent to hell will only have to bear those horrible torments until the "end of times," which is very similar to the Muslim and Christian descriptions of the end of times. The major Zoroastrian difference is, when this happens, evil will be eliminated, all souls, including those who have been suffering in hell, will be purified and rejoin those from heaven. Devils and demons will be destroyed, and everyone will live happily ever after in a perfect world.

Incidentally, if anyone remembers the old Sunday comic strip, *Hatlo's Inferno* by Jimmy Hatlo, you might notice the tortures designed in Hatlo's version of hell, each designed for particular sins, have a real Zoroastrian flavor.

I usually brought up Zoroastrianism in class for a day or two before I began Judaism, Christianity, and Islam, since threads of Zoroastrian philosophy and theology seem to run through all three. There are interesting Zoroastrian practices such as the sacred flame and burial practices, but the principle that sums up what the essence of Zoroastrian teachings is all about is: "good thoughts, good words, and good deeds."

52

BAHA'I

"The well-being of mankind, its peace and security, are unattainable unless and until its unity is firmly established."
- Gleanings from the Writings of Bahá'u'lláh, CXXXI

Many students, even those who are rock solid in their own faith, develop a respect for Baha'i after learning something about it. It seems to have the most politically correct world view, and is certainly one of the newest world religions. The following is a list of major beliefs.

1. Independent Investigation of Truth
2. Elimination of Prejudice of Every Kind
3. The Oneness of Humanity
4. One Essential Foundation for All Religions
5. Religion Should Cause Love, Affection, and Joy
6. The Harmony of Science and Religion
7. A Universal Auxiliary Language
8. Universal Compulsory Education

9. Gender Equality
10. Establishing a World Parliament
11. The Abolition of the Extremes of Wealth and Poverty
12. The Non-Involvement of Religion With Politics
13. Human Rights for All[1]

This is a most interesting agenda for making the world a better place. But, is it realistic? Can it ever be achieved, as long as those implementing these goals have to be human beings? I'm not optimistic. But I am also not optimistic Jesus' ideas in the Sermon on the Mount will ever be seriously implemented either. However, maybe because I went to college in the 1960's, I can't help but admire idealism in worthy causes.

Though Baha'i comes out of Islam, it is not part of Islam. In the middle of the 19th century, a Persian Muslim who called himself the Bab (aka The Gate) said he was preparing the way for a new messenger from God. Talking about a new prophet in a devoutly Muslim country, where everyone believes there are no prophets after Muhammad, could make one very unpopular, and it did. The Bab was executed in 1850. However, one of his followers, who took the name Baha'u'llah, said he was that messenger and went on to found the Baha'i faith. Over the years, he and his followers were persecuted and imprisoned all around the Middle East. While imprisoned, Baha'u'llah wrote many letters and books, and directed missionary work to spread Baha'i. After Baha'u'llah died, leadership passed to his son, and then to his grandson, until his death in 1957 when the religion then came under the control of an elected body of Baha'is from all over the world.

While the Bahai's are very liberal with the rest of the world, they do require more of themselves. Going over a list of beliefs and practices, there is a whiff of the same sorts of personal religious values, including daily prayer, scripture reading, prohibition of alcohol, an annual fasting period, and an emphasis on the importance of the family, which are also the mainstays of day-to-day Islamic practice. Like Islam and Christianity, Bahai's promote traditional values of monogamous, heterosexual relationships, and couples who wish to marry should have the permission of both sets of parents.

Divorce is allowed, but only in extreme cases. Homosexuals may join and participate in Baha'i without prejudice, as all people are to be treated with respect and dignity. Bahai's do not seek to promote or oppose gay marriage. Homosexual behavior is disapproved of with the same level of intensity as premarital sexual activity, but Baha'i disapproval ends with theory. It leaves personal morality up to the decisions of the individual, and does not become involved in private lives.

Baha'i House of Worship, Wilmette, Illinois (photo by author)

Despite their small numbers, Bahai's are very active in community outreach and other practices. While there are approximately seven million Baha'is in the world today, they probably have a much higher ratio of "active" members, than more populous faiths with larger gross numbers, but a significant percentage of members who are inactive or lapsed. Though Baha'i's have been persecuted in Iran, Baha'i is a fast growing religion, and one of the most widespread world religions with congregations just about everywhere.

53

SIKHISM

"Sikhism emerged as a ray of hope for the people of India who were stuck in obscurity – who craved for a way out from the rigorous battle between Hindu and Muslim orthodoxy."
- Abhijit Naskar

There is always a historical question when a new religion is founded by a prophet who claims to have been inspired by God. Who really came up with the idea for the religion: God or the prophet? Muslims will say Muhammad did not design Islam to have similarities to Christianity and Judaism, this is the design ordered by God. Likewise, Sikhs would say Guru Nanak did not design Sikhism as a compromise religion between Islam and Hinduism, but was instructed to do this by God. However it came about, Sikhism is a religion that has within it, elements similar to both of those religions.

Guru Nanak was inspired at the beginning of the 16th Century, in northeast India, where Muslim invasions and control had been frequent. It is believed God told him "there is no Muslim and there is no Hindu," so he preached a religion of unity which stated God was one and indivisible, as the Muslims believed, and the process of karma and reincarnation is how the afterlife worked, as the Hindu's believed. When a person dies, God decides if that person should be reincarnated again, or should be united with God.

The fact that we exist as human beings shows we are getting close. Human beings are *one* people, and God's highest and most profound creation. All people, men and women, are considered equal in every way. They should not use alcohol, tobacco or drugs. Rites and rituals are believed to be a waste of time, for the most part, so Sikhs are encouraged to meditate, and read from their own scriptures, to develop a close and loving relationship with God.

Even though Guru Nanak was a profound pacifist, Sikhs lived between Hindus and Muslims, each of whom found things in Sikh beliefs to disagree with. Eventually, the Sikhs gained a reputation as fierce fighters. After Guru Nanak died, they were guided by a series of nine Guru's, each appointed by the one before, each believed to be a reincarnation of Guru Nanak. When the tenth Guru came along, he declared there would be no more human Guru's, but the Sikh collection of hymns and scriptures, the Adi Granth, would serve as the permanent Sikh Guru.

Sikhs have traditionally been recognized for the Five K's, clothing and grooming practices, which are required for men and give them a very distinctive look. These are Kesa- long hair, which is never cut, and the turban that covers it; Kangah- a comb in the hair; Kacha- short pants; Kara-a metal bracelet; and a Kirpan; a ceremonial dagger. It is also part of their original teaching to support the free practice of all religions and to support political rights for all men and women.

There are about 25-30 million Sikhs in the world and while most of them still live in northwest India, there are also about 450,500 in the UK, 500,000 in Canada and 700,00 in the U.S. There are smaller populations in many other places[1]. Some of these Sikhs, as happens to any culturally based religion that spreads beyond its native territory, wish to compromise certain of their traditional cultural requirements (Five K's) in order to more easily fit in with the larger society. This has caused some concern within and between congregations.

Occasionally the fact that adult males wear turbans causes confusion among the ignorant in this country. Sikhs have faced discrimination and death threats when hate groups assume they are Muslims. While there are a number of Muslim communities in the Middle East where turban or turban like headgear is worn, most turbans seen in the U.S. belong to Sikhs.

54

INDIGENOUS PRIMAL RELIGIONS

"Humankind has not woven the web of life. We are but one thread within it. Whatever we do to the web, we do to ourselves. All things are bound together. All things connect."
- Chief Seattle

No one knows how religion began. At what point did the earliest human beings begin to consider there were forces in the world they could not duplicate or control? Did God speak to them, or did they just begin inventing ideas that answered their questions? What were those primal beliefs? There are a lot of theories floating around, everything from "we made this up to make us feel good," to the belief that people became aware of the spiritual world a long time ago, in ways they could not explain. Burial remains from 35,000 years ago show some concern and care in placement of the body and items included in the grave, but does this reflect a widespread system of beliefs and practices, or was it an anomaly? While we know a lot about human religious practices after people settled down and began to grow crops, raise animals, build cities, and leave records, we know almost nothing about what human beings believed as hunter-gatherers.

This is an extremely important area to research. Over maybe two million years, homo sapiens evolved to become hunter-gatherers. From whatever we were before, to whatever we are now, our brains have changed. Whatever genetic changes took place, whatever behaviors, instincts and attitudes we developed, these were burned into our genes and culture during this time. If we want to understand why we behave the way we do as a species today, the hunter-gatherer time period is the one we need to understand. In the last 10,000 years, we have developed extensive technological cultures, but in all the millennia before, our development was influenced primarily by natural selection. Natural selection's measure of success, applied to any species, was whether or not an individual's genes made it into the next generation. Behaviors that helped this happen were passed on, while behaviors that did not help were not saved. Since this was the only goal of natural selection, it did not matter if successful strategies made us happy, caring, and rational, or miserable, mean, and neurotic. Evolutionary psychologists have suggested that the answers as to why humans today often seem to be violent, irrational, and selfish are found in the behaviors we developed as hunter-gatherers. Given our very different world, these behaviors don't work as well today.

Hunter-gatherers lived in small bands, moved frequently and did not leave many durable artifacts, besides tools, for archaeologists to dig up and analyze. In addition, there was often a lot of diversity in stories and spiritual details developed from one group to the next. We also can't learn as much as we would like from surviving Hunter-gatherer groups, since their life style, and even existence, has often been traumatized and changed by contact with European. Even in the remaining deepest jungles and most remote areas, we know of no tribal group, that has not had some degree of "contamination" from the modern world. There is also the theory that we can never be free from our own prejudices in our analysis and evaluation of the evidence we do find. Even so famous an anthropologist as

Margaret Mead has been criticized, and accused of bringing her subconscious wishes and desires to her analysis of Samoan society. So, we have limitations on what we can say we know for certain, but we move forward and do the best we can.

While there undoubtedly was wide variation in beliefs and practices between tribal groups, there are a few broad generalizations we can make. As I mentioned earlier, an author of a textbook on Native American religions lamented the diversity of beliefs he found. He pointed out he would have to write an incredibly long book to cover the specifics of each tribe, or he would have to generalize. So it goes.

In my classes, I taught Native American, African indigenous, and Australian Aborigine primal beliefs as examples of this earliest spiritual awareness. Even though these groups are very different in some ways, they each lived directly with nature, and therefore have characteristics in common, reflecting the type of existence all humans lived before the development of agriculture. Modern studies have suggested hunter-gatherers generally spent about 20 hours or less a week, hunting or gathering food and other necessities. They had a lot of leisure time to make tools, chat, sing, stare at the stars, tell stories and enjoy the company of their small group, which was probably the only other people they knew. Their general belief was that the physical and spiritual elements of nature, the visible and the invisible, are all interconnected parts of the larger whole. The physical world was seen as a front, a symbolic representation, for the more real spiritual world. In people's everyday lives, there was no separation between spiritual actions and those that were not spiritual. They were all connected.

A group might have a member, a shaman, who seemed to have a special sensitivity to the spiritual and could help mediate with it. Each group had stories and rituals to solidify their relationship with spirit. The shaman advised people about how they should act, and to ease the passage from one stage of life to the next. They believed there was a spiritual force of some kind that provided them, through nature, with everything needed for life. Along with rituals, were holy places and objects, taboos, those actions or things to be avoided, and a deep respect for, and sometimes fear of, their dead. Every spiritual aspect they practiced still exists, in some form, in the world of modern religions.

Huston Smith, in *The World's Religions*, identified three primary traits of these group's beliefs and worldview. First was the oral nature of their cultures. While writing things down is what we do, this has a tendency to make those thoughts and ideas permanent, and difficult to change. However, not being literate, hunter-gatherers used expanded memorization to a level hard to imagine, reciting their funny stories, songs, and mythological tales of deep meaning aloud. And, because each speaker was part of that culture, the telling always reflected the speaker and his society. Rather than reading from a page, the "teller" drew the story out of his own memory, and couldn't help but interact with it. The "wisdom" in the stories was instinctively appropriate to the needs of the group.

Second, because they saw themselves as a part of the larger whole of nature, and understood they literally existed only because they were able to tap the resources in the environment around them, they saw their homeland, where they were created and lived, as sacred. Their "place" was not seen as something divisible among individuals, or as a commodity to be exploited. To them, dividing the land would be as senseless as trying to divide the air.

Finally, their concept of time was always "now." There was a past time of creation and ancestors. There were cycles of existence, such as seasons and lifetimes everyone could recognize. But time for these people was not coming from someplace or going somewhere, it was always now. This reflects the primal understanding that their relationship with the spirit world involved what is needed for their survival now. "We need more animals to hunt now. We need to find more nuts now. This man needs to be cured of his wounds now." Compare this to modern religions where there is often interest in things or services needed now, but, ultimately and most importantly, their primary concern is focused on salvation, or a good rebirth, or an honorable status, not here, but in the next world (Smith, 368-374). It is almost impossible to figure out how many human beings still practice indigenous religions. There might be more than 200 million people in Siberia, India, Africa and the America's who either live the hunting-gathering life or, like many Native Americans, still try to hold on to their ancestral beliefs while living in a modern, technological society. Others, like some groups of South American Indians who are nominally Catholics, have developed local religions that combine both their ancient gods and modern beliefs.

I have always been fascinated with our primal ancestors and wish we knew more about them. They lived successfully for hundreds of thousands of years, and it was in this state that we evolved into human beings. Our physical, mental, intellectual and spiritual selves derive from this time, and it seems if we really want to understand who we are as a species, and what we are all about, this is a great place to be looking.

55

MODERN PAGANISM

"I don't love Nature because I'm a Pagan, I'm a Pagan because I love Nature."
- John Beckett

Modern or "Neo" Paganism was the last religion, among those I taught, that I had to work hard to figure out. It was tough getting into and understanding the core of beliefs and differences in practice that makes this system coherent to its followers. But, as is often the case, I found a "guru" who made it clear to me.

Most people in the Neo-Pagan movement believe in a goddess, many believe in the god and goddess combination, and some believe in their own miscellaneous collection of gods and goddesses. Some believe gods and goddesses are metaphors for various forces of nature, and some believe the gods and goddesses are actual discrete spiritual beings. Some groups within the larger movement seem to be following Native American beliefs, while others are Wiccans, Druids, Feminist Wiccans, Pagans, followers of ancient Norse religions, and other groups I had never heard of. They seem to be all over the map about what they believe and what they do. I could not find the common belief or action that would help it all make sense. That is, until I found my class a speaker on Neo-Paganism, Dan Holgrieve. He, a Wiccan, illuminated my understanding as he spoke to my classes over a number of years.

Historically, pagan was the term used to describe those Europeans in the late Roman Empire, who had not yet figured out the right religion was Christianity, and persisted in worshipping all those old time gods and goddesses. Since city people were the first to convert to Christianity, and country people generally dragged their feet, the word pagan had a very pejorative meaning, something like hayseed, redneck, hick, country bumpkin. After the Roman Empire in the west went down, and the Roman Catholic Church was the dominant European institution, widespread conversion to Christianity continued slowly over hundreds of years, with various degrees of cooptation, coercion, and persuasion until all but the most recalcitrant country people had come around. Then things got nastier.

In Europe, the time between the 15th and 18th centuries have been called "the burning years." Anyone suspected of being a witch had a good chance of being burned at the stake. Some of these people were probably pagan holdouts, others were women who might have used herbs, or "spells" to innocently cure people or create love potions, and probably some were just "uppity" women who offended someone in power. At least 40,000 and 60,000 people, mostly women, although some say many more, were killed for this "crime" during this time. Wiccans point out that all of the scary, evil stories of witches, still pervading popular culture in Halloween, films, and TV, are fiction, invented by the Church and government officials, to justify these killings. If there were still remnants of the old pagan faiths at that time, they were probably either totally wiped out, or driven so far underground, that they eventually died out. I know of no credible evidence that claims any ancient European pagan groups survived intact to modern times.

The philosophical base of modern day paganism stems from a variety of literary and religious sources, but Neo-Paganism came to life primarily because of the work of an Englishman, Gerald Gardner, and the books he published in the 1950's. He said he received his information from the last coven of witches surviving in England, though many people think he made that up. He developed a detailed methodology of practices to re-create the magical rituals covens of witches had, he said, invoked in the past. This movement gained a certain amount of notoriety and popularity. Some people were spiritually intrigued by the concept, while others thought it would just be cool to become witches.

From this beginning, and over the next several decades, groups freely adapted Gardner's rules and rituals, evolving into a number of different sects, usually identifying, more or less, with various historical ancient beliefs. This grew, developed, and spread from England to America and other places around the world. Some groups try to be as historically spot on to an original group of Pagans, but that is really hard because not much information has survived the centuries. I have been told that the majority of Neo-Pagans don't try for that degree of authenticity because, while it might be fun to dress up in costume and use ancient languages, it really isn't necessary. Something else is thought to be going on that makes these practices work.

There is a story about an American college in the 1960's, that required all students to attend a chapel service each week. It didn't matter which religion's chapel service they attended, but each student had to go once a week. Some smart boys decided if they had to go to chapel, why not be Druids? That would be so cool. They would dare the college to turn their "religion" down. The college said, "OK, but also said you Druids have to have regular services and you have to be serious. You can't use this time for monkey business." The students called their bluff, researched the subject and developed the details for a regular service. Then....something happened. It is reported the students felt, when they performed their services with seriousness and intent, something spiritual was taking place. They weren't sure what was happening, but they kept doing it because they felt they were getting results.

This is the report that comes back from Neo-Pagan groups. In their rituals, something is happening. The majority theory is that results occur because there are many ways to access the spiritual, and this is one of them. Our Wiccan speaker Dan said his group's meetings were great for socializing, but when they got down to it, the rituals they devised were bringing, they felt, palpable outcomes. Their belief is that the connections to the divine they experience, and the rituals they have created to bring about these outcomes, called magick (spelled differently to distinguish from stage magic), are available to all human beings. You just have to learn how to harness your abilities to do it. An old friend of mine often told me that "thoughts are things," meaning when we focus our minds correctly, we can bring about a tangible, real outcome. This seems to be a great description for what the Neo-Pagans claim is happening.

In theory, modern paganism works like this. Even though Gardner's Wiccans were very strict, and had many rules about procedure and process, people found results could still happen when they ignored the "rules" and free lanced their rituals. There does not seem to be only one method that works. This is one reason for the increase of diversity in the Neo Pagan movement. Holgrieve says what works is creating rituals with meaning for you and your group. Anyone who has read about magick knows that in the Wiccan cannon there are a number there of objects, prayers, and ritual practices with deep symbolic meaning. However important these concepts might be though, they are not essential. Those particular items in the standard format can be added to, or deleted from by any group, since the important thing is to end up with a ritual which has meaning for those performing it. Then, when conducted with sincerity and focus, it is believed the ritual works, the spiritual realm is touched, and the wishes of the group are released into the universe. It is expected the universe will respond, and they believe it does.

According to Holgrieve, the old Hindu story of the elephant and the seven blind men best explains how this fits into the larger spiritual picture. An elephant comes to town, and the seven blind men each grab a part of it and begin to describe the elephant, by reference to whatever piece they have. "An elephant is like a big wall," says one, who has the elephant's side. "An elephant is like a rope," says one who has the tail. "An elephant is hard, sharp and pointy," says the one who has the tusks, and so on. Everyone thinks their piece, as they perceive it, is the correct description of the elephant. So the spiritual realm, or God, or the Tao, or whatever you want to name it, is the elephant and we are the blind men. Many religions have a piece of the elephant, including the Neo-Pagans, but the elephant is just too big, and our senses too limited, to accurately describe it. The Neo-Pagans figure they have their piece of the elephant, which might seem different from yours, but it is part of the elephant none the less, and therefore no less valid.

Many traditional religious folks believe prayer brings a response. Neo-Pagans believe their focused rituals also get results. The ritual is the tool the mind uses to focus. It doesn't matter what ritual is used as long as it helps to connect us to the spiritual. And, it doesn't matter whether there are many gods, one God, feminine gods, masculine gods, or just a diffuse spiritual force; it's how you approach spirit that makes the connection. Pick the story that resonates with you and go with it.

There are a number of reasons why some people are drawn to this diverse collection of practices. For one, there is a widespread belief in the Goddess presence, which might appeal to those who feel alienated from a God, generally defined and discussed by traditional religions, as male. This God seems to be supportive of traditional patriarchal societies that historically have downplayed equality for women. There is also a strong "earth reverence" nature theme in Neo-Paganism, which might draw environmental activists who prefer to understand God as nature, or Gaia. For whatever variety of reasons, the one thing that keeps them coming back is the experience.

While all this variety first confused me, it became clearer when I understood Neo-Paganism is a non-doctrinal religion. There is not a list of things you have to believe. There are a small number of ideas a majority shares, but it is the experience, not specific, required articles of faith or beliefs that is most important. Participants might have contradictory beliefs, but that really doesn't make any difference to what happens when a group meets and conducts a ritual together. Dan explained how his views had evolved over time to include three different gods, yet he said he knew of Neo-Pagans who were atheists, and came back for the experience. Even they believe that in their services and rituals, something happens.

The Neo-Pagans I have met are generally a fun loving and ethical people. One of the few beliefs most Pagans hold in common is some variation of karmic law. If you do bad things, that will blast you back. Don't harm people, don't do spells that harm people, and don't do spells for people unless they ask. Also, for the rest of us, don't confuse Neo-Pagans with Satanists. Religious Satanists have this veneration of Satan/anti-God thing going, which is their own particular response to Judeo-Christian theology. There are many types of Satanists, including atheistic ones, who use Satan as a metaphor for free thought and expression. Pagans don't believe in absolute evil, and they see themselves as outside of the whole Judeo/Islamic/Christian, God v Satan worldview; it annoys them when people get that confused.

In response to student questions Holgrieve said, in this area [Washington, DC metro], he had never come upon any prejudice or discrimination over the fact he was a Wiccan. He has heard stories of Neo-Pagans, who live in parts of the country with a large fundamentalist Christian population, who, because of biblical antipathy to witches, choose to keep their religious beliefs "in the closet." Neo-Pagans almost never proselytize, figuring if this practice is right for you, you will find them. There are at least one million Neo-Pagans in the world today, most in the U.S. and Canada, though there may be a larger number of "closet" sympathizers. Neo-Pagans do not hold still long enough to be counted or defined easily.

PART 4

A QUESTION OF FAITH

"If you look for truth, you may find comfort in the end; if you look for comfort you will not get either comfort or truth only soft soap and wishful thinking to begin, and in the end, despair."
- C.S. Lewis

In this writing, I have laid out my understanding of the beliefs of the major religions of the world. Obviously, this effort could be neither absolutely exhaustive nor totally universal. Since there are so many religions, and so much history and different points of view for each, it is impossible to know everything. But I don't think we have to know every detail about each religion to do them justice, when it comes to understanding. To be fair, we can study them closely enough to get a sense of their underlying philosophies and their fundamental beliefs about life, the universe, and everything. If we do this honestly, we can let a universe of cultural differences, history, details, and trivial facts go. If we want to see the forest, at some point we have to stop counting trees.

I began this process to share what I learned as a high school world religions teacher because I feel strongly the world would be a better place if we had a sympathetic understanding of each other's religions. This is still a strong motivator for me but, as I reviewed my notes, another process, emerging in my mind, took me by surprise.

What I found was, as I edited, rewrote, and researched for more current information about each religion, I was simultaneously, but somewhat unconsciously, comparing them to each other, and to my own spiritual understanding. As a religion teacher, one of my most important goals, regardless of my own opinions, was to be scrupulously fair and neutral in the teaching of religion to my students. I wanted to present each one as if I was a member of that faith, not in a proselytizing way, but in a rational, straightforward, and objective way. I always told the students, "if you can determine my beliefs by the way I teach this class, then I am not doing a good job."

Now I am not teaching, and it has slowly dawned on me I do not have to be so discreet. I am writing to discerning readers here, so it is OK for me to have a point of view as I examine, analyze, and comment more deeply on the religious world. What this means is I must jettison some of the religion teacher, and become more of a philosopher. If my goal is to find the truth, I must use the tools of fact and mind at my disposal to discover what it is. Questions must be asked and answered.

As I mentioned earlier, a long time ago, when I was in high school, I attended Catholic Sunday school for kids on Tuesday night. While most of our instructors followed the lesson plans without deviation, we had a teacher one year who was going to be cool and with it. He asked what we thought about the Catholic faith. This may have been a mistake. I don't remember the whole conversation, but I do remember asking why we believe this stuff (Church doctrine). His answer was, what the Church tells us is true. I asked, how does the Church know this is true? He answered, the Church is always right in matters of faith. I asked, how do we know the Church is right? He answered, because we have faith. I asked why do we believe our faith is true? He answered, because the Church tells us it is. I sensed we were starting to go in circles so I ended it. This seemed like an unsatisfying way to determine the answers to important questions.

Since then, I have warmed to the notion there has to be a better way to determine, if not the truth about religion, then, at least, more satisfying answers. My atheist friends have opted for the easy way out by declaring God's non-existence. End of story. My most religious friends don't need to search, because their various faiths tell them their answer is the right one, and everyone else is some degree of wrong. End of story. Neither view makes me happy. I need to ask some questions. Of myself.

56

KEY QUESTIONS ABOUT RELIGION

"In all affairs it's a healthy thing now and then to hang a question mark on the things you have long taken for granted."
- Bertrand Russell

It is time to ask some basic questions that a seeker of the truth has to answer, when considering the veracity of religious beliefs. I don't want to spend the rest of my life as an agnostic and would like to come to the best conclusion I can.

Always trying to be a good philosopher, I want to work through this in a rational and logical manner. I will suggest possible answers, and make it clear which I like. You are welcome to discover additional or different answers.

1. Do you think there is the possibility of a transcendent, purposeful, intelligent, force or entity (let's call it God for short) running, guiding, or significantly influencing some combination of the universe, our world, and our lives? The scope of this force/

being could range from the total universe and beyond, in existences we do not know about, to a singular entity or force within this universe.

NO- THIS MEANS you believe there is no God. Your questioning ends here since you agree with the atheists, believing that there is nothing going on in the universe except mindless natural processes.

YES- OR AT LEAST THE possibility of yes, then continue. The universe has the narrow range of qualities that have produced processes for the development of life and consciousness. From the Big Bang to the present, every step in the universe's evolution has led to the next step, and so on, until we have us. This makes me wonder if this chain of events is purposeful or just a wacky accident.

2. If there is God, and we do participate in whatever the spiritual process is, does it make any difference to God what we say, do, or believe? In other words, is our current or future status in God's system affected by our actions or beliefs?

NO- WE CAN CONTINUE to question God's existence but it is just academic. After all, if there is nothing we can do to affect things, we are just going along for the ride. Our beliefs, and actions have no impact on our situation. If our status in God's system is predetermined, the result is the same, nothing we do makes any difference. In this scenario, the atheists are wrong about God's existence, but it doesn't matter since religious belief has no extrinsic meaning or value.

YES- THEN CONTINUE. This answer implies we do have an interactive, affective role in the universe, in some way or another.

Our actions might result in giving us a happier/ unhappier life, or perhaps it means we will have a significantly positive or negative afterlife, or something else. I prefer this answer over "No" because this answer gets everyone involved. I like to give God credit for some originality.

3. If actions and/or beliefs do matter to God, what are they? How do we know what to do? It has been suggested that one, or a combination of the following activities, may be required to affect our status in God's system. Maybe you can think of additional nominees.

A. Being a good person (save the argument on what that means for later).

B. Being a very good person ("A," plus significant outreach to helping others).

C. Holding particular beliefs and sacred texts to be absolutely true through our faith.

D. Worshiping God, through required services or mandated life style actions.

LET's take a deeper dive into this question and analyze different ways people respond to it.

A. Good actions or correct beliefs?

Hinduism, Buddhism, and **Judaism** are primarily concerned with our actions. Certain activities such as meditation, following mitzvah in Conservative and Orthodox Judaism, religious services, and studying scripture are considered by many to be helpful for us to focus our lives on performing good actions, but are not essential to be spiritually successful. While some people in these faiths might insist certain specific beliefs or practices are required, the overwhelming majority would, I believe, agree spiritual progress is best measured by actions.

Hindus and Buddhists have an enormous volume of religious scriptures but, for the most part, adherents feel these are inspired writings, or the collected sayings of a historical person, like the Buddha. While it is thought by many that studying scripture can help us be better people, doing so is not required. Actions are what count.

Traditional Chinese beliefs of maintaining a correct relationship with heaven and society is all about proper actions to insure harmony and balance in life, whether as a Confucian, a Taoist, or a follower of ancestral folk beliefs. Since many religious Chinese also follow Buddhism, they are covered there.

Christians and **Muslims**, as much as they disagree on important points of theology, have similar answers to this questions. Historically, and perhaps in majorities today, both hold that correct beliefs are the only, or at least the most important, determinant for God's favor.

Protestants have traditionally held that only those who believe in the salvation, provided by the death and resurrection of Jesus as the Son of God, will have a good afterlife. Many believe good actions are a byproduct of faith, but are not essential for salvation.

Roman Catholics hold that belief in Jesus, plus good actions, help us acquire merit in heaven. The grace and sacraments obtained from the Church are also required for salvation. My impression is, that opinions on the weight of each of these factors in determining salvation, varies widely depending on whom you ask. There are many Catholics who do not feel disbelief, by itself, condemns a person to hell, but there are conservative Catholics who disagree.

In the **Orthodox Churches,** faith in the teachings of Jesus is first and most essential. Good works are said to help us fight the tendency to sin, and align our lives with the gift of salvation. My impression is that these actions are seen as important to help adherents keep their faith strong and on the right path, without being absolutely required.

In **Islam**, since God makes all decisions about the afterlife, there are no guarantees. Certainly, faith is involved. However, I have heard from some that the belief in both Muhammad's prophecy, and in one God, are essential. Others think that belief in one God is sufficient. Good practices and works are strongly encouraged to build up merit, as we try to have our good deeds outweigh our sins, for God's consideration. God is merciful, but God looks at your total package after death, and then decides.

B. Sacred scripture-

Jews have the Hebrew Bible (Old Testament), and Christians have that, plus the New Testament, while Muslims have those (where they do not contradict the Qur'an), plus the Qur'an, the Hadith, and the sayings of Muhammad. While almost all believers in these faiths feel these are important documents, there is wide disagreement about interpretation, and how literally scriptural injunctions are supposed to be believed and followed.

C. Atheistic humanists-

do not believe in God, but do believe that being a good person (or a very good person) is an ethical goal everyone should follow. Humanists who do believe in the spiritual possibilities, agree being good is all that is needed to be right with God. They say this is what God is concerned with, and different religious beliefs and practices are a matter of personal, family, or cultural preference. Those might provide us with helpful teachings and familiar rituals, but are not essential in themselves.

D. Does worshiping God make a difference?

My Catholic school catechism says God created us because He loves us. I guess I can buy that in an abstract way, but the notion we were created to worship God seems like a sad reason for our existence and a knock on God. The practice of worshiping God, like any discipline, may have inherent psychological benefits for us, but I can't imagine this is something God needs or desires.

Now that we've explored these topics, let's go back to the Q and A and our next question.

4. How can we know which, if any, of these actions and/or beliefs we are supposed to do? We might have been raised in a certain faith but how can we know it is correct? Is it possible to really know the answer to this question?

If we can't know the answer with some degree of reliability, then questioning ceases because trying to figure out what God wants is a crapshoot, given that the religious world has so many different points of view. Therefore, we can become either agnostics or sign up for the faith of our culture or family. Then, even if we can't be sure our family faith is the right one, at least we will all face our fate together.

5. If God wants us to be or act in a certain way, why doesn't he just tell us in some unambiguous way?

My atheist friend always asked this question, and I never had a satisfactory answer. Recently, re-reading a Bill Moyers interview with Huston Smith I found one. Smith points out what Soren Kierkegaard says, "That's what we think we want, but if we had it, we would realize that's not what we really wanted, because if it told us the answer it would take our freedom away from us." Meaning, we would be like puppets passively accepting that answer and doing as we were told. The way it is now, we have our free will.

6. What if I don't want to give up on knowing just because it seems impossible? If I can't know for certain in a scientific sense, I still want to get closer to the truth. How should I proceed to get useful results?

a. Rational thinking- Rational people looking at the same facts, often disagree in their interpretation of what they mean. Atheists say there is absolutely no empirical evidence demonstrating that anything being discussed here is more than an illusion. End of questioning? Not so fast. There are many topics in science we know about today, for which there was no empirical evidence in the recent past. Many other phenomena remain unexplained. Maybe God is behind some of that. Shouldn't we maintain an open mind until all the facts are in?

b. Divine revelation- As my Hindu guru Dr. Nene said, "If Mario can go up the mountain and come back with a book, so can Luigi." I know people of faith who will tell you that if you read their scripture with an open mind, the truth of what it says will seem obvious. I have read some of those scriptures and I didn't get that result. The Buddha said if what he preaches works for you, follow it. If it doesn't, don't. Perhaps we should take "revealed" information at face value, but strain out what seems hard to believe. Thomas Jefferson made his own version of the *New Testament* by keeping the teachings of Jesus and excluding miracles. Otherwise, besides the dictates of family or culture, how do you know which book to follow, Luigi's or Mario's?

c. Anecdotal spiritual experiences- There have been many people throughout history, in all religions, who claim to have had spiritual/paranormal experiences. These include such things as hearing voices, seeing apparitions, near death experiences, past life memories, miracles, communication, through dreams and mediums, with the dead, speaking in tongues, and a host of others. While some of these claims have surely been fraudulent, seriously mistaken, or caused by aberrant human psychology, can that be said for all of them? To broadly rule out every instance of this evidence seems irresponsible. Dr. Ian Stevenson did an extensive study of past life memories, and his team at the University of Virginia is still investigating the paranormal. I have spoken to several people who claim such experiences. They may be mistaken, but I don't think they were lying.

d. First hand intuitive experiences- It is one thing to discuss the spiritual experiences other people claim to have had, but much more meaningful if it happens to you. I am not sure how to define what counts as a spiritual experience, or even if those experiences are really spiritual or some type of natural phenomena, we cannot yet explain. My atheist friend has said he has never had such an experience, but I might have had one. Another friend who is searching for answers told me she would be happy to have Jesus, God, or the Buddha speak to her, but it hasn't happened yet. So the validity of this criteria is personal, hard to share, and difficult to assess or assert unless of course it happens to you.

As mentioned earlier, writer and atheist Barbara Ehrenreich had an unexplainable experience when she was younger. She suggested that perhaps we share this planet with non-corporeal intelligences, and it was a meeting with them she experienced. Take your pick.

e. FAITH- Shouldn't faith have something to do with our religious choice? I grew up thinking it was essential, and wondering why I didn't have it. If you have it, you probably already belong to a religion. But what if you don't?

Faith is the belief in something when there is insufficient empirical data to prove it is true. I used the example earlier that if my wife says she is going to the store, I have faith that this is true, even though I cannot prove she is not meeting a lover or buying cocaine instead. However, I have had thousands of experiences that compel me to support that trust. Life and religion both rely on faith, to some extent, since they accept "truths" that cannot be empirically demonstrated.

Most people in the world acquire and accept their faith through culture/family, which is a powerful tool to mold our minds and thinking. It makes me pause and be suspicious of my own thinking, when I consider this phenomenon. Would our views be different if we were raised in another culture? How can I be sure of my faith, if I know other people acquired their different faith in a similar way? How can I know which is true? I have watched my little niece sing,

"I will always follow Jesus," but she probably wouldn't be singing the same song if she had been raised Hindu.

The problem is people belong to many different religions and have faith in many divergent concepts. Not all of them can be true. At some basic level, they are either all correct, or they are all wrong, or one is right, and the others wrong. Or it doesn't matter, and being a good, compassionate person is what matters, if anything does.

How can we know what is correct if, as some believe, our eternal fate rests on figuring out the right answer? Clearly, relying on faith alone creates a very confusing system. Since I do not have faith in any particular religious belief, faith doesn't help me as a criterion of truth.

I've decided to take logic and rational thinking as far as I can, to try to get closer to an answer. Perhaps I can at least eliminate some possibilities.

7. Other than selecting an existing religion, what are my options?

If we want to find a belief that makes sense about God and religion, why should we be limited to picking from one of the choices currently on the world religions shelf? In the novel *The Life of Pi*, by Yann Martel, young Pi is a Hindu, and then becomes a Christian, and then a Muslim, without quitting his previous faiths. He selects and combines aspects from each religion that are meaningful to him, ignores the contradictory parts, and develops a syncretistic explanation (his own point of view) about religion that appeals to him. Pi feels agnostics miss out on the benefits of a belief system, and that he has more in common with atheists who, lacking evidence to support their position, have selected a story (mechanical, purposeless universe) that makes sense to them.

8. What is the Problem I am having with Religion?

Hmmm.

How to approach the question of God and religion? As I stand outside looking at the sky trying to find this answer, it once again becomes clear that if I am relying on my own intuition, I do not know. However, I do want an answer.

My question (Does God exist?) has two possible answers, God does exist or God does not exist, one of which is certainly true. To address this dilemma, I believe it is not illogical or irrational to start with the answer that most appeals to me. I may be wrong, but in the spirit of Pi, I will make a choice. God, in some form or another, exists. However, since this is a decision based on reason, not faith, I am willing to change my mind if new evidence, or better arguments arise. This is my first assumption.

Second, I will assume that as undefinable and unknowable as God is, God is also rational and compassionate. This seems like a no-brainer, if the alternative is an irrational God who is heartless or indifferent to us. This leads to my third assumption.

Since God has these qualities, God has implemented a long-term spiritual system which involves all of creation for its ultimate benefit. My bet is that if we use our will properly, making good decisions, we will have spiritual success, whatever that is. I don't say this because God told me or I read it in some book of spiritual revelations. I say it because it is a point of view that makes sense to me, given my assumption that God exists.

Religion is another problem. We developed religion to help us deal with our existence, the fact of our eventual death, our purpose, and our relationship with whatever caused this all to happen. The result is that our world is loaded with religions. I have always been able to find something I liked about every religion, and very often, something I have disagreed with. I see three systemic problems with most religions. First, despite their wide diversity, religions often engage in groupthink, which discourages creative thinking or differing interpretations, and encourages everyone to go along with the groups' decisions and traditions.

Second, the two most popular religions, Christianity and Islam, have long traditions of exclusivity, believing only their point of view is correct and unbelievers are doomed. This has sometimes led to an arrogance, which has promoted outbreaks of prejudice, intolerance and violence. Again, because of the wide diversity of beliefs within each faith, many Christians and Muslims do not agree with this exclusivity. Nevertheless, a significant number of believers in both faiths do share the idea that their religion alone is correct.

Third, some of our existing religions have been used by zealots and political leaders to incite and justify some horrible actions. Despite the good religion achieves in many areas, on a day-to-day basis, history paints a bleak picture of religious violence.

Overall, I feel more comfortable with Pi's "pick and choose" process. I have decided I do not want a religion package. I have decided to follow my thinking until I can find/construct a belief system that makes sense to me.

57

THE PI PROCESS

"To choose doubt as a Philosophy of life is akin to choosing immobility as a means of transportation."
- Pi Patel from *The Life of Pi*, by Yann Martel

For most of my life, I have been stymied trying to come up with an understanding of God and religion that made sense to me. Perhaps because of my upbringing, my universe of religious brainstorming could not get beyond the standard Judaeo-Christian model for many years. This was a barrier to creative thinking, since that model generated most of my questions. I couldn't think my way out of the box to find satisfactory answers. Then, some things happened.

First, because I was lucky enough to teach a world religions class, I had to revisit and research what I thought I knew about world religions. I knew the facts from college, but with fresh motivation, the deep research I did throughout my career, and the insights provided by my guest speakers, something like scales fell from my eyes. In researching both Eastern and Western faiths, I found clearer understanding and value in many of them. I felt I was better able to see through the cultural differences and abstruse terminology, and came to appreciate aspects underlying each one's beliefs. I loved these new ideas, but for years, I couldn't figure out how I could deal with the contradictions and differences between these faiths, and differing cultures, to arrange them into a system that would work for me. I was a man without an answer. Then, years later, I read *The Life of Pi*.

Pi taught me I didn't need to find a religion "package." Born with what he describes as "a germ of religious exaltation," Pi rejects the idea there is only one correct way to know God. He finds meaning by creating his own spiritual story, an explanation of God and religion, including beliefs and practices, that appeal to him. I realized I could do as he did, and create my own syncretistic religion, mixing beliefs from various faiths and other source to make a combination that makes sense to me. I had been puzzling over this question for a long time and cannot explain why this didn't occur to me sooner.

Along the way, I learned that many people within every religion are already doing this to some degree. In an evolutionary manner, adherents of the same faith, separated by time and distance, tend to diverge in what they believe and how they practice their faith. In their day-to-day religious choices about beliefs and practices, they may make decisions that are different from their fellow adherents who live far away, perhaps in a different culture, making their own daily choices. Over time, these differences add up. For both groups, this does not require a major revolution in thought because they are generally choosing within acceptable parameters of their local family or cultural faith. In the past, this could be chalked up to a lack of global communication and connection. Each separated local group simply decided and went their own way.

Today, with information more widely available, and strict cultural and family control waning in many places, some people have become religiously adventurous, more likely to choose at least some beliefs which make more sense to them. For instance, a majority of American Catholics disobey the Church doctrine forbid ding birth control. Also, a recent Pew survey said that 69% of American Catholics do not believe the bread and wine used for Communion actually becomes the body and blood of Jesus Christ, which is a central teaching of the Church[1]. Many Christians reject the idea of hell, and the notion that only believers in the salvation provided by Jesus, will be saved. Among American Muslims, 64% believe there is more than one way to interpret the Qur'an.[2] These differences, from the strictest interpretations of their beliefs to the most liberal, demonstrate the reality shown by the spread of dots on each faith's scattergram.

However, most adherents do not want to stray too far from the tenets of their faith. The idea of critically examining their whole belief system from the ground up would make them more than a little nervous. Not me. Since my childhood religious upbringing apparently did not stick, I am intrigued and excited by the idea of going further. I know what I select for me may not be true, but no one, atheists, or those from any faith, can demonstrate a religious claim that can be proven. So, I have decided to use Pi's syncretistic method. Perhaps when I am finished, I will feel, at the very least, that if the spiritual world is not actually ordered in the way I think, then it should be. I will have a belief, but it will be based on rationality, not a faith that would encourage me to declare it to be the only truth. If you try this, your results may differ.

Now I have to spill all of my religion Lego pieces out on the floor and figure out how to build this thing. The first step is to identify the underlying philosophy of my ideal spiritual system. What are my basic assumptions about God and religion? Following my assumption methodology, it is clear that I have decided God exists and is both rational and compassionate. In my religion, all life has an interactive relationship with God that will help us to reach our ultimate spiritual goal (Heaven? Hell? Nirvana? Something else?). I will fill in the details as I work it out.

As we've discussed, in the world's religions, the most popular views about how to successfully advance spiritually fall roughly into two belief camps, correct faith and good actions. Spiritual progress through faith generally requires we believe certain dogma, alleged historical events, and historical writings are true. Many faith adherents say if we don't believe correctly, we might be punished severely in a nasty afterlife. In these religions, the value of good actions is not ignored, but it is faith that counts.

My problem with faith as criteria for religious truth is that most people acquire their initial faith through family and cultural influence. Even though Pew surveys show that 44% of Americans do not currently belong to their childhood faith, many have gone through several congregation changes and, while some end up unaffiliated, most settle in another religiously adjacent denominations[3]. I suspect this pattern is less pronounced in more traditional countries, where culture is closely tied to one faith.

While some religions are somewhat to very tolerant of diverging views, others are not. There are many contradictions between faiths, and some hold that only *their* beliefs are the right ones. If there is actually only one belief system approved by God, and all other beliefs are wrong, what does this mean for the majority of the world's population that does not share it? From this point of view, the faith of those who follow other beliefs is mistaken, not true. Some religions would say, despite their sincere beliefs, these otherwise possibly good people, who picked, or were born into, the wrong religion, will be eternally punished for having faith in a false set of beliefs. With deference to my more evangelical and fundamentalist Christian and Muslim friends, I have a lot of difficulty with this idea.

If I was contracted to design a spiritual system for sentient beings, is this the way I would do it? No. I can't find any reason why a compassionate, rational God would implement a requirement that would punish such a large number of people for being born in the wrong culture or for guessing wrong about faith. This seems to be a cruel way to run a spiritual system. I can only conclude that God did not create this rule. The requirement for a specific faith belief for salvation must have been the invention of humans, who figured this would be a great way to scare people into their religion, and keep them from leaving.

From this, I conclude God's actual spiritual system counts, if anything, not faith, but actions. After all, it is what we do on a day-to-day basis that is most telling about our spiritual state. For me, faith is off the table as criteria for deciding the truth about God.

When this realization first came to me, it was a seismic development in my understanding of God and religion. Curiously, I have always thought my religious problem was trying, as a person without faith, to find the right faith, the one that is correct, one I would recognize instantly. As it turns out, that is not my problem at all. My problem is that it took me so long to recognize the failure of faith as a way to find what is true. Religions that require absolute faith in a human designed system of beliefs, in order to win God's favor and avoid eternal suffering, are disingenuous and intellectually stultifying. They are doing God a grave injustice by emotionally blackmailing people into their churches, and using the threat of eternal damnation to keep them there. It is such an illogical and irrational way to think about a compassionate God, that only the fact it has been enforced by cultural and family pressure, and fear, can explain how it has been successful for so long. Before this revelation, it had never occurred to me that requiring such faith beliefs was contrary to God's nature, as I understand it.

In order to follow the Pi Process, I have to investigate and think about what we know to be true, what we don't know, and what theories and ideas might be helpful to consider. My goal is to discover a definition and understanding of God, and a spiritual system, I can believe in, that does not contradict the facts. I will believe it, not because I have faith it is true or have proven it true, but because it makes the most sense to me.

Obviously there are differing points of view on the value and legitimacy of creating syncretistic, Pi-like, religious beliefs. This is illustrated in the interview "Am I a Christian?" between Nicholas Kristof, an op-ed writer for the *New York Times*, and Pastor Timothy Keller, an Evangelical Christian Pastor and best-selling author, that was published on Dec. 23, 2016. The discussion started as follows:

. . .

KRISTOF: Tim, I deeply admire Jesus and his message, but am also skeptical of themes that have been integral to Christianity — the virgin birth, the Resurrection, the miracles and so on. Since this is the Christmas season, let's start with the virgin birth. Is that an essential belief, or can I mix and match?

KELLER: If something is truly integral to a body of thought, you can't remove it without destabilizing the whole thing. A religion can't be whatever we desire it to be. If I'm a member of the board of Greenpeace, and I come out and say climate change is a hoax, they will ask me to resign. I could call them narrow-minded, but they would rightly say that there have to be some boundaries for dissent, or you couldn't have a cohesive, integrated organization. And they'd be right. It's the same with any religious faith.

I think Keller is wrong, because it is not the same with every religious faith, and I am becoming more certain, contrary to his assertion, that our religion should be absolutely what we choose it to be. Religions that believe we make spiritual progress only through our actions, generally believe in reincarnation, and do not require specific faith based beliefs. They know it is our good efforts that count and demonstrate our quality. Why can't you have the teachings of Jesus without the virgin birth or miracles? I can understand why Pastor Keller wants to keep Christian belief as a monolithic whole. But to customize our religious beliefs, we have to use a little intelligence and creativity. We have to realize the truth about the major religious assumption in the West; that spiritual success relies solely on belief in one particular faith story, is not rational.

Keller is clearly against the type of religion I have been talking about using the Pi process. He likens religious diversity in a church to different points of view in an organization, such as Greenpeace. I don't think that makes much sense. If I want to be a member of Greenpeace because I support one of their programs, they won't throw me out if I don't support all of the others. Every religion already has adherents with different points of view, often in small ways, sometimes in large ones. That's why every large faith has many denominations, and people within those denominations have different points of view. Those splits from within happen for a reason.

Syncretistic religion, borrowing ideas from different sources to create a unique set of beliefs, is not an odd or dangerous way to think about religion, but an innovative and creative process to discover the religious views that have most value for each of us. It is a way to approach religion that has a proven track record, makes sense, and, if practiced more widely, would eliminate large groups of people insisting that only their way was right. Reducing religious beliefs to individual points of view, rather than large groups, would make the world a more peaceful, happier place. It is better for us all if we admit when we do not know the truth, but are willing to rationally speculate, rather than insist on the unprovable, illogical belief that our view alone is correct.

Established religions have used syncretism, to a degree, in the past. Every faith evolved from some beginning point, and added bits and pieces from the concepts believers came up with, or borrowed from existing religions, to flesh out beliefs and practices as it grew and developed. Buddhism grew out of Hinduism, and Zoroastrianism, Judaism, Christianity and Islam, share much in common. As Christianity spread in Europe, it absorbed some pagan worship sites, beliefs, and practices. Sometimes a pagan god became a saint and, over time, popular pagan practices were adopted. Halloween, Christmas, and Easter traditions are filled with pagan lore and beliefs. In the ancient world, a virgin birth, resurrection from the dead, or speaking to God, can be found in the mythology and beliefs of extinct religions.

Pastor Keller's position defends the exclusionist point of view for Christianity, and I am sure many Muslims, if questioned from their religion's perspective, would agree with him. On the belief spectrum from "All good people will be saved" to "Only those who believe will be saved," both faiths still have many adherents close to the latter end of the scale. For these believers, creating a "mix and match" religion would not be tolerated. Everything must be believed. If one belief is not true, maybe all beliefs are not true.

In an exclusionist religion, the belief that religious success is determined by correct faith has to be maintained at all costs, and the notion that there might be other worthy views, cannot be considered. Unfortunately, this type of thinking creates a zero sum religion game. For your faith to be right, the other guy's different faith has to be wrong. If he is right, you lose. There can be no negotiations or compromise when the stakes are heaven or hell, and you are 100% right and the other side is 100% wrong. Since every conversion to another faith means one more person who won't be saved, differing views are the enemy. Adherents know if they stray from the faith, they are going to hell and so are too fearful and psychologically locked-in to contemplate alternatives. As close as most religions seem to come on questions of ethics, it is unproven faith differences that keep them apart. Suppose I have a faith that tells me there are certain things I must believe and do to get into heaven. I buy that, and am working toward that goal, and ensuring that my family is working toward that goal. However, I am a tolerant fellow, and have friends and colleagues from many religions. I know some of them, even if they are good people, will not be saved, because of incorrect beliefs, but that is their choice. We work and socialize together and just don't talk about religion. Suppose my kid innocently asks the neighbor across the street about his different religion. Perhaps he gives my kid informational answers, and later the kids brings up the other religion at dinner. Maybe he sounds interested. I lose my cool. My kid is not going to hell! I storm across the street and punch that guy in the nose, and tell him never to talk to my kid again. I begin looking in the ads for houses in neighborhoods with people of my faith. So it goes.

As a religious syncretist, you want to select beliefs and practices that make sense to you, but also lead you to actions that help you become a better person. It makes sense to me that it doesn't matter to God what your faith or lack of faith might be, but that God prefers good results to beliefs. The real question is, what works best for your personality, or your age, or your station in life, or other important personal factors? You might choose to attend worship services in a church, or maybe in the forest, you might choose to study holy books, you might choose to help others, you might choose to meditate, or you might choose to do nothing. Later you could change your mind, as your situation changes. There might be choices that don't help you much, but there is no wrong selection on this path, if the question you answer is always, "What works best for me to be a good person in my day-to-day life?" This is the core of the Pi Process.

PART 5
THINKING ABOUT...

1. WHAT DO WE KNOW?

"One does one's thinking before one knows what one is to think about."
- Julian Jaynes

In finding religious beliefs that make sense to us, we have to make sure they do not violate the findings of science. Science can be wrong, but, over time, it is self-correcting. While we do find the most verifiable thinking available about what is true, science still has a way to go.

During the past few decades, science has figured out the main details in the creation story of the cosmos and of human beings. The universe was not created in six days. We now know that a series of important steps, each one developing in a way to bring about the next, brought about the emergence of the universe, from the Big Bang event to the present day. This process is continuing. We can also say a lot about the history and evolution of life on earth, from one-celled organisms, to multi-celled ones, to us. It turns out that all life on earth is genetically related at the cellular level. We don't know all of the details, but we know what happened, and about when it happened. Eventually we will fill in the finer points and make corrections, but for now, the overall direction and chronology of events is clear.

It is important to know this so we can decide what makes the most sense about God, and the spiritual role of humans in the universe. Science does not prove or disprove God, but any opinion we have about God or religion, while still speculative, should obviously not contradict established science, to be credible. This does not happen in the creation accounts that come to us from traditional religions. The suggestion to foster a rational relationship between science and religion was introduced to me in the *Journey of the Universe* by Brian Thomas Swimme and Mary Evelyn Tucker. These authors demonstrate a scientifically based way to understand our new creation story, the real story of us, according to science.

All ancient cultures had creation stories, which explained, through the actions of God or gods, how and why we are here, and how we should live our lives. These were often different from each other, and were passed on orally through many generations. Eventually they were written down and widely accepted by the cultures who inherited them. They seemed like timeless wisdom from the ancestors, explaining the answers to everything, so were accepted. There were also no available alternative explanations, except some other group's account. As religions globalized over time, many peoples turned in their old stories for what seemed to be better ones. After a while, Zeus was out, and Adam and Eve were in.

Because of this, everyone in the Abrahamic faiths thought the universe was created in six days. In that story people, birds, and trees were created exactly as they are today. The universe consisted of the earth in the center, circled by the Sun, Mercury, Venus, Mars, Jupiter and Saturn. Beyond that, there were a lot of twinkly lights decorating a big black something beyond the planets. Things moved in this universe, and annual cycles continued but, in the largest sense, it was believed to be complete and unchanging. People felt that if scripture says Joshua asked God to stop the sun in the sky so he would have time to win his battle, and God did so, it was pretty clear that it was the sun that was moving, not the earth (Joshua 10:12).

The Hebrew creation story in the Bible is probably the most popular such account in the world still thought by some to be literally true. In Judaism, Christianity, and Islam, there are those who believe this, as the word of God, and is without error. According to a Pew Trust study, 42% of Evangelical Protestants say humans have always existed in our present form[1], which contradicts the scientific account of evolution. Different beliefs folks have about scripture range from, "these are God's words" to "these are important lessons inspired by God, but not always literally true," to "interesting stories from various ancient Middle Eastern cultures, adopted and adapted by a wandering desert people." Regardless of its veracity, no other creation account has had as much impact on world history. Given that there is no physical evidence to support them, these stories, and others like them, if they are supposed to be literally true, are religion's weakest link.

Can we switch from these stories from the past, to a new story based on science, that validates the events in the formation of the universe, our solar system, and us? From the very beginning, the universe has gone through a number of significant evolutionary changes. The physics of each change had to happen within a narrow parameter of possibilities, or the universe would cease to exist or fail to produce life. At every stage, events played out to select for complexity, creativity, and the opportunity for further development. I am struck by the many things that could have gone wrong in this process, but didn't. It couldn't have worked out better for us if it had been planned.

Science's creation story is both fascinating and provocative because it explains what had to happen for us to exist. You can examine this story and think, "What an amazing number of arbitrary, random, coincidences to happen in a mindless, uncaring universe, to bring about life." Or, you could wonder, "What does the result of a succession of precise, successful, evolutionary cosmic events across billions of years, resulting in intelligent life, mean for us as human beings?"

This creation story begins with the cosmic expansion (aka: the Big Bang), which happened about 13.8 billion years ago (BYA) for reasons we can only guess. Early galaxies coalesced from atoms, and later conglomerated into larger galaxies. Early stars formed and became massively explosive supernovas, creating chemical elements in their cores, before blasting them throughout the galaxy. Those elements became essential ingredients in all later formations, including life. Stars, people, worms, and trees were not created complete in the form they have now. About 4.5 BYA our sun formed and acquired a set of planets. The first one celled life appeared on earth 4 BYA, and evolved into multicellular creatures that eventually filled the sea, land and sky. Early on, life developed a way to pass on what it learned through DNA, as it changed and adapted to meet new conditions. Eventually, there was us and, still, the process of universe emergence continues. Could this creation be purposeful?

Copernicus' idea of a sun centered solar system, and Galileo's identification of the Milky Way galaxy were part of a difficult struggle to find the truth. In the late 1920's work by Georges Lemaitre (a Catholic priest), Edwin Hubble, and others, proved there were other galaxies, and they were all moving away from us. Lemaitre first proposed that the universe started with a massive cosmic expansion (called the Big Bang). By the mid 1960's this model had won over the bulk of the scientific community and, while there is still discussion about the details, is virtually unchallenged today. Rather than the idea of a finished universe, which inspired so much early religion, we now know our universe has been evolving and changing dramatically over the last 13.8 billion years.

We have been gifted, by luck or purpose, with a planet uniquely suited for life. It is not too close to the sun, nor too far away. Our hot core generates a magnetic field that protects our atmosphere from solar wind. There is enough change over time, through plate tectonics, and complexity in nature, to encourage species to evolve to meet new challenges. Also, even as the sun's temperature has increased

25% in the last 4 billion years, somehow the earth has responded by reducing the amount of CO2 in the atmosphere, thus protecting us.

Whether this process was the result of purpose or coincidence, the question to answer is, "What role do we humans have in this story?" Understanding what is happening today with our rare and precious planet is critical to our future. For our own good, we should obviously be doing everything we can to preserve plant and animal life, balance the climate, and stop poisoning the land, water, and air. We don't want the human experiment to fail, but I do not know if we are smart enough, or brave enough, to save it. These days it doesn't seem wise to underestimate human greed and stupidity. Maybe our brand of intelligence does not lead to long-term survival. Of course, there are religious groups who believe that since God promised Noah he would never again destroy the earth (Genesis 8: 20-28), we don't have to worry about climate change or other environmental disasters. They've been told God won't let that happen.

Is there intelligent purpose and direction evident in this evolutionary process? Examining what has happened, it seems possible, at least circumstantially, that this is so. Something seems to be happening, in the formation of the universe, as each step helped to bring about life and consciousness. This is not just happening here, but everywhere. It's a big universe.

In looking at how much more we know today compared to the past, we are also discovering how much we don't know. When everyone based their knowledge on scripture, they felt like they had the answers to everything. Where did the universe come from? Where did life come from? How should we live our lives? What is God? It was all answered in scripture. Now, because we know so much more, we are beginning to realize how much we still don't know. This might be an unintended law of science, but it seems every time we learn something new, we expand the mysteries that need further investigation. Neil DeGrasse Tyson has said, "We don't know what we don't know and this leaves me awake at night. I lose sleep over this." *(The Late Show* with Stephen Colbert 1/6/2018*)*

For instance, we derived the Big Bang Theory as our answer to how the universe was created, but we don't know why or how it happened. This theory also does not account for dark matter or dark energy, which apparently make up the vast majority of the cosmos. We can't see it, so we call it dark. We know it's there because of its gravitational effects, but beyond that, we don't have a clue. We also don't know why both general relativity and quantum theory seem to work in their own realms (the very big world of stars and galaxies and the very small world of elementary particles) to make the universe happen, but are theoretically incompatible with each other. Maybe the truth about God will be found in the solution to these or our next round of profound scientific questions.

2. WHAT REALITY IS

"A few years ago, the city council of Monza, Italy, barred pet owners from keeping goldfish in curved bowls... saying that it is cruel to keep a fish in a bowl with curved sides because, gazing out, the fish would have a distorted view of reality. But how do we know we have the true, undistorted picture of reality?"
- Stephen Hawking

"Reality is merely an illusion, albeit a very persistent one."
- Albert Einstein

Einstein was correct. Reality is a very slippery critter. We think we grasp it, but we always take it for granted because there are two things we keep forgetting. First, the reality we think we perceive does not exist outside of our minds. Using our limited senses, our brain manipulates our perceptions and creates "our" reality. We can only know the reality our mind presents to us. Does this mean we can perceive 100% of reality, as it actually exists or 5%? We don't know. Theoretically, all humans should be able to share the same reality, but no two of us have had the same sense impressions, experiences, and interpretations. While most of us can agree when the sun is up, we disagree on lots of other things, such as how we should live our lives.

Second, if we can't perceive phenomena, we will never know it is there. Our senses, by themselves, tell us the sun revolves around the earth, and that there is nothing living in a drop of water. Telescopes, microscopes and other scientific technology have immeasurably expanded our sense abilities, but this has also made us more aware of our limitations. We now know we can only see a narrow band of light in a much larger spectrum. We know bats can hear many things we cannot, and a dog's sense of smell creates a reality for them we can barely imagine. Humans, dogs, and bats evolved the senses they needed to best survive in their environmental niches. Likewise, for every creature in the universe, there will be a different reality created for it, by its' unique combination of sensing abilities. We look at the world we think we know and say, "Well, that's it." However, really, we don't know for certain.

Some scientists thinking about the Big Bang, and the suggestions from some religious folk that this is evidence for a purposeful creation, have suggested that reality is not just a universe, but a multiverse. This idea of parallel or multiple universes has sometimes been seen in science fiction. The theory, in this iteration, asks us to imagine that millions of universes have popped up over time, but with random settings for their physics constants. Because these settings are all over the map, almost every one of those universes fizzles out for one reason or another. However, even with an infinite number of possible combinations, eventually one universe will emerge where everything works. So according to this notion, that's where we are, in the one that stuck. No God or purpose needed, just natural stuff happening, so one might conclude, our universe is the product of mindless randomness. Why did this occur? No reason, it just happened. So, either the universe occurred because of some purpose, or it happened due to blind, mindless, random chance. My atheist friends vote for the second choice, and my religious friends, for the first.

There is a third theory, considered by scientists with wildly varying degrees of seriousness. Simulation Theory holds everyone and everything in the universe is not reality, but virtual reality. In this hypothesis, our universe is really a computer program being run by God, or aliens so intelligent they might as well be God, or maybe an artificial intelligence that has taken us over. This is what we saw in 1999's *The Matrix*. Living in the matrix, most people think reality is as they perceive it, the way you and I think we live every day. However, that life is a false reality. Except for a few freedom fighters, the human race exists in pod-like artificial wombs, their lives, families, and jobs existing only in their dreams

To what degree could Simulation Theory be true? Elon Musk is a believer, and Neil deGrasse Tyson suggested "better than 50-50 odds."[1] Harvard theoretical physicist Lisa Randall put the chances at "effectively zero." Later she wrote in an email: "At this point, we cannot prove that we do or don't live in a simulation. More to the point, there is no reason to believe that we do. However, we can pretty much be sure that people will do amazing things and they will also mess up in spectacular ways."[2]

This discussion is not really science, since no one can set up an experiment to prove/disprove this idea, though one bright person did suggest that we should all go off and live exciting, interesting lives so "they" are entertained and don't turn off the program. Since each of these is possible, but I can't know which is true, and since I don't like being agnostic about this, I am going to choose the one that best fits the facts we do know. Of these three, I will assume the universe/Big Bang theory is correct because that aligns with the science we know, and with my understanding of the actions and motivations of a compassionate, intelligent, purposeful God-like force. If we ever find any evidence that one of the others is true, I might change my mind.

Now that I've settled that, my next question about reality is to figure out the relationship between God and the rest of the universe. Abrahamic religions believe in theism. This version of reality consists of two distinct, separate, aspects, God and God's creation (including us). In my third grade Catholic school religion book, God was graphically displayed, seated on a big square throne, in the clouds. With long white robes, long hair, and white beard, he looked like Gandalf's older brother, and he did not seem happy with us. It wasn't a mean look, but stern, very stern. His direct gaze into our eyes told us that he knew exactly what we had done and thought we could get away with. All these years later, I am sure that whatever God is, God does not exist in the form of a person, but I will never forget that picture.

Some philosophers and Eastern religions support various definitions of either Pantheism (everything that exists in the universe equals God) or Panentheism (same, but God also exists outside this manifestation). Buddhists are nontheistic, with no divine creator, God, or supreme being. Yet many Buddhists do believe that powerful spiritual forces can help us out. There may also be a few old time polytheists out there, but my hunch is that most of those see their various gods as different ways of understanding aspects of the one God, much as Hindu's do. Other than the hardcore atheistic view of no God in any format, I don't know of any other rational choice.

While I have no definitive evidence for one of these theories over the other, the notion that God transformed into the physical manifestation of everything in the universe appeals to me the most. Science does tell us that ultimately, below the level of atomic particles, everything in the universe is some form of energy. I like the idea that we are all an aspect or manifestation of God, but just don't realize it. This makes reincarnation more attractive to me, because it is a process where we use our progression from lifetime to lifetime to grow in the realization that, in some way, we are part of God, and should learn to act in a more God-like manner.

Try this metaphor. What if the whole universe is the entity and we are like cells in its ongoing spiritual growth and development? I have cells in my body chugging away to my benefit which communicate with each other, think, create more cells, fight off invaders, etc. I don't believe most of them grasp the big picture.

If God created the universe, might there be an ultimate purpose for the whole undertaking? In 1953 Arthur C. Clarke wrote a great science fiction novel, *Childhood's End*, where the human race had reached a certain point in its evolution, was given a little push through outside help and, in a generation or two, left the physical world behind and joined the universal "Overmind." Humans became "one" with a particular fictional definition that might be God. This is an example of universal evolution, from the creation of the universe, to the first spark of life, and to a logical conclusion. That certainly shows purpose but it is also fiction. Could some sort of evolutionary afterlife be true for us?

3. IF THERE IS AN AFTERLIFE

"The day I was born I made my first mistake, and by that path have I sought wisdom ever since."
-The Mahabharata

The most basic and fundamental tenets of every religion is that our good actions and/or spiritual beliefs will yield a positive outcome in the afterlife. As mentioned earlier, I assume good actions, not particular beliefs, if anything, is what counts with God. However, we don't need a religion to act in a good way. A faith, by itself, is not an absolute criterion or guarantee for spiritual progress. Religion may help some folks be better people, and that is good, but if correct actions are the criteria, it does not ultimately matter what our religious beliefs may be. In this light, many atheists and Ethical Humanists already have the search for right behavior going for them, since their goal is to live as good people. As Kurt Vonnegut once said, "Being a Humanist means trying to behave decently without expectation of rewards or punishment after you are dead."[1] This sounds like a great attitude for all of us. How could God object to that?

For those of us who do feel there is a reasonable chance God exists, we should want to focus our lives and actions on being an active part of God's evolving creation. Going to a religious service once a week and believing a set dogma, without good actions the rest of the week, may not bring spiritual success. What we do becomes the evidence of our religion, whether we worship in a cathedral or ponder existence in our private moments. However, whatever articles of belief a religion of millions, or a faith of one, may hold, if its membership is not becoming better, kinder, and more compassionate, that religion is failing.

What keeps us from doing better? Maybe it is our personal combination of ignorance, selfishness, uncontrolled emotions, trauma, brain or hormone malfunctioning, or the perception that our lives are unsatisfactory or full of suffering. As Robert Wright pointed out in *Why Buddhism is True*, some of this may be the result of how natural selection "selected" human qualities, as we evolved to make us successful gene spreaders, but not necessarily happy people. In today's world, this problem is exacerbated by the inability of natural selection to keep up with the fast-paced changes to our lives, brought about by cultural evolution, over the last ten thousand years. Societal change is happening faster than we can adapt through evolution, so we are forced to react to today's situations with whatever mental tools and strategies we inherited to survive in an earlier world. Wright recommends we follow the Buddha's suggestion, to meditate to help us learn to understand our actions and reactions.

There are historical examples of religion gone bad, and there are current adherents whose interpretation of their faith and subsequent actions would make Jesus and Muhammad weep. Despite such negative outcomes, religion is important for the deep allegiance it commands from so many people, and for its institutional potential to turn people away from bigotry and hatred to do good.

I can't know if the good we do only impacts us in this life, or pays off in an afterlife, but I choose the possibility of an afterlife to be my working hypothesis, as part of the Pi process. It seems like an easy call, to want to continue my consciousness in some way after bodily death, as opposed to no further existence. Besides, if there isn't an afterlife of some sort, there is not much to talk about, and we can all go back to the Humanist web page, and read about being good people while enjoying our one life.

Other than being agnostic about the afterlife, there are two major schools of thought. One view, most popular in Christianity and Islam, is the "live one life-be judged-go to heaven or hell (maybe purgatory)-stay there for eternity" model. Specific beliefs about this vary widely within each religion.

A final judgement after only one lifetime seems, well, judgmental, and does not allow do-overs or further opportunities to learn to be better. It's as if you study for your one and only final exam, and if you fail the test, you are failed for all eternity. All good teachers would say this is a bad system. What if everyone can eventually pass the test, but some people are going to need a lot more remedial time than others? Wouldn't it be compassionate to give them more opportunities to learn and succeed? In the more literal descriptions of the heaven/hell scenario, what happens is certainly not fair or compassionate. I can't imagine God created us, knowing most of us would suffer for eternity. Whatever sad mind devised this model, I am certain it was not God.

A second school of thought has to do with some sort of rebirth or reincarnation, most popular with Asian religions. As mentioned earlier, I liken this to a K-12 school, but one where advancement is individual, not as a member of an age cohort. Many lifetimes give us many lessons based on what we need to learn, and our actions set up later lives through karma. Our passing from one "grade" to the next is totally decided by our own efforts. When there are no more lessons to learn, we don't come back again. Then we become "one with God," or reach "nirvana," or "go to heaven," or some other option we haven't thought of yet. From this view, we are not separate from God now; we just think we are, since everything in existence is a different manifestation of God. This second school of thought makes a lot more sense to me.

My impression has always been that there is minimal belief in reincarnation in the U.S. However, there is a famous country music song, *Highwayman* (written by Jimmy Webb, recorded in 1985 by Willie Nelson, Johnny Cash, Waylon Jennings and Kris Kristofferson, and recently covered by Judy Collins) about the existence of one consciousness. He is a highwayman who is hanged for his crimes and says, "But I am still alive." He is then a sailor killed on a ship, a dam builder who falls into the wet concrete, and a starship captain flying across the universe. After each of these, he is still alive. Listen to it. If that doesn't sound like some idea of reincarnation, I don't know what does.

Whichever theory suits you, in every minute of our lives, we make decisions that determine our direction, and the qualities that will make us who we will be later in this life, or in future lives. In this regard, we are as free and independent as we want. We can believe that we are locked into ways of being and doing by forces beyond our control, but we don't have to believe that. Whatever limitations we think we have because of our situation, we can always pick another option because we have free will. Right?

4. IF THERE IS FREE WILL

"Free will is an illusion. People always choose the perceived path of greatest pleasure."
- Scott Adams

Can we really make independent, meaningful, decisions that will change our lives? Do we have free will? Scott Adams seems to be saying that there is no free will, because we will always mindlessly choose whatever we perceive to be the biggest pleasure, like a machine without discretion or decision. But how does this negate free will? Whenever we make a choice, isn't it always for what we perceive to be the best result? Why would you freely make a choice that did not benefit you? One reason might be, because the not so obvious choice might not get you a prize now, but will set you up to get a better prize later.

This reminds me of those psychology experiments with little kids and a marshmallow. Here is a marshmallow. You can eat it now but if you wait until I come back in ten minutes, you can have two marshmallows. Some kids gobble their marshmallow right up;

others do not. They hold out for two marshmallows. Sounds like free will to me. For some reason, the marshmallow eaters could not understand they would get more pleasure if they waited a bit. Why is that? Did they learn that at home, or is there some sort of delayed gratification gene they don't have? The types of kids who can reasonably delay gratification and get the extra marshmallow, seem to do better in school, have fewer behavioral problems, and score higher on the SAT.[1]

Therefore, Scott Adams is right in predicting that we always make the choice which will get us the biggest reward. The catch is we don't necessarily agree on what that is. We might see that choice "A" is not as good as choice "B" right now, but will pay off much better in the future. Will some people always take the reward right now, and always forego the opportunity for a bigger or better reward later? If so, why would they do that? If we are overwhelmed by our emotions or needs, we might pick the biggest reward right away, but if we can control that compulsion, we would be better off. If we decide to change our diet (choose to have only one good donut each week instead of donuts every day), and start exercising to enhance our long-term health and pleasure, wouldn't that lead to a bigger reward?

Maybe free will is just making the smart choice about what is best for us in the long term, rather than grabbing something shiny right now. Suppose all of humanity makes massive sacrifices in the near future to produce a world, 100 years from now, that is not plagued with climate change, pollution, poverty, or energy problems, where people are free, happy, and in harmony with the planet? Wouldn't that be a big prize? We can be like "Homer Simpson" automatons and always choose, "Eat donut now!" but we don't have to. If we choose to utilize our free will, we can stop, think, and determine what is really best. When we learn to discipline ourselves, we can make the most advantageous choice in almost every aspect of our lives.

In our day-to-day lives, what motivates our thinking about our choices? So many influences go into making our "free will" that sometimes it looks like we're on autopilot. But what is there? If we think introspectively, what do we find? As our mind has evolved over millions of years, it has been programmed by evolution with reactions that helped our ancient ancestors survive, and then those were passed down to us. Unfortunately, there are many emotions and unthinking responses locked in place, that do not necessarily serve us well in today's world. We like to think that we are rational and sometimes we are, but the raw material for our rational mind comes from those deep ancient layers that can often fool us into making choices that are not in our best interests today. To best help ourselves, we should develop the ability to step back and challenge our own thinking, prejudices, and explicit and implicit biases. We need to ponder more and react less.

What is that "self " that is making our decisions? I had questions about this even before I saw The Matrix. The only ones, with free will, as you will remember, were those who took the red pill and were freed from the illusion. Is our will an illusion? I have a friend who says that if you know everything about someone's life, you can predict what they will do in any given situation, because we are totally molded by our experiences, culture, family, and environment. Unfortunately, there is no way to prove or disprove that. I've read others who believe that our genes set the stage for our decision making process. Some folks might believe that a combination of these is what is really in charge, not our "selves," whatever that is. Are we locked into a role, to some degree? Sometimes our upbringing sets boundaries for us that were meant to protect us, but they can also limit our options by narrowing the box in which we are thinking. If I had been raised to believe that certain types of actions are good, while others are bad, I will probably be much less inclined to do what I have been told is bad. If I have been raised to not trust my own judgement, I won't. If I have been born with certain mental, emotional, or physical conditions or limitations, I might look at the world and make decisions that reflect those circumstances.

If I believe I am a certain type of person, one who is, for example, angered by certain things and pleased by others, how do I know that is actually who I am? Have I created a self-fulfilling prophecy by thinking I am this one way? Can I decide to be a different type of person, or am I programmed into being who I think I am now? Which is the real me? To what degree can education, experience, or a wiser, more nuanced self-awareness increase my potential to make unbiased free choices? It might take a lot of will power to get beyond such limitations. How flexible are we to change?

In her book *Quiet: The Power of Introverts in a World That Can't Stop Talking*, Susan Cain examined the work of Dr. Carl Schwartz, as it affects the existence of free will. Cain found that Schwartz's work suggests we all have varying degrees of ability to change and adapt our personalities. Obviously we have the genetic and cultural/family baggage we are born with, and into, but we also have a degree of "elasticity". We can stretch to bring about change in ourselves. Was the dramatic change in Eliza Doolittle in *My Fair Lady* a real possibility, or just made up?

For adherents of religions that believe in God's judgement, believing in free will is essential, because we must have it in order to be responsible for our decisions. If God is going to judge me on my actions or beliefs for either reward or punishment, I cannot claim I didn't want to steal the big donut, but couldn't help myself. God knows I can't say I didn't have a choice. These folks believe God knows our minds and souls ,and exactly how much responsibility we carry. According to believers, God's knowledge is always perfect and the judgement is always just.

A view that doesn't recognize limitations on the freedom to exercise our will, is the philosophical approach of existentialism. Existentialism begins with the idea that our existence precedes our essence. This means, we exist as free human beings before we become covered with the personal and societal labels that tell everyone, and ourselves, who we are. This also means we were not created as a part of "God's plan." We choose our purpose and path in life, not God. Existentialists believe our decisions and actions create the person we become, and all of that is our responsibility. Most importantly, we are always free, so we can change our minds at any time.

As we are not bound to what a God thinks about us, or what society thinks about us, we are also not bound to our past decisions. Our will is not decided by God or our genes, and cannot be dictated by society or family. It is ours to exercise. As free beings, we are totally responsible for all of our decisions. We can pretend there are outside (or inside) forces requiring us to act in a certain way that we are helpless to change, but we would be lying to ourselves. We may succumb to pressure, we may do as we are told, we may pretend to give up our freedom, but we are still responsible. We cannot give away our freedom. It is always our choice and our responsibility. There is no one else to blame.

There is no guarantee free will means we are smart, just free. But how much flexibility to change does each of us have? Dr. Adrian Raine, writing in his book, *The Anatomy of Violence*, found indicators that predispose people to making criminal or violent choices. Many of these have to do with environmental factors, like lead paint poisoning, abusive family life, bad nutrition, and poor pre-natal care. In addition, he found biological factors such as genes from parents who were criminals, various medical issues, and abnormal brain structures, in violent criminals. While having a combination of these factors might seem predictive of future violent behavior, Raines discovered, in the course of his research, that he not only has an abnormal brain pattern, but realized he had grown up suffering from many of these negative environmental criteria. Yet he became an eminent scientist, not a criminal. He suspects the support of a loving family was the factor that kept his life in check. However, if a person has these negative factors, no redeeming family or other positive support, and does turn to crime, to what degree is that decision inevitable or a choice?

Trying to figure this out becomes complicated very quickly. My inclination is to believe there are a lot of people who, through the good luck of a life filled with favorable qualities and experiences, are able to truly exercise free will. Others of us, who have a somewhat mixed bag of qualities, grow into our ability to use our will through the lessons of experience and maturity. "Why did I make that bad choice?" I ask. "Oh yes, I'm stupid." One more lesson there. If I am able to learn from my errors, that is an important quality to develop. By doing this, perhaps we can grow into knowing our will.

Who is making these choices? However, the sausage is being made down in my brain factory by the combined efforts of the evolutionary, emotional, genetic, cultural, and rational departments, the answer eventually comes out of my mouth, and that is me. For good or ill, that's my free will.

5. PRAYER AND GOD

"Prayer is less about changing the world than it is about changing ourselves."
- David Wolpe

If we believe we are in relationship with God, can we meaningfully communicate with God? Prayer seems to be in the news all the time. I will admit to being disappointed with the announcement from Congress, and others a few years ago, that they were sending their thoughts and prayers to the victims and families of a mass shooting. This seems to be the standard answer to any tragedy but, if Congressmen actually do take the time to pray and think about the victim's families, does it do any good? Recently, I came across a tweet from the science guy of this generation, Neil DeGrasse Tyson. He wrote, "Evidence collected over many years, obtained from many locations, indicates that the power of Prayer is insufficient to stop bullets from killing school children." This made me stop and think. Is prayer really a thing? Can it make a difference?[1]

There seems to be, as usual, two points of view on the efficacy of prayer. One view comes from my atheist friends who see absolutely nothing spiritual about prayer, since there is no God or other powerful force listening. They might grudgingly agree that prayer may have some placebo value, if someone thinks God is paying attention, or hears that many people are praying for them in their difficult situation. On my Facebook feed recently, I found an older post where someone was asking for everyone's positive energy to help with a tough situation. Today she said, "Thank you all so much. It worked!" Transfer of energy to her through God, because of those prayers and wishes, or placebo effect?

The other view is that prayer is real and does work. Some religious friends have examples of healings and bad situations that turned around after prayer. They believe in the power of prayer, but most also believe that sometimes God says "no." I was in college when a monster hurricane was barreling down on Virginia Beach. I think it was Pat Robertson on his TV show, who asked everyone to pray that the storm might miss Virginia. The storm did turn north, and slammed into Long Island and Cape Cod. I guess God didn't like those folks as much. Maybe they didn't pray enough?

My problem with prayer is that I don't understand how it is supposed to work. Prayers seem to be granted sometimes, but often are not. Thousands of people pray for a little girl with leukemia, but she dies. My friend's grandmother is miraculously cured of blindness when she was a girl. How would God decide this? Did the leukemia girl do something wrong? Can God be swayed? I hope it is not the quantity of prayers, or the sincerity per prayer, that God is measuring before acting. If the predicted outcome, or even the surprise outcome, is in accordance with "God's Plan," then it should just happen, and prayer should have no impact. I cannot think of a single good reason why prayer would change God's mind about what had already been decided. Maybe God was going to move that hurricane anyway, but wanted to see how much we wanted it? Nah. That doesn't make any sense.

If there is no "God's plan," and everything just happens randomly, then would God interfere in the randomness, to bring about a certain outcome, if moved by people's prayers? If so, that makes a little more sense, but still doesn't explain why one situation would motivate God to act, but not a different one. Since I have assumed God is rational, there should be a reason for one choice over another, but I can't figure it out. Does God like some people more than others? I wouldn't think so if God is as compassionate as I understand God to be.

Is prayer part of a wider world of "spiritual power" that is accessible to human beings, and works to bring about desired results? My old friend Jack used to say that thoughts are things. By this, he meant that our intentions can bring about real results. You might say he was echoing the Power of Positive Thinking, but I think Jack had something a little more metaphysical in mind. The Wiccan speaker who came to my classes for a number of years, and spoke about the success of their group rituals, might agree with Jack. Maybe there is another way to think about how things can happen through focused spiritual efforts, including prayer.

Wiccans meet in small groups and perform rituals that have meaning for them, which they believe bring about tangible results. When conducted with sincerity and intent, the ritual is supposed to release those wishes to the universe, and they believe the universe responds. Some also believe this is a power all humans can harness if they learn to put their minds to it properly. That would make sense if we are all, indeed, physical manifestations of God, and find the way to work our bit of "Godness."

There are some Buddhists, Hindu's and New Age folks who believe great masters, who have meditated deeply for years and reached enlightenment, understand the true nature of reality, and have developed supernatural spiritual powers. However, these powers are not limited to particular religions, but are available to anyone who has achieved the appropriate deep spiritual cultivation. Are these folks fooling themselves with wishful thinking and illusions, or are they on to something? Is there more to what makes events happen than textbook physics?

People have been searching for authentic extrasensory powers for a long time. I have mentioned Dr. Ian Stevenson who founded the Division of Perceptual Studies (DOPS) at the University of Virginia, spent which has spent decades applying the scientific method to such questions. As detailed in *Mind Beyond Brain: Buddhism, Science, and the Paranormal*, DOPS has investigated near death experiences, out of body experiences, past life memories, precognition, and a long list of other psychic and spiritual phenomena with scientific rigor. In every area, there definitely seems to be something going on which cannot be explained away. This challenges current scientific assumptions about the total physicality of the mind/body relationship. These authors believe the scientific notion that consciousness can be totally explained through processes of the brain and body is in " deep trouble". New evidence suggests the brain does not create consciousness, but provides a sort of operating system for its functioning.[2]

This says to me that there are alternative possible explanations for what mainstream science says can't possibly be so. Could our mind exist outside of our physical body, and use the brain as a tool to transmit elements of our consciousness into the physical world? It's time for more scientists to get to work examining these phenomena that could shake the world up more than Darwin did.

6. THE PROBLEM OF EVIL

"No evil can happen to a good man, either in life or after death."
- Plato

"It is a man's own mind, not his enemy or foe, that lures him to evil ways."
- Buddha

Some of the most telling arguments atheists have used to question the existence of God are through the problem of evil. David Hume, the 18th century Scottish Philosopher, who helped make atheism trendy back in the day, quoted Epicurus in the following argument. "Is he [God] willing to prevent evil, but not able? Then he is impotent. Is he able, but not willing? Then he is malevolent. Is he both able and willing? Whence then is evil?" (Hume's *Dialogues Concerning Natural Religion*, Part X, 63)

In other words, Hume is saying God either allows evil, or can't stop evil, because we certainly have evil in the world. Or, God doesn't exist. Since Western religions have always maintained that God is all good and all powerful, how can we explain the existence of gratuitous evil? This is a tough nut to crack. The two reasons I have heard most often, to justify God in this situation, are a bad argument and a slightly better bad one. The bad argument is that whatever happens, however evil, is all part of God's plan. Even if it doesn't make sense to us, we should have faith and trust God has everything under control, and that events will all work out for everyone's benefit in the end. You'll see. If you live long enough. Perhaps you can understand why I labeled this the bad argument. It is based on ignorance, and using ignorance is a hard way to win an argument, at least with people who have more intelligence than faith. The slightly better bad argument is that God has given us all free will, and it is important we are allowed to exercise it so we can be held responsible for our actions. According to this view, evil is created by humans who choose to exercise their free will for evil purposes. God doesn't like it, but what can God do, and have the free will system still work? It's not God's fault. It's ours.

The problem with these explanations arises when we consider that natural phenomena are often responsible for horrible situations. Are these not under God's control? Earthquakes happen, volcanoes erupt, tsunamis wipe out communities, tornadoes and hurricanes slam us, diseases spread, and all of these create death and suffering. Many people believe God can decide if these events will happen, because someone is always praying to God that the latest disaster will go away. These events do end, but it usually seems to be in their own sweet time. Others proclaim some calamity is God's punishment for our sins. When that big asteroid hit earth 66 million years ago, it wiped out the dinosaurs, but cleared the way for the fuzzy little mammals that were always scurrying out of their way. Bad for the dinosaurs, but very good for the fuzzy mammals, and ultimately, for us. Was that part of a plan?

Can we come up with any other answers to explain the relationship between God and evil in the world? Some apologists for God have tried to explain how God can exist with evil. Many people believe there is a force for evil, with active agents operating all around us.

This would be the Russians. No, just kidding! That force is Satan and his minions. After all, if God created Satan, he must have known how that was going to turn out. The belief is that God allows Satan and his minions to fly around, whispering in our ears and tempting us to be bad, so we can choose to be good. While some people see the whole Satan/devil thing as metaphorical, many others believe it to be real. In the old sitcom *Family Matters*, I remember one episode where Steve Urkel has a good Steve angel advising him on one shoulder, and a bad Steve devil whispering on the other. I don't think this actually happens to us, but many folks buy the concept.

My atheist friends have the easiest answer when they assert that God doesn't exist. There is no good force and no evil force. Some people are good and some people are bad. Nature is amoral. Whether you wake up tomorrow with a tumor the size of a basketball, or an earthquake swallows your house, or an asteroid strike blots out your species, there's nothing personal involved. Sometimes bad stuff just happens as part of life in the universe. End of discussion.

Is there another explanation? Let's try this. Imagine a universe where consciousness never actually dies. Bodies die, stars die, galaxies collide, and random stuff happens, but consciousness always lives on. Conscious beings may inhabit a body, but when the body gets a tumor, or is swallowed up by an earthquake, or is blotted out by an asteroid, the consciousness survives, and works its way to another life, to continue its growth, development, and learning. I have no proof this occurs, but if consciousness is important to God, there should be some way to cultivate it, in opposition to the "one life and done theory," so it can grow and develop further.

I think learning has to be the key to this system. What happens to those who do bad and evil things, or even those who cause pain for others, and are unable to control themselves? In one system, after one lifetime, the bad suffer for all eternity in never ending pain. Some hold that everyone except true believers wallow in never ending pain because that's what they deserve. A second view says there is no system. When something dies it is "not only merely dead it is really most sincerely dead." End of discussion. In a third system, consciousness is preserved and reborn into lives where there is a chance to learn from past mistakes. We do this by living through new situations, and finding opportunities to make the right choice, or do the correct action, rather than the wrong one. It may take many lives to learn the lesson, but when it happens, it's on to more advanced lessons. Perhaps the universe is not set up on the basis of severe punishment, but on the basis of compassion and learning. Perhaps it is more like a school, where everyone advances lifetime after lifetime, at their own pace, rather than a prison where everyone is tortured daily, and twice on their birthday. When all of the lessons have been learned, maybe there is no need to return for more lessons. What happens then? Perhaps our consciousness merges with God, or perhaps there are other levels of existence to explore. Only God knows.

Looking at this third system, you can understand why the atheists are right to a point. Bad stuff does happen and the universe, on the physical side, seems amoral. Some people choose to be good and some choose bad. We have some very advanced, kind, generous, compassionate people among us, and some who seem like pure evil on steroids. There is nothing in the system that can change this in a moment. But maybe, in the ultimate sense, consciousness never dies, it just changes its state of being and continues on its path of improvement.

Once you've looked over these systems which one would you prefer? Which sounds more like the spiritual system created by a compassionate God? Can you guess my choice? Frankly, if the only selections were an afterlife where most people might burn in hell forever, or one with no God, and no afterlife, I would pick the second view. When you die as part of that scenario you are just gone. I would much rather there be nothing afterwards, than the existence of eternal suffering and vindictive punishment. Who would choose that? Why?

7. IS GOD IN OUR FUTURE?

"Science without religion is lame, religion without science is blind."
- Albert Einstein

Everything I've been discussing about God and religion sounds so conditional because there is very little in that realm we can prove to be true or false. Almost every religion lays the basis of its beliefs in the past, when there was no science, and so no way to analyze what was true. Maybe that's the problem; perhaps we are looking in the wrong chronological direction. Maybe the truth is not in the past, but is more likely be found in the future. I recently read the three books cited in the following discussions and found they opened my mind to a new way of thinking about religion. Let's look to the future.

John Haught, *The New Cosmic Story: Inside our Awakening Universe*

John Haught looks at new science and old religion in a different way. Haught proposes an innovative understanding of God which takes into account the latest discoveries in science, making his thesis both spiritually compelling and scientifically friendly. Rather than seeing God's creation as a completed process, we should consider that the universe, and everything in it, is continuing to evolve. God's creation is not finished, it is still unfolding, and perhaps the best is yet to come.

Science and religion are sometimes at loggerheads, if science happens to contradict a religious belief. Many religious folks are able to live with those differences, seeing scripture as more metaphorical than literal. However, not everyone agrees with that view. I was once told by a believer that God put all of those dinosaur bones in the earth to test our faith in the literal biblical creation account, so if we fall for the bones, it proves our faith is shot, and we are doomed.

Haught embraces the science behind human and cosmic evolution, and uses it to describe a new way to understand God. He works within the framework we have already established, beginning with a Big Bang, followed by the evolution of the universe, life, and consciousness. From those first incredibly unique moments, to the present day, the universe has continued to evolve.

Haught points out that very early on, human beings developed a religious/spiritual consciousness. In ancient times, we worshipped and sacrificed to gods so they would give us benefits, and/or not mess with us. Everyone knew there were many gods, initially the gods of tribal groups, and then later of a city, or a country. From their mythology, we have learned that these gods didn't always act well, often feuded amongst themselves, and often got humans involved, but we continued to give them worship and sacrifices. Other than loyalty to them, the gods rarely made any ethical demands on us. However, from roughly 800 BCE to 300 BCE, during what is called the Axial Age, all major religions and schools of thought, in a unique paradigm shift, changed from following this "selfish god" model, to the belief that God, however we understood the concept, wanted us to focus on being good people, practicing what Haught calls "rightness."

Many believe there are certain actions that are morally and ethically "right" for human beings. Inquiring into this concept became a new direction in human thought in the Axial Age. Greek philosophers began to explore what it meant to be a good person, and Hebrew prophets asserted that God expected us to love our neighbor, and take care of the widow and orphan. In Iran, Zoroaster (maybe before 800 BCE) preached personal responsibility and accountability for our actions, that would be weighed upon our death. These ideas were later extremely influential in the development of Christianity and Islam. In India, Buddhism and Jainism arose as ethical and spiritual alternatives to Hinduism, which itself began to change, understanding there was ultimately one Brahman, and one spiritual process. In China, Confucianism and Taoism, complementary opposites distilled from traditional thought provided different directions, but were both ways humans could live in harmony and balance, for the good of heaven and of earth. Most people don't think about the similarity of these worldwide changes today, but this shift in thinking happened in many places during this time, and, as far as historians can tell, independently. Even though religions have occasionally strayed from "rightness," this remains the ideal.

Haught contends these Axial Age developments were not random events that just happened, but part of a continuing universal evolutionary process. Since the Big Bang, one event has brought about another, which brought about the next. Religious consciousness developed in early humans, and became based on "rightness" during the Axial Age. Religion leads us to philosophy, which leads us to the scientific method, that has us staring at the universe wondering what is going on. Perhaps we can find God in a universe wide evolution, growing toward life, consciousness, spiritual yearning, and deeper understanding. The evolutionary aspect of Haught's thesis is supported by science. What he says makes sense, may be true, and therefore could be an excellent vehicle for understanding God.

Every particle that exists is part of the universe, including us. We are the part of the universe that has come to life, consciousness, religion, science and curiosity; the part of the universe that is aware of itself, and is trying to find answers. Evolution seems to be a fact of life. To say that we have evolved to these qualities is the same as saying the universe has evolved to these qualities. I don't know if consciousness is developing elsewhere in the cosmos, but it sure is here. After billions of years, something is happening. The universe is waking up and in this process, Haught sees God.

If this makes sense, how do we deal with it? Haught uses the term "anticipation" to describe how we should approach this new view of religion. God didn't create the universe finished and complete, as many religions have traditionally believed, but as a process that is still unfolding. He suggests we should assist in this process by trying to spread rightness.

"There are many questions...which, so far as we can see, must remain insoluble to the human intellect unless its powers become quite a different order from what they are now."
- Bertrand Russell

J.L. Schellenberg, *Evolutionary Religion*

Charles Darwin opened a lot of doors for us when it came to understanding our place in time and space. Published almost 160 years ago, *The Origin of the Species* supported the radical idea of plant and animal evolution. Since then, this concept has swept through science and society, changing the way we view almost everything.

In the last several decades, science has advanced in more directions, with more complexity and sophistication than most of us can grasp. We seem to be in the midst of an accelerating scientific and technological revolution. In line with this development, philosopher J.L. Schellenberg has written a thought provoking book, *Evolutionary Reli-*

gion, that explains how and why it is desirable for our religious focus and speculation to shift from the past to the future.

Evolution is the way the universe works, whether we are talking about the development of the cosmos, or about plant, animal, and human life. Not long ago, we thought in time frames of decades, centuries, or a few thousand years. We lived in a world where we believed species never changed, and creation was relatively recent and complete. For the most part, we have recovered from the cultural shock administered by Darwin. Except for fundamentalist irreconcilables, we are comfortable discussing and comprehending events that have taken place over the past 14 billion years. This includes the Big Bang, the beginning of life on earth, and the whole process of plant, animal, and human evolution. At the same time, many religions still look to their ancient scriptures for answers about God and man. It is clear, that unless we are reading those scriptures in a metaphorical way when they contradict science, not everything that follows, including religious beliefs based on the literal accuracy, is true.

While we have made great strides in understanding the past, Schellenberg suggests that the past is not going to provide us with any verifiable truths about religion. To do this, he says in agreement with John Haught, we need to reverse our perspective on time, so we are looking not to the past, but to the future.

Schellenberg suggests, that even though beliefs espoused by present day religions based on ancient scriptures are incorrect, the basic premise that there is an intelligent, benevolent, transcendent force behind the workings of the universe could be true. A rational skeptic finds both the atheist, and religious points of view, to be equally suspect, since neither position has been proven. Looking to the past cannot answered this question. Only in the future can this happen.

Scientists tell us that some day the earth will become uninhabitable, because the sun will get too hot to sustain life here. Anyone still on earth, who can't get off, will die. Estimates are this will happen in about one billion to 2.3 billion years. When I recently googled this question, it came up as 1.75 billion. Being very conservative, let's say for the sake of discussion, that the earth will last about one billion more years. What this means is, that unless we wipe ourselves out, or earth is hit by a planet killing asteroid, human beings will continue to live, learn, and evolve on this planet for a long, long time. That is a lot of time to look forward to and think about, when considering what knowledge our descendants might discover in the deep future.

It takes a lot of work to know things. In just the past few hundred years of serious scientific inquiry, we have increased our knowledge at a geometric rate. Yet how much do we really know? Consider Immanuel Kant who said we can never know the truth about a thing in itself. We have our senses and brainpower, but these tools are a product of the very system we are trying to study. Are there perceptions we can't pick up? Are there truths in the universe we could never fathom? Even with the machines we construct to help us, which improve the quality and quantity of our information, we still cannot be certain how much we know, and how much we do not know. However, even over a small slice of the next billion years, we are extremely likely to learn a lot more. Within that time, we will discover new information, become smarter, and may even evolve, biologically or culturally, in ways impossible to predict.

What will we learn in another 1000, 10,000, or 10 million years? Given enough time, it is almost certain we will eventually be able to answer the big question- is there an intelligent, benevolent, transcendent force (God) behind the workings of the universe? The answer might be yes, or it might be no, or it might be an answer so revolutionary and unexpected that we never could have guessed it. But, is there any reason we should not expect a great expansion of knowledge in the deep future?

"A knowledge of the existence of something we cannot penetrate, of the manifestations of the profoundest reason and the most radiant beauty - it is this knowledge and this emotion that constitute the truly religious attitude; in this sense, and in this alone, I am a deeply religious man." - Albert Einstein

Even given a lot of time, it is going to be tough to prove or disprove the existence of a God like force in the universe. If a first grade student is given a calculus problem to solve, she might mumble and stumble and invent some sort of answer, maybe something a friend told her. She might believe whatever answer she came up with, but there is no way she can know if she is right or even close. What is certain, is that one day in the future, if she studies, she will figure it out. One day in the future, we will know the answer to our question about God. And by that time, we may be able to understand the answer.

If we were a species with 100,000 years of experience in documented scientific inquiry, and no convincing evidence had yet arisen to suggest the validity of religious/spiritual beliefs, we could say, with a reasonable degree of certainty, that it isn't going to happen. But that is not our situation. We don't know what we need to know to make that call now, and won't for the foreseeable future. This will be a long-term project, and, everyone, now and in the future, can be focused on trying to find the answer.

In the meantime, we should reorient the way we think about God. Religion can be a valuable aid to human life and development. Focusing on God can help give our lives meaning and purpose, set us on the straight path to being good people, and teach us to work towards laudable goals cooperatively with others. However, while religious beliefs should always be demonstrated through benevolent actions, that hasn't always been the case. Religion sometimes shows a tendency to violence and emotions have combined with religious zeal to bring out the worst in people. Maybe, with a focus on the future, different sorts of religious practices can help eliminate the root causes of those "us versus them," no-win situations.

A religion, based on an evolving understanding, can entice both our hearts and our minds, and invite us to use creativity and imagination to speculate about what might be discovered in the future. We should learn to look forward to discovering the truth someday, rather than looking back and hitching our beliefs and actions to ancient myths. A religion, based on an evolving understanding, can entice both our hearts and our minds, and invite us to use creativity and imagination to speculate about what might be discovered in the future. We should learn to look forward to discovering the truth someday, rather than looking back and hitching our beliefs and actions to ancient myths.

As a way to do this, Schellenberg introduces the concept of ultimism, the hypothesis that we will eventually find there is an accessible "ultimate good springing from something in reality and value..."[1] Not a religion or a way to worship, this position claims that there is the possibility of an ultimate spiritual source of good. What this might be, we can only imagine. Being good skeptics, we have to say there may be nothing there, but we also know there may be "something" therefore, it is valid for us to contemplate the existence of a compassionate, transcendent reality. I can consider this hypothesis likely, without believing it to be absolutely true, through what Schellenberg calls "beliefless acceptance." This means that even though I cannot say it is so, such a religious claim is possible, would be beneficial for us if true, and I assert a "pro-attitude (103)" towards it. I hold this position because of rational thinking not faith. What will this future spiritual reality be? We can't know yet, but can use what we do know, and will discover through science, to devise rational hypotheses that fit the facts. Of course, unlike many of today's faiths, we have to be prepared to change our minds in the face of new evidence. How close my answer or your answer will come to what we eventually discover, will only be known in the future.

Schellenberg says ultimism is not a religious faith, but can be a religious hope. A man in a dangerous position might not know whether or not he will survive, but he hopes he will. That hope will carry him forward in the face of many obstacles, but he will not know until later whether his hopes were well founded or in vain. Why do I have a hopeful pro-attitude towards this concept? I don't know anyone who, if they had a genuine choice, wouldn't pick a universe that reflects intelligence, purpose, harmony and compassion, where life doesn't end with physical death, but might continue in other ways.

Isn't that better, more positive and hopeful, than a universe that does not have those qualities? I completely understand the universe may only consist of mindless physical processes that have brought about life, intelligence, and a religious sensibility through random coincidence, but that is not the answer I would tie my hopes to.

If we can hold to the possibility of ultimism being true, associating with this positive view of reality can be good for us. We can choose to reflect compassionate ultimistic values in our lives, which would align us with what we hope to be the deepest nature of reality. If we believe this transcendent force is on the side of compassion, and not indifferent to our deepest needs, we can deduce its guiding principles, and decide to live without giving up rational doubt about its existence. Schellenberg suggests that, "Imaginative religious faith, understood not as a stop-gap measure, but as an attitude with vital integrity and vibrancy of its own, might be precisely the right attitude to direct toward ultimism at our present stage of development…(105)." Our long-term inquiry, if successful, could bring us to the understanding that the universe is religious in nature.

Evolutionary religious faith is designed for the long haul. While many contemporary religions look for an escape from this world, some even anticipating its end during a time of tribulation and suffering, evolutionary religion would have us favor the future, looking forward, with determination, to the answers yet to be discovered. Evolutionary religion relies on science, knowledge, and rational thinking, realizing if we don't know the answers, it is dishonest to make something up and say it is true. While leaving behind the detailed faith based dogmas of many current religions, evolutionary religion recognizes the underlying premise of those religions (God, in some definition) may be true. It also invites us to use our imagination and creativity to devise, share, and debate rational ideas from our continuing inquiry into what the universe is all about.

"Religion will not regain its old power until it can face change in the same spirit as does science." - Alfred North Whitehead

Michael Dowd, Thank God for Evolution

To be credible today's religions must ensure their beliefs conform with what we know from science and, as scientists do, be prepared to change their views as new evidence and better interpretations become available. Buddhism is on-board with this. As the Dali Lama has said, "If scientific analysis were conclusively to demonstrate certain claims in Buddhism to be false, then we must accept the findings of science and abandon those claims."[2] Also, for about the last seventy years, the Roman Catholic Church has held that there is no intrinsic conflict between Christianity and evolution, as long as members believe that God did the creating, and also gave us souls.

Why this change is needed, and how to integrate these new ideas with long held religious beliefs is the subject of *Thank God for Evolution*, by Michael Dowd. Dowd explains how our growing understanding of science, specifically the evolution of the universe and life on our planet, can be understood in a modern religious format. By considering a view of religion that is aligned with science, the door opens to spiritual concepts that are both rationally and spiritually appealing.

Even though we know evolution is the continuing activity by which major changes in the universe occur, there are some religions that maintain this is not true. These are faiths Dowd refers to as "Flat Earth" Religions. They were established before humans developed science and began to learn about the universe, so their scriptures and theology often reflects this disparity. Until more modern times, all that human s knew about the world came from observation, and stories passed down from their ancestors. For instance, everybody knew that the sun revolved around the earth. This was self-evident from observation since, on any sunny day, we could tell the earth was definitely not moving but we could see the sun was. In trying to explain the natural world and our place in it, our ancestors did their best but only much later did we discover the truth. As Arch-bishop James Ussher famously calculated, using biblical data, creation occurred on October 23, 4004 BCE. That was incorrect.

This type of insistence is what Dowd would suggest needs to be updated based on science.

Every faith should go back through their beliefs and scriptures to re-evaluate them on the basis of what we know from science. The creation story in Genesis should be downgraded to an interesting historical/religious artifact/metaphor, as many non-fundamentalist Christians, Jews and Muslims have already done. Certainly the damage done to women throughout history, by the blame directed at Eve for being easily turned to sin by the serpent, tempting Adam to also sin, and thereby destroying a perfect system, should be rejected. Also, prejudice against those with alternative sexual orientations, people accused of witchcraft and other noxious claims based on biblical injunctions/interpretations should end. There is wisdom to be gained from the Bible, but it should not be tainted by the belief that scientifically incorrect information is literally true. Dowd provides ways Christians, as a model for all faiths, can adapt their beliefs to this new way of thinking about God and religion.

Agreeing with science does not harm God, but increases our understanding. God, in whatever existence He might have, is the origin of our creation and evolution. Because we don't know more, it is legitimate to speculate about God's qualities. From a religious point of view, God could be seen as a desired, but still theoretical, compassionate, creative force. If we want, we can hypothesize about souls and the existence of an afterlife, in terms of reincarnation, or a return to God in heaven, or whatever seems reasonable to us. As Dowd points out, the valuable, ethical teachings, and wisdom of Moses, Jesus, Muhammad, Confucius, the Buddha, and others can be understood to align with our beliefs about this ultimate reality.

The important point is that the ideas we might infuse into our concept of God should be the wishes, hopes, and speculations that make sense to us, but don't contradict science. This supports the Pi Process. We don't know enough to say anything for certain, and so will have to be satisfied living without a proven truth. However, we can still speculate, reason, and discuss our views. While the day of faith based religions, where all elements must be believed, is on the way out, the door is now open to wider participation in religious discussions and the development of rational interpretations. As we learn more, evolutionary religions will adapt their beliefs to the best new view of reality. Maybe someday science will be able to explain it all and we will then understand the true nature of God, the Universe, and us. Or not.

8. GOD'S PLAN

"Math, Science, History, unraveling the Mystery, it all started with a Big Bang."

- Theme song from *Big Bang Theory*

I WAS RAISED to believe that everything that happens is part of God's plan, and I spent a lot of time as a kid trying to figure out what that plan was. When I was miserable in math, being pushed around by a bully, or forced to mow the lawn, I couldn't see how my suffering, presumably ordained by God, was helping bring about anything good.

In the long run, things have worked out just fine for me. But, as I watched the news and learned more about the world, I saw a lot of death and suffering, not just from man's inhumanity to man (and animals), but from natural disasters too. Were the deaths of each of those people killed by tornados in the Midwest last spring part of a plan? If so, I don't understand it. It seems arbitrary. I cannot justify that God plans out every occurrence that takes place. More likely, God put systems in motion and here we are.

I have more success looking for evidence of any discernible pattern or plan, if I focus on the long sweep of time and events, to find purpose in the evolution of the cosmos and consciousness. My preferred start for such speculation is the Big Bang, followed by the evolution of the cosmos and of life on earth, which started as single cells but gave way to multi-celled organisms, that evolved into all plants and animals (including us). The leading theory for life not sticking as single cells, is that cells which cooperate, are better able to adapt to environmental changes than cells that go it alone. Complexity achieves success.

Over time there have been a number of mass extinctions, but whenever they happen, X millions of years later, life always returns and nature refills all available environmental niches. The most interesting extinction to me is the asteroid strike that wiped out the dinosaurs around 66 million years ago. That was very bad for them, but very good for the mammals, who went on to fill the niches the dinosaurs left vacant. Some of those mammals were our ancestors and we are very lucky they were able to survive until the ecosystem regenerated. Then, over time, they evolved into every type of modern mammal, including us.

Natural selection brought our evolution to historical times, but is too slow to bring about sufficient adaptation in short periods of time. The new driver of change for us is cultural evolution. When we were living as hunter-gatherers, new ideas were few and far between, only slowly diffusing from one group to the next. Once we began agriculture, approximately 11,000 years ago, and moved into villages and then cities, our social/technological expansion really began to take off. Life became a lot more complicated, and we became more dependent on each other, but this new complexity brought about a lot of success. Our species' population of some five million people 10,000 years ago has skyrocketed to more than seven billion today.

It's clear we are the current winners of the "Smartest Critter on Earth" award. If we look back, we can see we won because we were lucky. Many times our ancestors could have been rubbed out by chance and circumstances, and we could still lose our spot on the winners' podium. This century will bring many big challenges. Aaron Bastani in his book *Fully Automated Luxury Communism*, has succinctly identified the major crises humans will face.

1. Climate change due to global warming.
2. Resource scarcity for minerals and fresh water.
3. Societal aging as birth rates fall and life expectancy increases.
4. A growing surplus of global poor who are not needed for industrial, military or technological growth and development.
5. A new machine age that will bring even greater unemployment as more physical and cognitive work is performed by high tech robots and artificial intelligence, not people.[1]

If he had written his book in 2020 Bastani might have put in one additional entry-

6. Worldwide pandemics.

If we are bright and perceptive, we are going to solve these problems and become a technologically advanced global civilization, where life will be pretty good for all. If we don't solve them, because of selfishness, greed, tribalism, stupidity or emotions gone bad, we will blow it. About 99% of all species that have ever existed are extinct today. Life, however, keeps pushing on, no matter what. If we depart the scene, natural selection will have time, and in a few million years, another species will get the luck, and seize the opportunity to be on top.

The Big Bang, and everything that has followed, might have been designed to bring about intelligent life. If there is a plan, this could be it. However, whatever God is, God clearly did not design this system just for us. There is a big universe out there, with undoubtedly many places for life to start, where we humans don't live. If this is a plan, it is designed for whatever lucky form of life is able to evolve the consciousness and intelligence to win the prize, and survive its own success. Given more time, some dinosaurs (like those clever raptors in *Jurassic Park* perhaps) might have developed more intelligence, but they were unlucky. Maybe we will be unlucky too. But if so, the evolutionary plan will continue to run, allowing the next potential winner the opportunity to break through.

In *Nonzero: The Logic of Human Destiny*, Robert Wright discusses this situation. He states, "We've been very lucky. The winner of a bingo game is also very lucky. But there's always a winner." The ultimate winner for planet earth may, or may not be, us.

Here's hoping our luck holds.

9. GOD'S WILL

"All things are artificial, for nature is the art of God."
- Thomas Browne

If there is only one thing I have learned from writing this, it is that we are not going to prove the truth about God's existence any time soon. Perhaps in thousands of years, science will be able to do this, one way or another, but that will not inform us today. We can use faith, and/or our rational minds, to come to an answer we might believe could be true, but we cannot know it is true.

What should we do when the answer to the most important question is unknowable? If we want to discover what is true, so we can align our lives appropriately, but cannot determine the truth, how do we proceed? Our best bet is to find an answer that makes sense to us, that we can believe in, but still be ready to adapt, if we find new information or a better argument. For many people, that will be to start with the religion they were raised in. This is an easy path because they don't have to look far, or think very hard about it.

Folks often find great comfort in the religious community they grew up with. One student told me that the actual tenets of her faith are not as important to her as the deep and meaningful feelings she has from her connection to the people and rituals of her church. It just feels right to her and she would never want to change. Still, we should be honest enough to admit that what we believe may not be true.

Those who were raised with or without religion, and wish to use their intellect to find a rational answer, often become atheists or agnostics. Based on their preferences, agnostics have opinions on the foibles of different religious systems, what those people believe, and how they act. However, they will not take a position on God's existence, because they have not found sufficient evidence to make a determination. Other folks will find that the atheist track appeals to them. Their belief is that God does not exist. Again, they cannot prove their position to be true, but accept it because they feel it makes the most sense.

However, being an agnostic leaves me unsatisfied, and intellectually restless. I want an answer, but one that is rationally possible and believable, without having to make a massive leap of faith I can't justify. Even if I can't prove it, my answer should be congruent with science and make sense (at least to me). The Pi Process provides this opportunity. Pi's advice to agnostics was to pick the religious or atheistic story you like best, one that resonates with you, that you can believe, even though you are aware it may never be proven true.

In thinking through these questions, I imagined I was a consultant for God, tasked with designing a religious system for humans, that best reflects the realities of the universe, and God's rational and compassionate nature. You might say it also reflects my view of the way the spiritual system should work, if it doesn't already. As a result of this process, I have derived a set of working assumptions that guide my daily beliefs and actions, and make sense to me. Your results may differ.

1. I cannot prove the existence of God or a God-like force, one way or the other. So, if I want to step beyond agnosticism, there is nothing irrational about selecting a scenario that does not contradict known facts. Therefore, I will assume God exists and our lives have meaning. If the atheists are right, I am wasting my time, but then, if that is the case, wasting time probably doesn't matter.
2. The universe has brought forth complexity, life, consciousness, and intelligence. What created the universe we can call God, and I choose to believe God planned to bring about those qualities. If this is true, I assume God values these qualities, which leads me to believe this is a God of creativity, rationality, and compassion.
3. If God is compassionate, I assume God would never set up a religious system that required people to select one correct belief from many choices, and, if they pick the wrong one, or don't worship him properly, subject them to eternal torture. It makes more sense that if God judges anything, God judges actions.
4. Since God created the universe, including us, and has instituted processes to bring about the evolution of life, I assume God wants us to have respect for this creation, which includes people, animals, and our planet. Our personal and group policy should be to treat all people with respect, treat all animals and lifeforms with respect, and to treat the planet with respect. If we ever find life elsewhere in the universe, we should treat that life with respect also.
5. Since God has created a consciousness-producing universe, I assume God has designed a way to preserve this consciousness so it has opportunities to grow further. The best answer I have found to explain the recycling of this, is some form of reincarnation. In this way, a consciousness that made decisions violating #4 in a past life, will have opportunities to learn and correct its actions in another life. I assume a compassionate God is a teacher, not a punisher.
6. Clearly, we are part of God's consciousness creating

project. I assume God prefers we assist his project by supporting #4 in every way we can as a group and as individuals. For instance:

a. If wealth and resources are going overwhelmingly to a few, while many are impoverished, suffering, and without opportunity, we must redress that imbalance.
b. If our unprovoked actions cause physical or psychological harm, or serious economic detriment to others, we must redress that situation.
c. If animals are suffering to provide us food and service, or are becoming extinct because of our actions, we must redress that situation.
d. If our planet's environment is being unsustainably damaged by our actions, to the detriment of life on earth, we must redress that situation.

I DON'T KNOW how we can reach these goals, if the world continues to operate as usual, in the political and economic realms. For change this broad and deep, and to really make things happen, it seems we would have to reconstruct the way the world of human beings works.

Here is an idea. Some Native Americans have suggested we should make important decisions in the best interest of all humans. This would not be just for us, our family, our country, or even for everyone alive now. We should make our decisions on behalf of, and to the benefit of, the next seven generations of humans to come. If we can't justify our actions based on those criteria, we shouldn't do it. Now that's wisdom.

As best I can determine, this is the will of God.

Of course, I could be wrong.

THE RELIGION TEACHER'S BOOKSHELF

"When the facts change, I change my mind, sir. What do you do?"
- John Maynard Keynes

Over the years I have spoken to many people about their religious beliefs. I cannot possibly remember all of these kind folks but they have helped me understand their faiths from the individual's point of view. As I mentioned earlier, most people don't mind talking about their beliefs if approached with sincerity and respect. Try it.

The following list does not pretend to cover the religious studies field, but these are the books, on my shelf, and other resources I have come across and learned from.

World Religions Textbooks

I have used (*) or have been recommended to me by teachers. There are probably later editions. Teachers, check carefully for student readability level.

Burke, T. Patrick, *The Major Religions: An Introduction with Texts*, ISBN-10: 140511049X

*Hopfe, Lewis M. and Mark R. Woodward, *Religions of the World* (12th Edition) [Paperback], ISBN-10: 0205158609

*Smith, Huston, *The World's Religions* [Paperback], ISBN-10: 0061660183 (I used this as a textbook but it is written for the general reader. There are no questions at the end of the chapter)

Fisher, Mary Pat, *Living Religions* (8th Edition) [Paperback], ISBN-10: 0205835856

Ludwig, Theodore M., *The Sacred Paths: Understanding the Religions of the World*, (4th Edition), ISBN-13: 978-0131539037

World Religions Reader

The only Reader I ever used in class. I am sure there are other good ones but this one is endorsed by Huston Smith.

Novak, Philip, *The World's Wisdom: Sacred Texts of the World's Religions*, Harper San Francisco, 1994.

Buddhism

Berry, Thomas, *Buddhism*, Anima Publications, Chambersburg, PA., 1989.

Chopra, Deepak, *Buddha: A Story of Enlightenment*, HarperCollins, New York, 2007.

H.H. Dalai Lama, *Beyond Religion: Ethics for a Whole World*, Houghton Mifflin, Boston, 2011.

Ethics for the New Millennium, Riverhead Books, New York, 1999.

The World of Tibetan Buddhism: An Overview of its Philosophy and Practice, Wisdom Publications, Boston, 1995.

Hagen, Steve, *Buddhism: Plain and Simple*, Broadway Books, New York, 1997.

Harris, Dan, and Jeff Warren, *Meditation for Fidgety Skeptics*, Spiegel and Grau, New York, 2017.

Harris, Elizabeth J., *What Buddhists Believe*, One World, Oxford, 1998.

Johnson, George, Book Review, *The Universe in a Single Atom: The Convergence of Science and Spirituality*, By the Dalai Lama, *The New York Times*, Sept. 18, 2005.

LeShan, Lawrence, *How to Meditate: The Acclaimed Guide to Self-Discovery*, Bantam Books, New York, 1975.

Mishra, Pankaj, *An End to Suffering: The Buddha in the World*, Picador, New York, 2004.

Naht Hanh, Thich, *The Heart of the Buddha's Teaching: Transforming Suffering into Peace, Joy, and Liberation*, Broadway Books, New York, 1998.

The Miracle of Mindfulness: A Manual on Meditation, Beacon Press, Boston, 1975.

Powers, John, *A Concise Introduction to Tibetan Buddhism*, Snow Lion Publications, Ithaca, New York, 2008.

Presti, David E., *Mind Beyond Brain: Buddhism, Science, and the Paranormal*, Columbia University Press, New York, 2018.

Renard, John, *Responses to 101 Questions on Buddhism*, Paulist Press, New York, 1999.

Salajan, Ioanna, *Zen Comics*, Charles E. Tuttle Co., Rutland VT., 1974.

Smith, Huston and Philip Novak, *Buddhism: A Concise Introduction*, HarperCollins, San Francisco, 2003.

T'sai, Chih-Chung, trans. Brian Bruya, *Zen Speaks: Shouts of Nothingness*, Anchor Books, New York, 1994.

Watts, Alan, *The Book: On the Taboo Against Knowing Who You Are*, Vintage books, New York, 1972.

Wright, Robert, *Why Buddhism is True: The Science and Philosophy of Meditation and Enlightenment*, Simon and Schuster, New York, 2017

Chinese Religion

Albert, Eleanor, *Religion in China*, Council on Foreign Relations, Updated June 10, 2015, http://www.cfr.org/china/religion-china/p16272

Blofeld, John, *I Ching: The Book of Change*, E.P. Dutton and Co., New York, 1968.

Bloomfield, Freda, *The Book of Chinese Beliefs*, Ballantine Books, New York, 1989.

Chuen, Lam Kam, *Feng Shui Handbook: How to Create a Healthier Living and Working Environment*, Henry Holt and Co, New York, 1996.

Confucius, *The Analects of Confucius*, translated and annotated by Arthur Waley, Vintage Books, New York, 1989.

Fung Yu-Lan, *A Short History of Chinese Philosophy*, The Free Press, New York, 1966.

Hoff, Benjamin, *The Tao of Pooh*, Penguin Books, New York, 1982.

Hogan, Ron, *Getting Right with Tao: A Contemporary Spin on the Tao Te Ching*, Channel V Books, New York, 2010

Johnson, Ian, "Decapitated Churches in China's Christian Heartland," *The New York Times*, May 21, 2016.

Lao-Tzu, Tsai Chih Chung, illus., Brian Bruya, trans., *The Tao Speaks: Lao Tzu's Whispers of Wisdom*, Anchor Books, New York, 1995.

Levin, Dan, "China Officials Seek Career Shortcut With Feng Shui," *The New York Times*, May 10, 2013. http://www.nytimes.com/2013/05/11/world/asia/feng-shui-grows-in-china-as-officials-seek-success.html

Lin, Derek, *The Tao of Daily Life*, Jeremy P. Tarcher, New York, 2007.

Mitchell, Stephen, *Tao Te Ching*, Harper and Row, New York, 1988.

Page, Jeremy, "Why China Is Turning Back to Confucius," Sept. 20, 2015, *The Wall Street Journal*, http://www.wsj.com/articles/why-china-is-turning-back-to-confucius-1442754000

Page, Michael, *The Power of Ch'i: An Introduction to Chinese Mysticism and Philosophy*, Thorsons, London, 1988.

Puett, Michael and Christine Gross-Loh, *The Path: What Chinese Philosophers Can Teach Us About the Good Life*, Simon and Schuster, New York, 2016.

Thompson, Laurence G., *Chinese Religion: An Introduction (Fifth Ed.)*, Wadsworth Publishing Co., Belmont, CA., 1996

Watson, Burton and Mo Tzu, *Mo Tzu: Basic Writings*, Columbia University Press, New York, 1963.

Christianity

Bauckman, Richard J., "All in the Family: Identifying Jesus' Relatives," *Bible Review*, Vol. XVI, #2, April 2000.

Burstein, Dan,(ed). *Secrets of the Code: The Unauthorized Guide to the Mysteries Behind The Da Vinci Code*, CDS Books, New York, 2004.

Crossan, John Dominic, *Jesus: A Revolutionary Biography*, Harper San Francisco, 1989.

Dias, Elizabeth, "'Mormon' No More: Faithful Reflect on Church's Move to Scrap a Moniker," *The New York Times*, June 29, 2019, https://www.nytimes.com/2019/06/29/us/mormon-church-name-change.html

Droge, Arthur C., "Did Paul Commit Suicide?," *Bible Review*, Vol. 5 #6, December 1989.

Ehrman, Bart D., *Jesus, Interrupted: Revealing the Hidden Contradictions in the Bible (and Why We Don't Know About Them)*, Harper One, New York, 2009.

Lost Christianities: The Battles for Scripture and the Faiths We Never Knew, Oxford University Press, New York, 2005.

Misquoting Jesus: The Story Behind Who Changed the Bible and Why, HarperCollins, New York, 2005.

Truth and Fiction in the Da Vinci Code, Oxford University Press, New York, 2004.

Freke, Timothy and Peter Gandy, *The Jesus Mysteries: Was the Original Jesus a Pagan God?* Three Rivers Press, New York, 1999.

Gopnik, Adam, "What Did Jesus Do?: Reading and Unreading the Gospels," *The New Yorker*, May 24, 2010. Last accessed 3/21/16,

http://www.newyorker.com/arts/critics/atlarge/2010/05/24/100524crat_atlarge_gopnik?printable=true#

Granberg-Michaelson, Wesley, "Where is Christianity headed? The view from 2019," Written January 10, 2019, accessed in *Religion News Service*, June 28, 2019, https://religionnews.com/2019/01/10/where-is-christianity-headed-the-view-from-2019/

Hedrick, Charles W., "The 34 Gospels," *Bible Review*, Vol. XVIII, #3, June 2002.

Holy Bible, The: King James Version, New American Library, New York, 1974.

King, Karen L., *The Gospel of Mary of Magdala: Jesus and the First Woman Apostle*, Polebridge Press, Santa Rosa CA., 2003.

Kristof, Nicholas, "Am I a Christian, Pastor Timothy Keller?" *The New York Times*, December 23, 2016 https://www.nytimes.com/2016/12/23/opinion/sunday/pastor-am-i-a-christian.html

Life Application Bible: New Revised Standard Version, World Bible Publishing, Inc., Iowa Falls, Iowa, 1989

Moore, Christopher, *Lamb: The Gospel According to Biff, Christ's Childhood Friend*, Harper Perennial, 2003.

Meyer, Marvin W., trans., *The Secret Teachings of Jesus: Four Gnostic Gospels*, Vintage Books, New York, 1984.

Pagels, Elaine, *Adam, Eve, and the Serpent*, Vintage Books, New York, 1988.

Beyond Belief: The Secret Gospel of Thomas, Vintage Books, New York, 2003.

The Gnostic Gospels, Vintage Books, New York, 1981.

The Origin of Satan, Random House, New York, 1995.

Ranke-Heinemann, Uta, *Putting Away Childish Things: The Virgin Birth, the Empty Tomb, and Other Fairy Tales You Don't Need to Believe to Have a Living Faith*, Harper, San Francisco, 1992.

Rubenstein, Richard E., *When Jesus Became God: The Struggle to Define Christianity during the Last Days of Rome*, Harcourt Inc., Orlando FL. 1999.

Shorto, Russell, *Gospel Truth: The New Image of Jesus Emerging from Science and History and Why it Matters*, Riverhead Books, New York, 1997.

Stack, Liam, "Indianapolis Catholic School Fires Gay Teacher at Archbishop's Request," *The New York Times*, June 24, 2019. https://www.nytimes.com/2019/06/24/us/cathedral-hs-teacher-gay-marriage.html?module=inline

Strobel, Lee, *The Case for Christ: A Journalist's Personal Investigation of the Evidence for Jesus*, Zondervan Publishing, Grand Rapids MI.,1998.

Wills, Garry, *Saint Augustine*, Lipper /Viking, New York, 1999.

Wilson, Barrie, *How Jesus Became Christian*, St. Martin's Press, New York, 2008.

Wilson, Ian, *Jesus: The Evidence*, Harper and Row, San Francisco, 1988.

Hinduism

Cranston, Sylvia and Carey Williams, *Reincarnation: A New Horizon in Science, Religion, and Society*, Julian Press, New York, 1984.

Falerio, Sonia, "Saving the Cows, Starving the Children," *The New York Times*, June 26, 2015. http://www.nytimes.com/2015/06/28/opinion/sunday/saving-the-cows-starving-the-children.html

Hinduism Today, Editor, "Critical Collection: Downing Dharma is an ancient sport but few have amassed all the trading cards," Dec. 31, 1996. Last accessed 3/21/2016. http://www.hindunet.org/srh_home/1996_10/msg00225.html

"Ten Questions people ask about Hinduism and ten terrific answers," April/May/June, 2004. Last accessed 3/21/2016, http://www.hinduismtoday.com/modules/smartsection/item.php?itemid=1327

Kinsley, David R., *Hinduism: A Cultural Perspective*, Prentice Hall, 1982.

Nene, Dr. Vilas, T*he Logic of Hindu Thought*, Devan Publishing, Vienna, Va., 2000.

Patel, Sanjay, *The Little Book of Hindu Deities: From the Goddess of Wealth to the Sacred Cow*, Plume, London, 2006

Prabhavananda, Swami, *The Sermon on the Mount according to Vedanta*, Mentor Books, NewYork, 1963.

Yogananda, Paramahansa, *Autobiography of a Yogi*, Self Realization Fellowship, Los Angeles, 1985.

Man's Eternal Quest, Self Realization Fellowship, Los Angeles, 1985.

Islam

Ansary, Tamim, *Destiny Disrupted: A History of the World Through Islamic Eyes*, PublicAffairs, New York, 2009.

Aslan, Reza, *No God but God: The Origins, Evolution, and Future of Islam*, Random House, New York, 2005.

Armstrong, Karen, *Islam: A Short History*, Modern Library, New York, 2000.

Muhammad: A Biography of the Prophet, Harper One, New York, 1993.

Now: Society and Community, Transcript: Bill Moyers interviews Karen Armstrong, 3/01/02, *PBS*, http://www.pbs.org/now/transcript/transcript_armstrong.html

Dawood, N.J., trans., *The Koran*, Penguin Books, London, 1974.

Faul, Michelle, "Nigerian extremist says he approves of attacks on schools and teachers," July 13, 2013, *The Washington Post*, https://www.washingtonpost.com/world/nigerian-extremist-says-he-approves-of-attacks-on-schools-and-teachers/2013/07/13/1112d0f8-ebde-11e2-8023-b7f07811d98e_story.html

Hagerty, Barbara Bradley, "Some Muslims in U.S. Quietly Engage in Polygamy," *NPR*, May 29, 2008, http://www.npr.org/templates/story/story.php?storyId=90857818

Hazleton, Lesley, *The First Muslim: The Story of Muhammad*, Riverhead Books, New York, 2013.

Hubbard, Ben, "A Saudi Morals Enforcer Called for a More Liberal Islam. Then the Death Threats Began," *The New York Times*, July 10, 2016,

Ignatius, David, "Recapturing the Arab Muslim world's golden age," July 12, 2013, *The Washington Post*, https://www.washingtonpost.com/opinions/david-ignatius-recapturing-the-arab-muslim-worlds-golden-age/2013/07/12/e21d4bc8-ea68-11e2-aa9f-c03a72e2d342_story.html

Lippman, Thomas W., *Understanding Islam: An Introduction to the Muslim World*, Mentor Books, New York, 1990.

Manji, Irshad, *The Trouble with Islam: A Muslim's Call for Reform in Her Faith*, St. Martin's Press, New York, 2003.

Miller, Michael, "Killing Jews is Worship' posters will soon appear on NYC subways and buses," *The Washington Post*, April 22, 2015.

Nasr, Vali, *The Shia Revival: How Conflicts Within Islam Will Shape the Future*, Norton, New York, 2006.

Ramzy, Austin, "Brunei to Punish Adultery and Gay Sex With Death by Stoning," *The New York Times*, March 28, 2019, *https://www.nytimes.com/2019/03/28/world/asia/brunei-stoning-death.html?emc=edit_th_190329&nl=todaysheadlines&nlid=620063260329*

Rauf, Feisal Abdul, *What's Right with Islam is What's Right with America*, Harper, San Francisco, 2004.

Stoddart, William, *Sufism: The Mystical Doctrines and Methods of Islam*," Paragon House, St. Paul, Minn., 1985.

Wills, Garry, *What the Qur'an Meant and Why it Matters*, Viking, 2017.

Zep, Ira G., *A Muslim Primer: Beginner's Guide to Islam*, Wakefield Editions, Westminster Md. 1992.

THE RELIGION TEACHER'S BOOKSHELF

Judaism

Ariel, David S., *What Do Jews Believe?: The Spiritual Foundations of Judaism*, Schocken Books, New York, 1995.

Brooks, David, "The Orthodox Surge," *The New York Times*, March 7, 2013, http://www.nytimes.com/2013/03/08/opinion/brooks-the-orthodox-surge.html?_r=0

Cahill, Thomas, *The Gifts of the Jews: How a Tribe of Desert Nomads Changed the Way Everyone Thinks and Feels*, Nan A. Talese/Anchor Books, New York, 1999.

Glaser, Gabrielle, "What do you Mean I'm not a Jew?" *The Washington Post*, April 28, 1997. https://www.washingtonpost.com/archive/opinions/1997/04/20/what-do-you-mean-im-not-a-jew/424776fd-4857-40fd-b9d8-4302298efc65/

Jacobs, A. J., *The Year of Living Biblically: One Man's Humble Quest to Follow the Bible as Literally as Possible*, Simon and Schuster, New York, 2007.

Jews For Judaism, http://jewsforjudaism.org/knowledge/articles/answers/jewish-polemics/texts/christian-proof-texting/

Kosmin, Barry A., "The New American Jewish secularism," *The Washington Post*, Feb. 19, 2013. (http://www.washingtonpost.com/blogs/guest-voices/post/the-new-american-jewish-secularism/2013/02/19/23cfa7a8-7aae-11e2-9a75-dab0201670da_blog.html

Krueger, Alyson, "Bar or Bat Mitzvah? Hey, What About a Both Mitzvah?" *The New York Times*, March 27, 2019

Strassfeld, Michael, *The Jewish Holidays: A Guide and Commentary*, Harper and Row, New York, 1985.

Wilgoren, Debbi, "Brooklyn Visit Steeps Area Students in Unfiltered Judaism," *The Washington Post*, March 16, 1996. Last accessed 3/21/2016, https://www.washingtonpost.com/archive/politics/1996/03/16/brooklyn-visit-steeps-area-students-in-unfiltered-judaism/9ae928f2-4e7d-4ec2-bbe6-fb48ef2fb0d0/

Primal, Pagan Religions

Armstrong, Karen, *A Short History of Myth*, Cannongate, Edinburgh, Scotland, 2005.

Brown, Tom Jr., *Awakening Spirits: A Native American Path to Inner Peace, Healing, and Spiritual Growth*, Berkley Books, New York, 1994.

The Vision: The Dramatic True Story of One Man's Profound Relationship with Nature, Berkley Books, New York, 1991.

Campbell, Joseph, *The Power of Myth: with Bill Moyers*, Doubleday, New York, 1988.

Diamond, Jared, *The World Until Yesterday: What Can We Learn from Traditional Societies*, Viking, New York, 2012.

Harner, Michael, *The Way of the Shaman*, Harper San Francisco, 1990.

Narby, Jeremy, *The Cosmic Serpent: DNA and the Origins of Knowledge*, Jeremy P. Tarcher/Putnam, New York, 1998.

Neihardt, John G., *Black Elk Speaks*, Pocket Books, New York, 1972.

Thomas, Elizabeth Marshall, *The Old Way: A Story of the First People*, Farrar, Strauss, Giroux, New York, 2006.

Willis, Roy, General editor, *World Mythology*, Henry Holt and Co., New York, 1993.

Wolff, Robert, *Original Wisdom: Stories of an Ancient Way of Knowing*, Inner Traditions International, Rochester, VT., 2001.

Reference

Adams, Scott, *BrainyQuote*, https://www.brainyquote.com/quotes/scott_adams_385680

Bastani, Aaron, *Fully Automated Luxury Communism: A Manifesto*, Verso, Brooklyn, N.Y. 2019.

Cain, Susan, *Quiet: The Power of Introverts in a World That Can't Stop Talking*, Broadway Books, New York, 2013

Clarke, Arthur C., *Childhood's End*, Ballantine Books, New York, 1953.

Collins, Graham P., "Within Any Possible Universe, No Intellect Can Ever Know It All," *Scientific American*, March 1, 2009.

Dahlsgaard, Katherine, Christopher Peterson, and Martin E.P. Seligman**,** "Shared Virtue: The Convergence of Valued Human Strengths Across Culture and History," *Review of General Psychology*, September 1, 2005

Epictetus, and Sharon Lebell, *The Art of Living: The Classic Manual on Virtue, Happiness, and Effectiveness*, Harper, San Francisco, 1995.

Goff, Philip, *Galileo's Error: Foundations for a New science of Consciousness*, Pantheon Books, New York, 2019

Guiley, Rosemary Ellen, *Harper's Encyclopedia of Mystical and Paranormal Experience*, Castle Books, Edison, NJ, 1991.

Harari, Yuval Noah, *Homo Deus: A Brief History of Tomorrow*, Vintage, London, 2015

Hart, Michael H., *The 100: A Ranking of the Most Influential Persons in History, Revised and Updated*, Citadel Press, 1992.

Herman, Arthur, *The Cave and the Light: Plato Versus Aristotle and the Struggle for the Soul of Western Civilization*, Random House Trade Paperbacks, New York, 2013.

Hunt, Arnold D., Marie T. Crotty, Robert B. Crotty, *Ethics of World Religions*, Greenhaven Press Inc., San Diego, CA. 1976, Revised edition, 1991.

Landis, Benson Y., *An Outline of the Bible Book by Book*, Barnes and Noble, 1966.

Nohria, Nitin, "You are not as Virtuous as you Think," *The Washington Post*, Oct. 15, 2015, https://www.washingtonpost.com/opinions/youre-not-as-virtuous-as-you-think/2015/10/15/fec227c4-66b4-11e5-9ef3-fde182507eac_story.html?utm_term=.d67f7d58c991

Panati, Charles, *Sacred Origins of Profound Things*, Published by the Penguin Group, Arkana, 1996.

Pelikan, Jaroslav, Editor, *The World Treasury of Modern Religious Thought*, Little, Brown, Boston, 1990.

Pigliuuci, Massimo, *How to Be a Stoic: Using Ancient Philosophy to Live a Modern Life*, Basic Books, New York, 2017.

Presti, David, *Mind Beyond Brain: Buddhism, Science, and the Paranormal*, Columbia University Press, New York, 2018.

Raine, Adrian, *The Anatomy of Violence: The Biological Roots of Crime*, Vintage, New York, 2014.

Smart, Ninian, *The Religious Experience of Mankind, Third Edition*, Charles Scribner's Sons, New York, 1984.

Smith, Jonathan Z., ed., *The Harper Collins Dictionary of Religion*, Harper, San Francisco, 1995.

Stevenson, Jay, Ph.D., *The Complete Idiot's Guide to Eastern Philosophy*, Alpha Books, 2000.

Tresidder, Jack, *Symbols and Their Meanings*, Barnes and Noble, New York, 2006.

Tyson, Neil DeGrasse, *Astrophysics for People in a Hurry*, W.W. Norton and Co., New York, 2017

Walker, Barbara G., *The Women's Encyclopedia of Myths and Secrets*, Harper San Francisco, 1983.

Wright, Robert, *Nonzero: The Logic of Human Destiny*, Vintage Books, New York, 2001.

Religious History

Armstrong, Karen, *A History of God: The 4000 Year Quest of Judaism, Christianity, and Islam*, Alfred A. Knopf, New York, 1993.

_____*The Great Transformation: The Beginning of our Religious Traditions*, Anchor Books, New York, 2006.

_____*The Bible: A Biography*, Grove Press, New York, 2007.

_____ *Fields of Blood: Religion and the History of Violence*, Anchor Books, New York, 2015.

_____ *The Lost Art of Scripture*, Knopf, New York, 2019.

Boyce, James, *Born Bad: Original Sin and the Making of the Western World*, Counterpoint, Berkeley, CA., 2015.

Fletcher, Richard, *The Barbarian Conversion: From Paganism to Christianity*, Henry Holt and Co., New York, 1997

Freeman, Charles, *The Closing of the Western Mind: The Rise of Faith and the Fall of Reason*, Vintage Books, New York, 2005.

O'Grady, Selina, *And Man Created God: A History of the World at the Time of Jesus*, St. Martin's Press, New York, 2012.

Rubenstein, Richard E., *Aristotle's Children: How Christians, Muslims, and Jews Rediscovered Ancient Wisdom and Illuminated the Middle Ages*, A Harvest Book, New York, 2003.

Solomon, Robert C. and Kathleen M. Higgins, *A Short History of Philosophy*, Oxford University Press, New York, 1996.

Stone, Merlin, *When God was a Woman*, Barnes and Noble, New York, 1976.

Wright, Robert, *The Evolution of God*, Little, Brown and Co., New York, 2009.

Religion in Today's World

Alexander, Eben, M.D., *Proof of Heaven: A Neurosurgeon's Journey into the Afterlife*, Simon and Schuster Paperbacks, New York, 2012.

Aslan, Reza, *Beyond Fundamentalism: Confronting Religious Extremism in the Age of Globalization*, Random House, New York, 2010.

Capra, Fritjof, *The Tao of Physics*, Bantam Books, New York, 1977, 2010.

Dowd, Michael, *Thank God for Evolution: How the Marriage of Science and Religion will Transform your Life and Our World*, Plume, New York, 2009

Eck, Diana L., *A New Religious America: How a 'Christian Country' Has Become the World's Most Religiously Diverse Nation*, Harper, San Francisco, 2001.

Ehrenreich, Barbara, "A Rationalist's Mystical Moment," *The New York Times*, April 5, 2014.

Griswold, Eliza, *The Tenth Parallel: Dispatches from the Fault Line between Christianity and Islam*, Farrar, Strauss and Giroux, New York, 2010.

Haidt, Jonathan, *The Righteous Mind: Why Good People are Divided by Politics and Religion*, Vintage, New York, 2012.

Hart, David Bentley, *Atheist Delusions: The Christian Revolution and Its Fashionable Enemies*, Yale University Press, New Haven, 2009.

Haught, John F., *The New Cosmic Story: Inside Our Awakening Universe*, Yale University Press, New Haven, 2017.

Haynes, Charles C. and Oliver Thomas, *Finding Common Ground: A First Amendment Guide to Religion and Public Schools*, First Amendment Center, Nashville, 2007.

Holt, Jim, *Why Does the World Exist?: An Existential Detective Story*, Liveright Publishing Corp., New York, 2012

Kristof, Nicholas D., *Religion and Women*, The New York Times, Jan. 9, 2010.

_____ and Sheryl WuDunn, *Half The Sky: Turning Oppression Into Opportunity for Women Worldwide*, Alfred A. Knopf, New York, 2010.

Lujan, Fernando M., "How to get Afghans to trust us once again," *The Washington Post*, March 2, 2012, https://www.washingtonpost.com/opinions/how-to-get-afghans-to-trust-us-once-again/2012/03/01/gIQAfhZ9mR_story.html

Martel, Yann, *Life of Pi*, Harcourt Inc., New York, 2001

Moreland, J.P. and Kai Nielsen, *Does God Exist: The Debate between Theists and Atheists*, Prometheus Books, Buffalo, N.Y., 1993

Nord, Warren A. *Does God Make a Difference?: Taking Religion Seriously In Our Schools and Universities*, Oxford University Press, New York, 2010.

_____ and Charles C. Haynes, *Taking Religion Seriously Across the Curriculum*, ASCD, Alexandria, Va., 1998.

Pagels, Elaine, *Why Religion?* HarperCollins, New York, 2018

Prothero, Stephen, *Religious Literacy: What Every American Needs to Know - and Doesn't*, Harper, San Francisco, 2007.

Ruenzel, David, "Revival," *Education Week*, March 1, 1996. Retrieved January 2, 2005 from, http://www.edweek.org/tm/articles/1996/03/01/06relig.h07.htmlquerystring=revival&print=1

Schellenberg, J.L., *Evolutionary Religion*, Oxford University Press, Oxford, U.K., 2013

Silk, Mark and Andrew Walsh, *One Nation Divisible: How Regional Religious Differences Shape American Politics*, Rowman and Littlefield Publishers Inc., Lanham, Md., 2008.

Smith, Huston, *The World's Religions*, HarperCollins, New York, 1991.

Why Religion Matters: The Fate of the Human Spirit in An Age of Disbelief, Harper San Francisco, 2001.

The Way Things Are: Conversations with Huston Smith on the Spiritual Life, Phil Cousineau ed., University of California Press, London, 2003.

Swimme, Brian Thomas and Mary Evelyn Tucker, *Journey of the Universe*, Yale University Press, 2011

Tsubaki Grand Shrine in America, Ch.9, *Shinto and the World's Religions*, http://tsubakishrine.org/kaminomichi/kami_no_michi_9.html

Valpy, Michael, "God is Big These Days," in *Shambhala Sun*, January 2005, last accessed May 9, 2013. http://www.shambhalasun.com/index.php? option=com_content&task=view&id=1415

Wade, Nicholas, *The Faith Instinct: How Religion Evolved and Why it Endures*, The Penguin Press, New York, 2009

Weber, Michael C., "Teaching Religion in the World History Class," *World History Connected* 4.1 (2006): 12 pars. 17 Mar. 2016 <http://worldhistoryconnected.press.illinois.edu/4.1/weber.html>.

Weiner, Eric, *Man Seeks God: My Flirtations with the Divine*, Twelve, Hachette Book Group, New York, 2011.

Williams, Mary E., Editor., *Opposing Viewpoints: Religion in America*, Greenhaven Press, 2006.

Films/TV Mentioned

Arranged 89 Min., Film **Movement**, 2007

Bill Moyers Special: The Wisdom of Faith with Huston Smith, PBS, 1996

THE RELIGION TEACHER'S BOOKSHELF

David and Bathsheba, *115 Min.*, 20th Century Fox, 1951

Dead Poets Society, Touchstone Pictures, 1989

Decoding the Past: Secrets of the Koran, The History Channel, A&E Television Network, 2006

Little Buddha, 123 Min., Miramax Films, 1993

Little Mosque on the Prairie, The Complete First Season, CBC Home Video, 2006

Long Search, The, BBC Documentary, 1977

Matrix, The, 136 Min., Warner Bros., 1999

Mulan, 87 min., Walt Disney films, 1998

Samson and Delilah, 127 min., Paramount, 1949

Solomon and Sheba, 141 min., United Artists, 1959

Spirited Away, 125 Min., A Hayao Miyazaki Film, Walt Disney Studios, 2002

Ten Commandments, The, 231 Min., Warner Brothers, 1956

Thirteenth Floor, The, 100 min., Columbia Pictures, 1997

Web Sites

These sites deal with current events and issues. Web sites relating to individual religions are too numerous to mention.

<u>Division of Perceptual Studies</u>, University of Virginia School of Medicine, https://med.virginia.edu/perceptual-studies/

Investigation of phenomena that challenge mainstream scientific paradigms regarding the nature of the mind/brain relationship.

First Amendment Center- Religion

http://www.firstamendmentcenter.org/category/religion

Current issues and research on all First Amendment concerns.

Journey of the Universe- https://www.journeyoftheuniverse.org

The award winning film, on-line classes, podcasts, and further resources to learn about our place and role in the evolution the universe.

MeaningofLife.tv - Podcasts. Robert Wright interviews a wide variety of thinkers about various religious, social, political and scientific topics having to do with the meaning of life and lays out some of his own ideas. I especially like Wright's own lectures at Union Theological Seminary posted a week apart from May 23 to June 20, 2016.

On Being with Krista Tippett, onbeing.org *On Being* opens up the animating questions at the center of human life: What does it mean to be human, and how do we want to live?

On Faith- Washington Post, http://www.washingtonpost.com/national/on-faith Weekly page of news and commentary on religious issues.

Pew Forum on Religion and Public Life, http://www.pewforum.org/ Current religious issues and questions are researched with impressive quality and depth.

Pew Religion News, http://www.pewforum.org/Religion-News/Straight-but-narrow.aspx Weekly newsletter on current events in religion around the nation and the world.

Religion News Service, https://www.religionnews.com News about religion, spirituality and ideas.

NOTES

Introduction

1. David Masci, "In U.S., familiarity with religious groups is associated with warmer feelings toward them." *Fact Tank*, Pew Research Center, October 31, 2019, https://www.pewresearch.org/fact-tank/2019/10/31/in-u-s-familiarity-with-religious-groups-is-associated-with-warmer-feelings-toward-them/

5. Making Sense of World Religions

1. Michael C. Weber., "Teaching Religion in the World History Class," World History Connected 4.1 (2006): 12 pars. 17 Mar. 2016 http://worldhistoryconnected.press.illinois.edu/4.1/weber.html.

15. The Buddha's Teachings I

1. David Brooks, "The Act of Rigorous Forgiving," *New York Times*, February 10, 2015, https://www.nytimes.com/2015/02/10/opinion/david-brooks-the-act-of-rigorous-forgiving.html

26. Religion in China Today

1. Dan Levin, "China Officials Seek Career Shortcut With Feng Shui," *New York Times*, May 10, 2013, https://www.nytimes.com/2013/05/11/world/asia/feng-shui-grows-in-china-as-officials-seek-success.html
2. Ian Johnson. "Decapitated Churches in China's Christian Heartland," *New York Times*, May 21, 2016. https://www.nytimes.com/2016/05/22/world/asia/china-christians-zhejiang.html
3. Ian Johnson, "This Chinese Christian Was Charged With Trying to Subvert the State," *New York Times*. March 25, 2019.
4. Jeremy Page, "Why China Is Turning Back to Confucius," *Wall Street Journal*, September 20, 2015. https://www.wsj.com/articles/why-china-is-turning-back-to-confucius-1442754000

27. Abrahamic Faiths

1. "Who's Afraid of Arabic Numerals" by Mustafa Akyol, June 4, 2019, New York Times, https://www.nytimes.com/2019/06/04/opinion/arabic-numerals.html

29. Practicing Judaism

1. Debbie Wilgoren, "Brooklyn Visit Steeps Area Students in Unfiltered Judaism," *Washington Post*. March 16, 1996, https://www.washingtonpost.com/archive/politics/1996/03/16/brooklyn-visit-steeps-area-students-in-unfiltered-judaism/9ae928f2-4e7d-4ec2-bbe6-fb48ef2fb0d0/
2. David Brooks, "The Orthodox Surge," *New York Times*, March 8, 2013, https://www.nytimes.com/2013/03/08/opinion/brooks-the-orthodox-surge.html

30. Who Is A Jew, Etc.?

1. Alyson Krueger, "Bar or Bat Mitzvah? Hey, What About a Both Mitzvah?" *New York Times*, March 27, 2019, https://www.nytimes.com/2019/03/27/style/gender-fluid-bar-bat-mitzvah.html
2. Gabrielle Glaser, "What do you Mean I'm not a Jew?" *Washington Post*, April 28, 1997

32. Rules and Holidays

1. "Noahide Covenant: Theology and Jewish Law, *"Jewish Understandings of the Other: an Annotated Sourcebook*, Boston College: Center for Christian-Jewish Learning. https://www.bc.edu/content/dam/files/research_sites/cjl/texts/cjrelations/resources/sourcebook/Noahide_-covenant.htm
2. Harriet Sherwood, "Europe's Jewish population has dropped 60% in last 50 years," The Guardian, October 25, 2020, https://www.theguardian.-com/world/2020/oct/25/europes-jewish-population-has-dropped-60-in-last-50- years

33. Christianity

1. President Russell Nelson, "The Correct Name of the Church," The Church of Jesus Christ of Latter-Day Saints, October 2018, https://www.churchofjesuschrist.org/study/general-conference/2018/10/the-correct-name-of-the-church?lang=eng
2. Elizabeth Dias, "Mormon No More: Faithful Reflect on Church's Move to Scrap a Moniker" *New York Times*, June 29, 2019, https://www.nytimes.-com/2019/06/29/us/mormon-church-name-change.html

34. What Christians Believe

1. Megan Brenan, "40% of Americans Believe in Creationism," *Gallup*, July 26, 2019, https://news.gallup.com/poll/261680/americans-believe-creationism.aspx
2. Barbara Bradley Hagerty, "Evangelicals Question the Existence of Adam and Eve," *NPR*, August 9, 2011, https://www.npr.org/2011/08/09/138957812/evan-

gelicals-question-the-existence-of-adam-and-eve

35. More Beliefs

1. "Many Americans Say Other Faiths Can Lead to Eternal Life,"Pew, December 18, 2008, https://www.pewtrusts.org/en/research-and-analysis/reports/2008/12/18/many-americans-say-other-faiths-can-lead-to-eternal-life

37. Biblical Scholarship

1. Arthur C. Droge, "Did Paul Commit Suicide?" *Bible Review*, Dec. 1989

43. The Big Split

1. Karen Armstrong, *Fields of Blood: Religion and the History of Violence*, Anchor, 2015, 329.

46. True Islam

1. Ben Hubbard, "A Saudi Morals Enforcer Called for a More Liberal Islam. Then the Death Threats Began," New York Times, June 10, 2016.
2. Michael Lipka "Muslims and Islam: Key findings in the U.S. and around the world," Fact Tank, Pew Research Center, August 9, 2017 https://www.pewresearch.org/fact-tank/2017/08/09/muslims-and-islam-key-findings-in-the- u-s-and-around-the-world/
3. Jacob Poushter, "In nations with significant Muslim populations, much disdain for ISIS," Fact Tank, Pew Research Center, November 17, 2015, https://www.pewresearch.org/fact-tank/2015/11/17/in-nations-with-significant-muslim- populations-much-disdain-for-isis/

52. Baha'i

1. "Baha'is Believe in the Essential Unity of All Religions," September 23, 2020. https://bahaiteachings.org/bahai-faith/.

53. Sikhism

1. "Sikhs." Wikipedia. Wikimedia Foundation, April 16, 2021. https://en.wikipedia.org/wiki/Sikhs.

NOTES

57. The Pi Process

1. Gregory Smith. Just one-third of U.S. Catholics agree with their church that Eucharist is body, blood of Christ. Pew Research Center. 5 Aug 2019. https://www.pewresearch.org/fact-tank/2019/08/05/transubstantiation-eucharist-u-s-catholics/
2. "Religious beliefs and practices." Pew Research Center. 26 July 2017. https://www.pewforum.org/2017/07/26/religious-beliefs-and-practices/
3. "Faith in Flux." 27 April 2009. Pew Research Center. https://www.pewforum.org/2009/04/27/faith-in-flux/

1. What Do We Know?

1. "Adults Who Say Humans Always Existed in Present Form" Pew Research Center, date accessed April 29, 2020, https://www.pewforum.org/religious-landscape-study/views-about-human-evolution/always-existed-in-present-form/

2. What Reality Is

1. Powell, Corey, "Elon Musk Says We May Live in a Simulation," NBC News, October 2, 2018, https://www.nbcnews.com/mach/science/what-simulation-hypothesis-why-some-think-life-simulated-reality-ncna913926
2. Purtill, Corrine, "A Harvard Physicist Explains the Problem With Believing We Live in a Simulation," Quartz, March 1, 2017, https://qz.com/921277/a-harvard-physicist-explains-the-problem-with-believing-we-live-in-a-simulation/

3. If There Is An Afterlife

1. Vonnegut, Kurt, Frequently Asked Questions, American Humanist Association, April 29, 2020, https://americanhumanist.org/about/faq/

4. If There Is Free Will

1. Cherry, Kendra, "Delayed Gratification and Impulse Control," Very Well Mind, May 11, 2020, https://www.verywellmind.com/delayed-gratification-why-wait-for-what-you-want-2795429

5. Prayer And God

1. Neil DeGrasse Tyson, NDT [@neiltyson]. (2018, February 16). Evidence collected over many years, obtained from many locations, indicates that the power of Prayer is insufficient to stop bullets [Tweet]. Twitter. https://twitter.com/neiltyson/status/964606017513410560

2. Presti, David E. Mind beyond Brain: Buddhism, Science, and the Paranormal. New York, NY: Columbia University Press, 2020.

7. Is God In Our Future?

1. JL Schellenberg, Evolutionary Religion, Oxford University Press, Oxford, U.K., 2013, 99.
2. Dalai Lama XIV, The Universe in a Single Atom: The Convergence of Science and Spirituality, Morgan Books, New York, 2005.

8. God's Plan

1. Aaron Bastani, *Fully Automated Luxury Communism*. Verso, June 2019, 316.

ABOUT THE AUTHOR

Jay Lamb taught world religion and philosophy at the Thomas Jefferson High School for Science and Technology for over 20 years. He lives in Virginia with his loving wife, a spoiled cat, and is the father of four adoring daughters. Trying to understand and explain various religious beliefs has been a major pursuit of his adult life.

www.ingramcontent.com/pod-product-compliance
Lightning Source LLC
Chambersburg PA
CBHW031402290426
44110CB00011B/241